· UNDERSTANDING ·

ROMAN
INSCRIPTIONS

turned or

D1338731

· UNDERSTANDING ·

ROMAN INSCRIPTIONS

· LAWRENCE KEPPIE ·

B.T. Batsford Ltd, London

© Lawrence Keppie 1991

First published 1991

All rights reserved. No part of this publication
may be reproduced, in any form or by any means,
without permission from the Publisher

Typeset by Servis Filmsetting Ltd, Manchester
and printed in Great Britain by
Courier International Ltd
East Kilbride, Scotland

Published by B.T. Batsford Ltd
4 Fitzhardinge Street, London W1H 0AH

A CIP catalogue record for this book is
available from the British Library

ISBN 0 7134 5692 2 (cased)
0 7134 5693 0 (limp)

CONTENTS

ILLUSTRATIONS

ACKNOWLEDGEMENTS

I am grateful to many friends and colleagues for their help on detailed points. In the first instance I must thank Dr Roger Tomlin for suggesting my name to Batsford as author of a book on this topic. Among those who wittingly or unwittingly aided my researches, I mention Professor Michael Crawford (University College, London); Mr P.R.Jeffreys-Powell (University of Glasgow); Dr Helen Whitehouse (Ashmolean Museum, Oxford); Dr John Patterson (Magdalene College, Cambridge); the late Dr Jaroslav Šašel (Slovenian Academy of the Sciences); Miss Lindsay Allason-Jones (Museum of Antiquities, Newcastle); Dr K.-V.Decker (Landesmuseum, Mainz); Professor Benjamin Isaac (University of Tel Aviv); Dr David French (British Institute of Archaeology, Ankara); Dr Emilio Marin (Archaeological Museum, Split); Mr Richard Brewer (National Museum of Wales); Mr Michael Dobson (University of Exeter); Dr D.J.Breeze (Historic Buildings and Monuments, Scotland); Dr Robert Matijašić (Archaeological Museum, Pula); Professor Jane Crawford and Professor Bernard Frischer (University of California); Professor A.A.Barrett (University of British Columbia); Lt.-Col. A.A.Fairrie; Prof. E.B.Birley; Dr Pierre Valette; Ivor Davidson and Margaret Robb.

Dr Miriam Griffin kindly agreed to read a draft version of the book, as did Miss Joyce Reynolds. In particular I benefited from the latter's unparalleled knowledge of epigraphic texts and secondary literature; her sharp eye and commonsense saved me from many errors. Those that may remain are the responsibility of the author. It is a pleasure to note that Miss Reynolds has recently completed a brief guidebook to Latin inscriptions, published by the British Museum.

The text was written partly in Glasgow and partly at the Institute for Advanced Study, Princeton, New Jersey, where the author enjoyed a happy and fruitful semester in the spring of 1989. During preparation of the book, I visited sites and monuments in Italy, Germany, Israel, Austria, France, Yugoslavia and Turkey. I enjoyed the hospitality of the Rheinisches Landesmuseum, Bonn, the Landesmuseum and Römisch-Germanisches Zentralmuseum, Mainz, and at various times had financial support from the University of Glasgow, the Johannes Gutenberg Universität Mainz, the British Academy, the Carnegie Trust for the Universities of Scotland and the Haverfield Trust.

Dr Graham Webster and Mr Peter Kemmis Betty made valuable editorial suggestions. The photographs were taken and the line-illustrations prepared by the author, except where acknowledged separately. For permission to reproduce photographs, author and publishers are grateful to: The Egypt Exploration Society (Fig. 1); Museum of Antiquities, Newcastle (Figs. 9, 51, 68); University of Durham (Fig. 11); Colchester & Essex Museum (Fig. 46); Corinium Museum, Cirencester (Fig. 76); National Museums of Scotland (Fig. 57); National Museum of Wales (Fig. 82); Rheinisches Landesmuseum, Bonn (Fig. 79); Rheinisches Bildarchiv, Köln (Figs. 47, 53); J.M.Arnaud and the Musée d'Aquitaine, Bordeaux (Fig. 56); Museo Archeologico, Aquileia (Fig. 40 and front cover). Arheološki Muzej, Split (Fig. 67); Museo Archeologico, Torino (Fig. 49); Institut français d'Archéologie orientale (Fig. 72); Prof. A.R.Birley (Fig. 21); Prof. D. Baatz (Fig. 50); Dr R.A.Knox (Fig. 13); Prof. S.S.Frere (Fig. 37) and Dr P.W. Freeman (Fig. 38).

Hunterian Museum
University of Glasgow
October 1990

1

INTRODUCTION

The value of inscriptions as historical material is so great that it can hardly be exaggerated. Apart from modern forgeries, which are rare and in general easily detected, they are contemporary and authoritative documents, whose text if legible cannot be corrupt, and whose cumulative value, in the hands of scholars accustomed to handling them in the mass, is astonishing. They are the most important single source for the history and organisation of the Roman Empire.
(R.G.Collingwood)[1]

The subject of the following pages is a substantial and ever-growing resource for archaeologists and historians of the Roman world. It can be estimated that over 300,000 inscriptions are known; this mass of evidence grows at upwards of 1000 items per year, and the volume of new discoveries shows no sign of diminishing. Inscriptions provide valuable confirmation and amplification of our often meagre and selective literary sources. They can provide details of events not reported at all by the Roman historians, or can attest the careers and activities of officials and officers otherwise completely unknown. Inscriptions of the latter type are a major source of material for the scholarly pursuit of prosopography, which seeks to reconstruct administrative hierarchies and family relationships, and thereby illuminate ancient society. Equally important, inscriptions cover a wide, though by no means complete, socio-economic spectrum of the community, bringing before us a vast number of people who have no place as individuals in the pages of the Roman historians. The evidence of inscriptions is especially useful in reconstructing the story of provinces far from Rome. Above all they provide an enormous reservoir of incidental information on the world of the Romans and the organization of their empire.

First, a definition. The term 'Roman inscriptions' is used in modern times to denote the texts inscribed on a variety of materials which have survived from antiquity. The study of inscriptions has come to be known as epigraphy, from a Greek word, *epigraphe*, meaning literally an 'inscription'. Latin terms for an inscribed text are *inscriptio*[2] and *titulus*,[3] the latter word encompassing both the text and the panel on which it is inscribed.

In Italy and the western provinces the language used was chiefly Latin. But it should be remembered that the common language of Roman provinces east and south of the Adriatic was Greek, which was the language of law and administration as well as the day-to-day *lingua franca* of much of the eastern Mediterranean world. Many 'Roman' inscriptions from these lands were inscribed in Greek. There are bilingual, even trilingual texts, in the manner of the well-known Rosetta Stone.[4] Local languages and scripts such as Punic, Thracian and Palmyran can be found alongside Latin and Greek. In the following pages, however, the emphasis will be on inscriptions in Latin. Sometimes the word 'inscriptions' is used to refer more casually to the stones or other materials which have been marked, written on, or chiselled with a formal message which the dedicator frequently intended would be seen, admired, and perhaps pondered on. Often the setting up of an inscription was a public act, for public consumption.

Not all inscriptions were, however, on stone. Bronze was an important medium, used often for legal documents.[5] After a fire had destroyed the Temple of Jupiter on the Capitoline Hill in Rome in AD 69, the new emperor Vespasian had a search made for copies as replacements for the three thousand bronze tablets, many relating to the early history of the Roman state, that had been lost.[6] The poet Horace claims in a well-known line that his poetry constituted a record *aere perennius*, even longer-lasting than bronze.[7] Nowadays inscriptions on bronze constitute a very small proportion of surviving texts; they were much more susceptible to damage, melting down and re-use in antiquity and after.[8] Where such documents survive, even in fragments, they preserve for us important historical information, such as laws, treaties, edicts, religious texts and dedications.

Wooden panels were employed for public notices. It was presumably on a painted wooden board that Julius Caesar displayed at his Triumph in 47 BC the simple but powerful text, VENI, VIDI, VICI (came, saw, conquered).[9] Such boards are shown, held by attendants, in the triumphal procession depicted on the Arch of Titus in Rome (below, p. 45).

Latin (or Greek) could also be written on metals, on baked clay tiles or bricks, on pottery, glass, wall plaster or in mosaic *tesserae*. All these texts come under the general heading of inscriptions, and often form a valuable corrective to more formal, official records on stone. It should be said at once that I here exclude two forms of documentary evidence from antiquity: coins and papyri, which constitute separate branches of study in modern times. Coins normally bear Latin or Greek texts often incorporating the names of an emperor, magistrates or other issuing authorities and other useful information; the texts can be instructively compared with those on stone. Papyri, a sometimes undervalued source, are found predominantly in Egypt. They give invaluable insights into the paperwork which an imperial bureaucracy generated, or report correspondence, business transactions or everyday activities which did not normally find their way on to stone (below, p. 110). Papyri, parchment sheets or wooden writing tablets served for day-to-day short-term transactions; they rarely survive in the western Roman provinces, but recent discoveries of wooden writing tablets from Vindolanda and elsewhere are pointers to how much we should know if they did (below, p. 90).

The Romans were not the first to inscribe texts. The impulse to do so is as old as writing itself. Cuneiform tablets from the end of the fourth millennium BC onwards recorded state events as well as the commercial life of Mesopotamia. Readers will recall the 'writing on the wall' at Belshazzar's feast, interpreted by Daniel.[10] Egyptian hieroglyphs decorated the tombs of pharaohs and nobles and the temples to the gods from about 3000 BC onwards. The Greeks made widespread use of inscriptions, in most of the major categories: building records, gravestones, dedications to the gods and public decrees. Greek settlers in Italy passed on a version of their alphabet to the Etruscans and others; soon the Romans had begun to inscribe texts, from at least the sixth century BC onwards.[11] As a medium of expression in the Roman world, inscriptions were being cut and erected over a period of one thousand years; the tradition of writing in Latin continued throughout the Middle Ages to modern times. Clearly therefore the surviving inscribed texts reflect and illuminate the changing vocabulary and grammatical structure of Latin over an extended period. A majority of the Latin inscriptions surviving from ancient times belongs in the first three centuries AD, i.e. from the time when Roman power was at its height.

The texts of inscriptions are frequently presented in books as neat lines of typescript. This gives a doubly false impression, firstly of a uniformity in script and lettering, and also of easy legibility, to produce a sanitized version of the text, which deprives it of much that would be interesting. The most important fact to remember about any Roman inscription is that it is inscribed *on* something. The text may easily not be the only decoration on the stone. The smallest and seemingly most insignificant slab can be set into the handsomest of monuments. The best place to study inscriptions is where they survive in an original location, or failing that, in a museum, preferably a museum with a large and varied collection.

This book has two aims: firstly to introduce the non-specialist reader to the subject of inscriptions and provide some guidance towards reading the Latin texts. Secondly, to get him or her to appreciate the significance of inscriptions as a resource for the historian and archaeologist anxious to know more about the Roman world. If this is the first book on inscriptions which the reader picks up, I hope it may not be the last. 'An inscription, to the scholars of those days [early nineteenth century], was like the sound of a bugle to a warhorse'.[12] Present-day epigraphists will know the feeling still! Nowadays, Latin is no longer a universal language, and is often employed in archaeological publications by those unfamiliar with its grammatical structure. Translations offered of Latin inscriptions in the following pages deliberately follow as closely as possible the wording of the originals, for better comparison with the Latin texts, though this may on occasion lead to some inelegance in the English.

It is not the principal intention here to provide another learned handbook to Latin inscriptions (for which, see Chapter 6 and Bibliography p. 148ff.). Nevertheless, it is difficult to avoid some of the standard features of such works, such as a list of Latin abbreviations, and a list of the names, titles and dates of Roman emperors (see Appendices, p. 136) The pages that follow are here intended rather as a demonstration to the non-specialist audience of the significance of this category of ancient evidence. It is hoped that no important aspect will have been ignored, but I have made no attempt to include every sub-category of texts. The Late Republic and the Early Empire receive the bulk of attention here, at the expense of early and later periods. A bias may well also be detected in the text and in the choice of illustrations towards categories which readers are most likely to encounter in a museum, or when visiting an archaeological site. One result should be to place Romano-British texts in a wider historical and cultural context.

A word of explanation, perhaps of apology, is necessary over the title of the book. 'Roman' is preferred to 'Latin', in accordance with common usage in British archaeological circles.

This is obviously a subject that lends itself to illustration, especially by way of photographs. The illustrations offered here are from Rome and Italy and from a wide spectrum of provinces. Some may be well known, but I find no value in avoiding texts which a small percentage of readers may find hackneyed, and to field a 'reserve side' merely as evidence of the author's ingenuity or wide researches. Inscriptions which seemed the best to illustrate a particular point are used here, whether familiar or not. Perhaps readers may look at even those familiar stones with new interest and awareness. Needless to say, many of these are the author's favourites, which he has found especially helpful in lectures over the years.

My own interest in this branch of ancient evidence was generated by a Roman history class taught at Glasgow University by A.R.Burn, the distinguished historian of ancient Greece, and also author of *Agricola and Roman Britain* (1953) and *Roman Britain: an Anthology of Inscriptions* (1932 and 1969). Each week the class (in my time about four students) sat with copies of that massive, then newly available tome *The Roman Inscriptions of Britain* (vol. 1), which we seemed to devour almost from cover to cover as the weeks progressed; particular stones, selected apparently at random, formed the subject of special scrutiny. The great bonus was Burn's ability to make even the apparently most uninspiring text seem interesting, and to draw out its unique contribution to our understanding of the ancient world.

It is to Robin Burn, now in his eighty-ninth year, that the present volume is affectionately dedicated.†

†A.R.Burn died in Oxford on 17 June, 1991, at the age of 88.

2

THE STONECUTTER
AND HIS CRAFT

Some idea can be formed, both from ancient literary references and from the surviving end-products, of a likely sequence of events involved in the commissioning and erection of an inscribed stone.[1] Firstly could come a decision on the part of an individual or group to have a permanent record made: a tombstone, altar or commemorative plaque of some kind. Presumably the text was then written out. A fragmentary sheet of papyrus from Oxyrhynchus in Egypt may represent a draft text written in large elegant capitals (Fig. 1). It is a dedication to the emperors Diocletian and Maximian by a [*v*]*exill*(*atio*) *leg*(*ionis*) *V* *M*[*ac*(*edonicae*)]. 'A detachment of the Fifth Legion *Macedonica*.' It must be very likely that this was a text from which the stonecutter was meant to work.[2]

After drafting, the text could be taken to a stonemason's workshop or yard (an *officina*), and an appropriate design selected for the stone itself. The stonemason is likely to have had a range of semi-prepared slabs and stones available for inspection. Marble came into use in Italy in the mid second century BC, and by the middle of the first was widely used in Rome, as it often was in the provinces, especially in the East. Local limestones or sandstones were also employed. Sometimes stonemasons had to work on uncompromising or difficult surfaces of whatever stone was available; the quality of the inscription suffers as a result.

Once the text had been drafted and details of cost agreed, the stonemason set to work. The front face

of the stone, assuming that this was the area to be inscribed, was smoothed off. Next the stonemason might chisel a series of horizontal lines across the stone to mark the top and bottom of each row of lettering. Sometimes such lines are still faintly visible on the stone. Occasionally it seems that the actual letter-shapes were lightly inscribed with a chisel. More often, they were probably marked in chalk, charcoal or paint. Something of the style of the chalked or painted lettering can be carried forward into the inscribed text. This process of preparation and arrangement is now termed *ordinatio*. The lettering of the text may start large and be reduced as the lines progress; the lettering may give prominence to certain elements, for instance the name of the deceased or the emperor. Some forethought was needed, so that important details were highlighted (See Fig. 16).

In some cases considerable attention has been paid to the preparation of the surface to be inscribed, the layout of the text and the placing of individual words. We may on occasion suspect that the text was perceived aesthetically as one element in an artistic whole, rather than merely a documentary record. However, such care was not universal. Sometimes the stonemason seems to have given little thought to the overall length of each line, or the length of the inscription in relation to the space available for it. Examples of such resulting irregularity occur particularly in the provinces, where tradition and experience in stonecutting must have been less securely based. The impression is occasionally gained of the sudden realization by a stonemason, say two-thirds of the way through his task, that there was insufficient room for all that had to be inscribed. Then follows some frantic abbreviation, or the linking up of lettering ('ligaturing', below, p. 20), or reduction in letter size. Even then the inscription can still spill over on to the side or bottom margins of the slab (see for instance Fig. 16).

The Latin term for a stonecutter was a *lapicida* or *faber lapidarius*, a 'workman in stone'.[3] One of the guests at *Trimalchio's Banquet* (as reported by Petronius, writing in the mid first century AD) was Habinnas, 'a priest and a stonemason [the word used is *lapidarius*], who's very good at doing tombs'.[4] Later Trimalchio gives Habinnas detailed instructions as to the decoration of his own tomb and the inscription to be cut on it (below, p. 100). Someone who inscribed a text was a *sculptor* (sculptor) or *scriptor titulorum* (writer of texts).[5] At Pompeii a certain Aemilius Celer signed

two painted electoral notices as their *scriptor*.[6] From Philippi in northern Greece comes a series of dedications, the sponsor of which claimed on one text that he had 'smoothed down the stone at his own expense', and on another that he had 'cut back the rock-face below, and made the panel on which he wrote (*scripsit*) and carved (*sculpsit*) the names of the worshippers'.[7] At Palermo there is a remarkable bilingual text on a stone panel, in Latin and Greek, which can be interpreted as a shop-sign (Fig. 2). The Latin text reads: *Tituli/ heic/ ordinantur et/ sculpuntur/ aidibus sacreis/ cum operum publicorum.* 'Inscriptions arranged and cut here, for sacred and public buildings'. The two Latin verbs are *ordinantur* and *sculpuntur*.[8] There is another such 'sign' from Rome: 'If you need inscriptions cut for tombstones, or any sort of stonework done, this is the place!'[9] The techniques of carving and the forms of individual letters have been the subject of detailed study. Recently, at Caerleon, Gwent, Mr Richard Grasby cut a full-size replica of one of the finest inscriptions in the

1 Papyrus sheet from Oxyrhynchus, Egypt, bearing a text in honour of the emperors Diocletian and Maximian. *26 × 23cm (10½ × 9in.) AD 295–96. (Egypt Exploration Society).*

2 Slab advertising stone-cutting services in Greek and Latin, first century BC? (Museo Archeologico, Palermo, Sicily.)

Legionary Museum; much was learnt about the techniques employed by his ancient counterpart.[10]

The stonecutter of Roman times was no more immune to errors and carelessness than his counterparts through the ages. Mistakes can occur in the grammar or spelling of individual words.[11] We cannot always be certain whether the error was made by the customer, in providing or dictating a text, or by the stonecutter through his ignorance of Latin, or was the product of carelessness. Occasionally an effort has been made to correct or disguise errors, but more often they must have remained visible.

Yet we must be cautious in detecting mistakes. An unusual spelling may be a guide to the pronunciation of the age, when syllables might be slurred over, just as today. As the Latin inscriptions of the Roman world cover a time-span of many centuries, inevitably within that period there were changes in spelling, vocabulary and grammar, all of which are reflected in Latin inscriptions.

The author Sidonius Apollinaris, in a letter to his nephew written about AD 467, reports his chance discovery at Lyon that the grave of his grandfather (an important imperial administrator) had been recently disturbed (also below, p. 109).[12] His remedial measures included the provision of a new slab. 'The verse inscription to go on it I composed that night, not a very polished one, as my mind was taken up with my onward journey. However worthless, please have it cut on the stone. But watch that the mason doesn't make a mistake on the stone. When that happens the malignant reader will ascribe it to me, as either deliberately done or from carelessness, rather than to the cutter himself.'[13] There was no opportunity for proofreading and, very clearly, Sidonius was concerned above all about his own reputation.

Getting the wording right was often very important. In 52 BC we know that Pompey was agonizing over the inscription to be placed on his temple to Venus Victrix (part of the complex known as Pompey's Theatre).[14] The inscription was to report his names and achievements, ending with a reference to his 'three consulships'. Should he write COS TERTIVM or COS TERTIO? (COS is the standard abbreviation for *consul*, from an early spelling of the word, in the form *cosol*). Having received conflicting opinions from 'experts', he turned to Cicero for advice. Cicero astutely suggested abbreviating both words, to COS TERT, so avoiding offence to any whom Pompey had consulted. As a footnote to this story, Aulus Gellius records that when the wall bearing this inscription collapsed many years later, and was restored, the word TERT was at that time replaced by the numerals III.[15]

Sometimes the tools used by the stonecutter are themselves represented on the stone, as a decorative feature.[16] This is especially common on a tomb monument to a craftsman. The most common are a chisel (*scalprum*) and a hammer (*malleus*). Most frequently the letters cut are capitals, whose form develops and changes as the centuries pass (below, p. 28). Under the Roman Republic the method of chiselling was usually frontal, producing a flat-bottomed groove, but by the mid to late first century BC there was a change to oblique chiselling, producing a V-section groove, which effectively changed the style of the letters being formed.

When the cutting of the letters was complete, they were frequently painted over in red, sometimes using cinnabar (Latin, *minium*) which can survive in the crevices of the lettering. According to the Elder Pliny, '*minium* is used in books and it makes lettering more visible, both on walls and on marble, and on tomb monuments as well.'[17] The sculptured details on the stone were also sometimes painted, in a variety of colours. Today we are accustomed to seeing inscribed stones looking rather plain and grey. In some museums, the lettering has been repainted. Not all would approve of this practice (below, p. 41), but it certainly helps the reader to decipher faintly surviving letter-forms, especially on a rough surface.

Many inscriptions are carved on slabs or panels completely devoid of other decoration or ornament. Others may have the incised text enclosed within a raised border. Sometimes the inscribed area is flanked to left and right by trapezoidal side-panels called *ansae* (lit., handles); such a panel is termed 'ansate'.[18] (See Fig. 34 for a bronze panel shaped in this way.) Occasionally the stone itself may be cut to represent the trapezoidal shape;[19] more often the outlines of the *ansae* are shown in relief. This layout is likely to have been carried forward from wooden tablets, such as those depicted on the Arch of Titus (above, p. 10). The shape also allowed such a panel to be mortised into a larger structure. A variant form employed the shape of a *pelta*, a crescent-shaped shield seen in profile.[20] These devices helped also to attract the eye and concentrate the reader's attention on the text itself. The inscribed panel may also be accompanied by decorative or sculptural details carved in relief: among them will be human or animal figures, the paraphernalia of military or civic service, or religious observance (e.g. on Figs 12; 14; 46; 47).

Many museum collections today contain altars or squared-off panels which seem to have been made ready for an inscription; but the text was never inscribed. Sometimes these can be seen as spare merchandise in a stonemason's yard that was never used, or proved faulty, and was later utilized as building material. At other times we can suspect that the letters themselves were simply painted on to the face of the stone, and not cut with a chisel. Obviously this was cheaper than having the letters cut; this method had a reasonable lifespan so long as the stone was not left exposed to the elements. A link could be assumed between the standard of lettering and the amount of money the customer was prepared to spend.

On some major monuments in Rome and cities elsewhere, the inscription was made up of individually cast bronze letters with tangs to permit their attachment to stone slabs. Often, as on the Arch of Severus in Rome (Fig. 21 and see also Figs 17, 23, 31), the outlines of each letter-shape were cut into the stone blocks to provide a bedding for the bronze letters, so that the texts can be read today even though the bronze letters themselves have disappeared. In other cases, the bronze letters were attached directly against the flat surface of the façade, so that all that now remains is a sequence of holes which once facilitated their attachment.

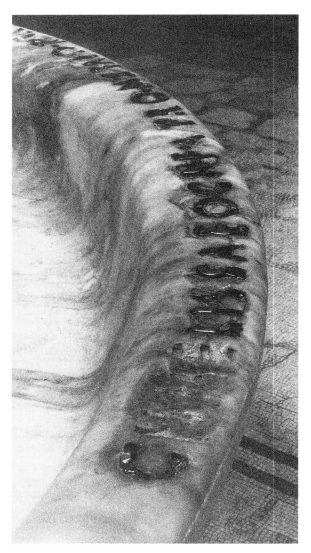

3 Bronze letters in situ, *on the lip of a marble basin, Forum Baths, Pompeii.* AD *3–4.*

However, the arrangement of the holes is often enough to reveal which letters were once placed there (below, p. 50). Sometimes the letters were gilded. The death of the emperor Augustus was said to have been foretold when the bronze or gilded bronze letter C, on an inscription below one of his statues, was struck by lightning and destroyed, leaving the letters AESAR, which meant 'god' in the Etruscan language.[21] Bronze letters could be used in other types of dedications, even on tomb monuments, for those who could afford the cost.[22] Occasionally, individual bronze letters which had become separated or had been removed from the monuments they decorated, survive in museum collections. Some surviving letters are not equipped with tangs but are perforated with nail-holes, for ease of attachment. Sometimes molten metal was poured into the inscribed letter-shapes, for added effect.[23]

It is only in the rarest of cases that the original bronze letters themselves remain *in situ*. In the Forum Baths at Pompeii is a marble basin, the rim of which bears an inscription in bronze letters recording its provision in AD 3–4 (Fig. 3).[24] Sometimes, where the original letters on a monumental façade have been lost, copies were placed in the surviving grooves during the nineteenth century, as for example, on the Pantheon (below, p. 24, Fig. 6).

3

READING
ROMAN INSCRIPTIONS

To the intending reader confronted by, or seeking out, Roman inscriptions on an archaeological site, in a museum or in one of the published collections (below, p. 36), there might seem to be a particular obstacle: the texts are inscribed in Latin. However, the task of deciphering the text need not require a university degree in the Latin language. It forms one of the present writer's annual tasks to persuade a class of archaeology students, mostly without any previous knowledge of Latin, and somewhat apprehensive of this new form of archaeological evidence with which they are expected to become rapidly familiar, to realize that the work of decipherment is not an insurmountable task. An awareness, albeit superficial, can be achieved quickly, with the aid of a list of the commonest words and abbreviations, so that they can at least determine to which general class of inscription a particular text belongs, and recover the gist of its message. However, a knowledge of Latin will always be needed if the inscription does not fall easily into a well-defined category, or if it is fragmentary, and an attempt needs to be made to restore its message.

It should be remembered too that the reading of the text is merely a first stage. The reader then has to interpret the information it preserves. This can only be achieved through a familiarity with a wide range of other epigraphic texts coupled with an awareness of the historical background and the socio-economic structure of the ancient world.

The Latin found on Roman inscriptions is often not the literary or poetic language of Cicero, Tacitus or Vergil. Indeed, even students of Latin may find an inscription intimidating or daunting. The terminology used may encompass, for example, the technical terms of the military establishment or the civil administration.

While I have claimed that a thorough knowledge of Latin is not a prerequisite for the reading of inscriptions, it is important to emphasize that a Latin inscription does not consist of a random assemblage of abbreviated Latin words, casually juxtaposed. The normal rules of Latin grammar applied. That is, the sentence will frequently start with a word in the nominative case (i.e. the subject of the sentence) or in the dative case (i.e. the person *to* or *for* whom the slab had been erected); sentences regularly end with a verb. Not every text will follow this outline, but it is important to remember that for the person erecting the text, as well as for the intended readership, the inscription was an expression of the spoken language they used every day.

THE ALPHABET

It is sensible to begin with a statement on the alphabet available to, and employed by, the Romans. It was an alphabet of 21 letters, adopted from Greek settlers in southern Italy (ABC DEFGHIKLMNOPQRSTVX).[1] To these 21 letters were later added Z and Y to express sounds in transliterated Greek words. Letters lacking in Latin were J (the consonantal version of I), U (the vocal version of V), and W. V stood for both u and v, so that the eye has to become used to words such as SERVVS for *servus* (a slave).

Most Roman inscriptions surviving on stone are written in 'Roman capitals' which are often considered to have reached their most perfect form between the reign of Augustus and that of Trajan (Fig. 4).[2] Changing styles in the carving of individual letters can be a guide to the dating of a text (below, p. 28). This type of lettering has been named *scriptura monumentalis* (script for writing on 'monuments'). It is important to remember, however, that other scripts were in use. When the medium was not the chisel but the brush, the strokes produced letters with more pronounced serifs. This form of writing is termed *scriptura actuaria* (writing for 'formal or public notices'), and predominates on painted plaster and the like. It was used also when texts were being cut on bronze panels, and came increasingly to be employed in formal texts on stone. The letters written in this way were often not square but more

upright, and narrower (see Fig. 10). For everyday, casual writing, where the writer was employing a stylus, simpler letter-forms were employed, consisting of sequences of straight and curving strokes. This script is known as 'cursive', and it is found on writing tablets, potsherds and papyri. Occasionally some letters carved in this way are found also on stone, when the stonecutter has carried forward the forms he found on a draft text written by hand.

ABBREVIATIONS

Latin inscriptions regularly make extensive use of abbreviations; that is, the words on the stone are shortened from their full grammatical forms to perhaps no more than two or three letters, even to a single letter (see Appendix 2). We too live in a world of abbreviations, acronyms and shorthand versions of words. Today we make frequent use of Latin phrases in abbreviated form such as Q.E.D. (*quod erat demonstrandum*), and more familiarly, A.D. (*anno domini*), a.m. (*ante meridiem*) and p.m. (*post meridiem*). But these phrases mostly have an origin in the Middle Ages or later, and have no

4 'Roman capitals'. The text commemorates Epaphroditus, freedman secretary to Domitian and earlier to Nero whom he helped to commit suicide in AD 68. ILS 9095. End of first century AD. (Rome, Museo Nazionale).

place either in Latin literature or Roman inscriptions.

For those setting up Roman inscriptions, the chief reason for cutting down on the length of words was often not speed or convenience, but the need to make the best use of the space available on the stone, and to maximize the information imparted on what was often quite a restricted area. Phrases which the dedicator expected would be familiar to the reader from long experience or usage could be presented in shortened form.

ROMAN NAMES

Space could be saved immediately on personal names. Under the Roman Republic every Roman had at least two names, his *praenomen* and *nomen* (forename and family name).[3] There were some 15 *praenomina* in regular use, for example M(arcus), Q(uintus), L(ucius), Cn(aeus) and Sex(tus). It can be assumed that the names Quintus and Sextus originally denoted sons who were fifth- and sixth-born, but they came to be employed indiscriminately. The *praenomen* Spurius was sometimes used of men whose birth had been illegitimate or whose fathers were not Roman citizens; tradition had it that the *praenomen* derived from the abbreviation s.p. (*sine patre*, father-less), placed after their family names in official lists.[4] Nowadays scholars are far from convinced of this argument. Less frequently employed *praenomina* include V(ibius), Ti(berius), N(umerius) and M(anius); the latter, when abbreviated, was written as *M′*, to avoid confusion with Marcus. The *praenomen* usually passed from father to eldest son.

The family name (*nomen*) was the chief distinguishing name outside the immediate family itself. Many thousands of family names are known; most end in *-ius* (e.g. Cornelius, Julius, Aelius, Aurelius), though a number of names of Etruscan or other Italic groups can have endings in *-enas*, *-enus*, *-anus* and *-ina* (e.g. Maecenas, Norbanus and Caecina).

Normally the forename (*praenomen*) and family name (*nomen*) of the individual are followed directly in an inscription by the forename of the person's father, for example in the form *M(arci) f(ilius)*, that is 'son of Marcus'. There was usually no need to repeat the *nomen* as this had already been stated; in most cases (apart from adoptions) it would remain the same. Such standard information could be reduced to the barest minimum.

Next may come the name of the voting-tribe (*tribus*) to which the person belonged. From early times Roman citizens were assigned to one of a number of tribes, eventually 35 in all, which formed the basis of voting in the assemblies of the Roman People (see Appendix 3); hence the regular description as 'voting-tribes'. As Roman power expanded, each new town was placed in one of the tribes, even though at increasing distances from Rome its citizens were less likely actually to vote in the city elections. The details of father's name and tribe were a formal part of the individual's nomenclature for legal purposes, such as a census. In the early first century AD the Popular Assemblies were abandoned; but new towns and their citizens continued to be assigned to one of the tribes, often the *tribus* of the reigning emperor, which people used on epitaphs and formal commemorative stones as evidence of their close links with Rome itself. But from the later second century AD, voting-tribes began to be omitted from inscriptions.

Next would come a surname (*cognomen*). Initially Roman citizens had not needed yet another name, but as their numbers grew it became necessary to have a method of distinguishing people in official records and in social life, so an extra name, sometimes initially a nickname, was added. The *cognomen* Scipio, for example, means 'a stick'; Cicero means a 'chickpea'. It became custom on receipt of an inheritance, or adoption, to take the names of one's benefactor, often in addition to one's own. Hence some people had a long sequence of names, especially during the Empire (see below, p. 72, for an example of such polyonymy). It was noted above that the father's *praenomen* was usually passed from father to eldest son, with other sons receiving different *praenomina*. However, from the early first century AD, it became common for the same *praenomen* to be given to all sons, who were distinguishable from each other by their different *cognomina*. A good example here is the emperor Vespasian and his family: Vespasian himself was T. Flavius Vespasianus, the *cognomen* deriving from his mother, Vespasia Polla. Vespasian's elder son bore the same names T. Flavius Vespasianus. (We know him better as the emperor Titus.) The younger son was T.Flavius Domitianus, with the *cognomen* here deriving from the name of his mother, Domitilla, the wife of Vespasian. In many families where our knowledge of relationships is inevitably incomplete, we cannot know whether the *cognomina* were selected for reasons of family tradition or at the whim of the parents.[5]

WOMEN AND SLAVES

The above guidelines refer specifically to males. Roman society, like so many others, was male-dominated, a situation reflected in the names of women and methods used to describe them. Women were not normally given a *praenomen*, but were known by a feminine form of the family name of their father; for instance Cicero's daughter was named Tullia from her father's *nomen* Tullius; Julius Caesar's daughter was called Julia. Most women had a *cognomen* too; sometimes the father's surname was transmitted in a feminine form; for instance the daughter of a Caecilius Metellus would be known as Caecilia Metella. This was obvious, clear, and satisfied family honour. When the girl married, she retained her name, and to it was added her husband's name in the genitive case – she now 'belonged' to him legally; so Caecilia Metella on marriage became *Caecilia Metella Crassi* (Caecilia Metella, of Crassus). Her husband, Marcus Licinius Crassus, was a son of Caesar's triumviral partner. (For her tomb monument on the *Via Appia*, see below, p. 102 and Fig. 63). Under the Empire husbands and wives can be found with the same *nomen*. This could result from the circumstance that the wife was a freed slave of the husband. Alternatively both might be freed slaves of the same master, or the descendants of such slaves. There seem to have been no regular words for Mr, Miss or Mrs, which were placed ahead of an individual name; but *domine* was employed in correspondence as a word for 'Sir' (see below, p. 125), when someone of superior rank or status was being addressed.

It is possible to read too much into an individual's names. Notice in this context a letter (of the second century AD) in Greek written home by an Egyptian called Apion, newly enlisted in the Roman fleet at Misenum on the Bay of Naples. 'As soon as I came to Misenum (home port of the fleet), I received my "expenses" of three gold coins from Caesar . . . My name is now Antonius Maximus.'[6] We cannot know why these names were chosen; at least it is clear that he had not been enfranchised by an M.Antonius or another member of this noble Roman family.

Slaves had a single name, given by a slave-dealer or their masters at birth or on acquisition, which was often retained for life. The names were frequently patronising like those given, in another age, in the American South. The owner's name followed, in the genitive case. If a male slave was given freedom – this was fairly common – he normally took the *praenomen* and *nomen* of his former master, in addition to his existing surname; so if a slave Verecundus was freed by a Marcus Favonius, he might become *M.Favonius M(arci) l(ibertus) Verecundus* – 'Marcus Favonius Verecundus, freedman of Marcus'; this is a known individual (see below, p. 81). If the slave had been freed by a woman, he adopted the notation Ɔ LIB i.e. *G(aiae) lib(ertus)*. The reversed C served as an abbreviation for Gaia, a female form of Gaius.[7] Gaia was not in use as a *praenomen*, but was a standard legal notation for 'a woman'. If a slave had served in the household of a Roman emperor, he would take the emperor's *nomen*; thus a slave of Trajan (M.Ulpius Trajanus), called Pacatus, became M.Ulpius Pacatus. He would not be known as *M.Ulpius M(arci) lib(ertus) Pacatus*, as of a private individual M.Ulpius, but *M. Ulpius Aug(usti) lib(ertus) Pacatus*, 'freedman of the emperor'.

Freeborn non-citizens in the Roman world, if enfranchised, took their patron's names or the emperor's. The client king Cogidubnus in Britain, enfranchised by the emperor Claudius or by Nero, became Ti(berius) Claudius Cogidubnus.[8]

Sometimes an inscription, if an epitaph, will offer no further information about an individual, beyond his place of origin and perhaps age at death (see p. 106). Occasionally, a profession or trade will be mentioned, or details of army service or a post in the Empire's administration. Here too abbreviation was particularly common (below, p. 78, 82).

LIGATURES, WORD-DIVISIONS AND ACCENTS

We have seen how space can be saved by abbreviating family names. It could also be saved by linking letters together, a procedure known as ligaturing. Mostly this was done to economize on space, but might also serve an artistic or aesthetic purpose. Three, four or even five letters could be run together; one letter can even be placed inside another.[9]

The divisions between words could be marked by dots, triangular incisions or, more elaborately, by ivy-leaf designs (*hederae*),[10] which can themselves become distinctive decorative motifs. These dots were placed not at the bottom of the line, as with our full stops, but were set halfway up the height of the letters. There was otherwise no punctuation, or the use of commas. One sentence followed another without any special notation, though the reader could be alerted by gaps left on the stone, a line division or the placing of verbs. On longer legal documents fresh paragraphs or sub-sections may be indicated by allowing the first word or part of it to project to the left.

The practice of using accents over some vowels, to indicate that they are long, may be mentioned. These accents (known as *apices*, sing., *apex*)[11] were usually slanted lines, like today's acute accents, though sometimes the line could be curving rather than straight. A 'long' I was sometimes indicated by lengthening the vertical stroke, so that it projected above the other letters (see Fig. 58, line 4) but some stonecutters used a tall letter 'I' merely for decorative effect.[12] Occasionally a sign similar to the acute accent or sometimes one shaped like a little sickle (and thus termed a *sicilicus*) was placed above a consonant to indicate that it was 'double' e.g. *oŝa* was written for *ossa* (bones), or *serŝs* for *servus* (a slave). Such markings form a rough guide to pronunciation, but great care needs to be exercised. (For the limited value of such notation towards dating inscriptions, see below, p. 28f.)

NUMERALS

If words could be abbreviated, so also could numbers, especially large numbers. Costs and distances are regularly mentioned in Roman inscriptions. A system was developed for expressing large numbers briefly. There were just seven symbols in everyday use: I (one), V (5), X (10), L (50), C (100), D (500) and ∞ (1000). There was no symbol for zero. Some symbols were adopted from Greek: L (evidently a form of the Greek χ) for 50

and ∞ (from the Greek Φ) for 1000. We are familiar with the modern use of M (abbreviated from *mille*) for 1000, but this was not used by the Romans in combination with other numerals. The thousand-sign (∞) was cut in half to produce a D, which served as the notation for 500. Similarly, the sign C for 100, which we might easily suppose was an abbreviation from *centum* (100), is thought to derive from Greek θ. Numerals were grouped in ways we would find familiar today, e.g. VIIII (as well as IX) for 9, LXIII (63) and so on; just occasionally there are some less familiar combinations, such as IIIIV for 9 (not $5-4=1$), and IIXX for 22, where addition is to be preferred to subtraction.[13] A bar across the top of a group of numerals may indicate multiplication by one thousand, e.g. $\overline{\text{III}} = 3000$. Since numerals occur in connection with indications of the cost of a monument, it is convenient here to consider the abbreviations for monetary values. The brass *sestertius* was indicated by the symbols IIS (i.e. II + *semis*, two-and-a-half bronze *asses*, a value it had before the end of the second century BC, though not later), with a horizontal bar across the middle of the first two numerals, to produce HS or (more confusingly) HS. The silver *denarius* was indicated by $\times$ (i.e. ten *asses*); the horizontal bar across the middle distinguished it from the letter X.[14] Numbers can also be written out as words.

FRAGMENTARY INSCRIPTIONS

The task of reading Latin inscriptions may be further complicated by the fact that many do not survive intact. The reuse of stone panels in later buildings, or some deliberate or accidental damage over the centuries (below, p. 30) may result in the survival of only a few words or lines, with the consequent loss of part of the message. Museums normally display only complete stones, or the most interesting, or the largest items they cannot put in store; such selectivity may not be obvious to the visitor.

Sometimes the information on a worn or missing portion of a stone may be lost forever, or at least until another part of the slab is discovered. At other times the information that does survive may be enough to allow a fairly confident restoration of at least some of the missing elements. This is one of the chief activities of the epigraphist, and requires knowledge of parallel or similar texts, enabling him to attempt a restoration. A knowledge of Latin grammar and vocabulary will be essential here. Sometimes such restorations have been proved correct by the subsequent discoveries of further fragments of the same inscription; at other times restorations may be thought hazardous, and have been shown to be wrong.

ERASURE OF LETTERS IN ANTIQUITY

There are some inscriptions where the loss of some part of the text is due not so much to damage over the centuries as to deliberate erasure in Roman times. This took place particularly after the death of an unpopular emperor who had suffered *damnatio memoriae* at the decision of the Senate.[15] Orders were given to erase his names from monuments and destroy any statues, or alter the portrait head. We must imagine that some inscriptions were removed from public view. In the University Museum at Philadelphia is a substantial slab once reporting road-building at Pozzuoli in Italy in the reign of the emperor Domitian. After his death in AD 96 the text was chiselled out. The slab soon found another use, with the reverse side turned to the front, as part of a sculptured frieze showing soldiers of the Praetorian Guard.[16]

Such erasing was not peculiar to the Romans: Egyptian pharaohs similarly caused hieroglyphic inscriptions of their predecessors to be erased or emended. The practice did not end with antiquity. It is still possible to see, in Italy and in coastal areas of Yugoslavia formerly ruled by Italy, inscriptions cut during the fascist era, which have been partly erased, with the removal of reference to the 'regnal years' of Mussolini as *Duce*.

Not only emperors and the imperial family were so treated. Prominent senators and governors, driven to suicide or disgraced after attempted rebellion or the suspicion of it, could suffer a similar fate. Dedications in honour of a cult might be defaced and even a legion could be 'damned'.[17] We may imagine that some inscriptions which were no longer acceptable, for whatever reason, were simply destroyed, if the panels could be detached from buildings and taken down. Often we have to remain unaware of the reason for disfigurement. One inscription can be cut on top of another; presumably red paint emphasized the revised version. The original inscription may be only partially erased, so that its wording can still be made out.

5 Gravestone in form of an altar, built into a building-frontage, Benevento, Italy. It commemorated Marcus Gavius Sabinus and his wife Nasennia Justa (CIL IX 1646). Second century AD.

6 Pantheon, Campus Martius, Rome. 27–25 BC, but completely rebuilt under Hadrian.

On tombstones commemorating several people the names of individuals can be erased. Where the inscription on a tomb or gravestone had been prepared in advance, we could think of family quarrels, or divorce; or the explanation may sometimes be that an individual was buried elsewhere.

THE MAIN CATEGORIES OF INSCRIPTION

When endeavouring to read a Roman inscription one may begin by establishing first of all the general category to which the text belongs. A number of major categories can be easily identified. These include: (1) Laws, treaties and other public documents, often on bronze panels. (2) Building inscriptions – texts commemorating the construction of some edifice. (3) Commemorative inscriptions, in honour of an individual, often placed on the front of a statue base. (4) Altars and religious dedications. (5) Gravestones.

Building inscriptions often name the emperor or the local magistrate who had authorized or overseen the construction work. Very often the text does not specify what was constructed; as the slab was normally erected on or beside a building, this was obvious enough. The texts on an altar or a bronze plaque attached to some offering at a temple, are likely to begin with the name of the god or goddess being venerated, and could end with some version of the formula *votum solvit laetus libens merito* (gladly, willingly and deservedly fulfilled his vow), normally abbreviated to the distinctive V S L L M. (below, p. 93). Gravestones and other funerary monuments may begin with the words *Dis Manibus*, 'to the Spirits of the Departed', abbreviated to D M, (below, p. 107); or end with the statement *Hic Situs Est* ('here he lies'), often abbreviated to H S E. The inscription may also include the age at death.

Sometimes the shape of the stone identifies it as belonging to one of these categories. If the slab is rectangular or square, and of no great thickness, it may well record the completion of some building or the achievements of an individual (see Fig. 9). If the stone is in the form of a squat, squared-off base with decorative architectural motifs at the top, it is perhaps an altar (below, p. 93 and Fig. 59). If the axis is vertical and the slab is fairly thin, it could be a gravestone (e.g. Fig. 48).

These categories, assigned according to the shape of the stone, may seem distinct and distinctive, but they are not exclusive and can be misleading. Milestones, with their distinctive columnar shape, belong among 'building stones'. A plain rectangular slab, with details of an individual's career, or bearing the names of a family and their freedmen, may have come from a tomb. Often a gravestone takes the form of a small altar (Fig. 5); on a grand scale, we can point to the tomb of Julius Classicianus, procurator of Britain, found in London (below, p. 77 and Fig. 44). What the inscription says will thus be a more valid indicator of its purpose than the shape of the stone on which it is inscribed.

The Pantheon, in the Campus Martius at Rome (Fig. 6), is a temple to 'all the Gods'. It bears a text recording its construction, which reads: *M(arcus) Agrippa L(uci) f(ilius) co(n)s(ul) tertium fecit.*[18] 'Marcus Agrippa, son of Lucius, consul three times, built (it)'. The inscription belongs in the second of the categories outlined above. If the structure itself had not survived, but only the slabs bearing the text, or some of them, we should not have been able to guess what was being commemorated.

4

DATING ROMAN INSCRIPTIONS

It will become clear that some inscriptions are capable of close dating by the information they contain; hence they are of particular value towards the dating of an archaeological site, or of a building whose erection they commemorate or the career of a particular individual.

However, very few inscriptions themselves bear an exact date, to the nearest day, month, or year, as we might expect to see today on the commemorative slabs in the walls of our Town Halls or Public Baths. Even tombstones, a category where we could suppose that exact information would have been important to the family and heirs, usually have no date. (But see below, p. 122.) This is not because the Roman world lacked an exact calendar or the means of expressing a date closely in relatively brief compass. The Roman calendar, of twelve months, originally began in March, hence *September* (the seventh month), etc. Later, at a rather uncertain date, the starting-point was changed, so that the year began in January. The names used for each month are familiar, except that until 44 BC the seventh month (originally the fifth) was known as *Quinctilis* (see Fig. 60), and until 8 BC the eighth month (originally the sixth) was known as *Sextilis*. The former was renamed *Julius* and the latter *Augustus*, in honour of Julius Caesar and Rome's first emperor. The individual months were divided into units according to the moon's phases, by reference to the *Kalends* (first day of month), the *Nones* (fifth or seventh day) and the *Ides* (thirteenth or fifteenth day); specific days were identified as being so many days before the Kalends, Nones or Ides, as appropriate. Naming individual days on a seven-day cycle is not attested before the Early Empire.

In the Roman world, each year was known primarily by the names of the two senators elected consuls at Rome. This form of dating can appear on inscriptions. The date was also calculated 'from the foundation of the city' (*ab urbe conditā*, abbreviated to A V C) which might have seemed a fairly easy method of calculation and conveniently expressible on stone. But this method is found only rarely.

A list of consuls inscribed at Rome down to the end of Augustus' reign survives in a fragmentary condition; it is known as the *Fasti Consulares*. The listings were resumed in more recent times, with nowadays the name of the Mayor (Sindaco) of Rome being added each year. Names of consuls survive too on calendars publicly displayed in individual towns. Some towns reckoned years in an 'era' which began from a mythical or known foundation date, and used the names of their own chief magistrates to identify the year. The phrase A.D. (*anno domini*) was not employed until the Middle Ages; the abbreviation B.C. (Before Christ) is modern.

We can also calculate dates under the Roman Empire from the names of the incumbent emperor, the known dates of his reign, and the details of his

7 Column of Antoninus Pius, Rome, showing modern bronze letters. AD 161–69. (Vatican Museums.)

titles and powers (see also below, p. 42). As an example, notice the inscribed base of the now destroyed Column of Antoninus Pius at Rome (Fig. 7). The text reads:

Divo Antonino Aug(usto) Pio | Antoninus Augustus et | Verus Augustus filii.[1] 'To the deified Antoninus Augustus Pius, his sons Antoninus Augustus and Verus Augustus'.

Antoninus Pius died in AD 161, so that the erection of the Column should belong soon after, during the joint reigns of his adopted sons Marcus Aurelius (here called by his adoptive father's name) and Lucius Verus, or at any rate before the latter's death in AD 169.

Towards even more exact dating, particularly valuable information is provided by the number of times the emperor had held the power of a tribune (*tribunicia potestas*), which was conferred on an annual basis. For most emperors of the first century AD, the tribunician power was renewed annually on the date of accession, but from the end of the first century most emperors, whatever the exact date of accession, had the tribunician power renewed on 10 December, the traditional day on which the tribunes of the Roman Republic came into office; thereafter a new emperor would be given the designation *tribuniciā potestate II* (and so on). Further precision may be possible when this designation of tribunician power is combined with a specification of the number of imperial salutations accepted. The latter (see also below, p. 45) can sometimes be closely datable, and on occasion they can be linked to a particular victory or event. The emperor Titus, according to the historian Dio, took his fifteenth salutation for Agricola's victories in Britain; the date is the second half of AD 79, but scholars are still arguing over which campaign was being commemorated.[2]

Reference to the number of consulships held by the emperor is also a helpful indicator. For example, Hadrian was consul for a second time (COS II) in AD 118 and a third time (COS III) in 119, but never held the office again, so that for the remainder of his reign until 138, inscriptions report him as COS III. Such a designation does not mean that the inscription was erected in the year 119, only that this was the number of consulships he had held up until the moment when the inscription was set up. In many cases, using such evidence, a fairly detailed chronology can be worked out for an emperor's reign.

It should be emphasized, however, that such evidence as this usually only serves to date some

IMP·VESP·VIIII·T·IMP·VII·COS·CN·IVL

O·AGRICOLA·LEC·AVG·PR·PR

8 Lead waterpipe, Chester, England. AD 79.
(Grosvenor Museum, Chester.)

construction work authorized or financed by the emperor. We seldom find such terminology used merely to *date* a dedication or gravestone. Occasionally inscriptions report that the text was inscribed in a certain year of the emperor's reign (below, p. 116); but the practice was evidently not widespread. The use of the consuls' names, or those of local magistrates, remained the official method; for example, sections of lead waterpipes from Chester (Fig. 8) bear a consular date for AD 79 and the name of Julius Agricola as Britain's Roman governor. The text reads: *Imp(eratore) Vesp(asiano)* $\overline{VIIII}$ *T(ito) imp(eratore)* $\overline{VII}$ *co(n)s(ulibus) Cn(aeo) Iulio Agricola leg(ato) Aug(usti) pr(o)*

pr(aetore).[3] 'In the ninth consulship of the emperor Vespasian and in the seventh of Titus, *imperator*, while Gnaeus Julius Agricola was legate of the emperor with the powers of a praetor'. The most familiar information, the names of Vespasian and his son Titus, is abbreviated to a minimum, while Agricola's names are written out.

DIFFICULTIES IN DATING

If an inscription names an emperor without additional information, the most that can be achieved is to date the inscription within his reign, which could be a period of twenty years or more. Building inscriptions from the provinces often

9 Building record from Hotbank milecastle, Hadrian's Wall. AD 122–24. (Museum of Antiquities, Newcastle.)

mention not only the emperor, but also the name of a governor whose tenure can sometimes be fixed fairly closely. A splendid example comes from a milecastle on the line of Hadrian's Wall (Fig. 9). The text reads:

Imp(eratoris) Caes(aris) Traiani | Hadriani Aug(usti) | leg(io) II̅ Aug(usta) | A(ulo) Platorio Nepote leg(ato) pr(o) pr(aetore).[4] 'Of the emperor Caesar Traianus Hadrianus Augustus, the legion II *Augusta* (*built this*), while Aulus Platorius Nepos was legate with powers of a praetor.'

A.Platorius Nepos held office in Britain between 122 and 124 AD (below, p. 72f).

But many, indeed most, Latin inscriptions do not offer any direct clues to dating, and recourse has to be made to other methods. Some hint may come from the information contained in the inscription itself; for example a soldier may mention a particular war in which he was decorated. In the specialized field of military inscriptions (below, p. 80ff.), the name of the army unit may offer a clue to dating, in that its various postings in the provinces of the Empire may be securely known.

The name of the dedicator or deceased may itself offer clues. For example, a man whose names begin with T.Flavius could well belong to a family who were given citizenship by Vespasian or one of his sons in the later first century AD (but see below, p. 129); here at least is a terminus post quem for the dedication. Similarly, a man with the names P.Aelius or T.Aelius is likely to have gained citizenship (or to belong to a family which gained it) under Hadrian (P.Aelius Hadrianus) or Antoninus (T.Aelius Hadrianus Antoninus, after adoption) respectively. Many citizens of the third century and beyond have names beginning M.Aurelius. Some will owe citizenship to the emperor Marcus Aurelius, but more are likely to have acquired that status when Caracalla (officially M.Aurelius Antoninus Pius) granted citizenship to the great majority of freeborn males in the Empire in AD 212 (below, p. 129).

The presence or absence of certain information, for instance reference to a father's name or voting-tribe, may be some indicator of date, such information often being omitted from the second century AD onwards. On tombstones, the use of the phrase H S E (*hic situs est*, he lies here) usually indicates a date before the end of the first century AD, whereas the appearance of *Dis Manibus* suggests a date not before the middle of the first century AD and more probably in the second or third centuries AD (below, p. 107).

LETTERS OF THE ALPHABET

Scrutiny of the lettering itself can lead to tentative conclusions on dating. It is common to observe four main phases in the carving of Latin inscriptions. Firstly 'archaic', from the earliest surviving inscriptions of the sixth century BC, often using letter-forms close to those used by the Greeks (with some texts written *boustrophedon*, having the lines inscribed alternately from right to left and left to right). The number of surviving inscriptions which can be placed in this category is very small.[5] Secondly 'Republican', from the fifth/fourth to the later first centuries BC, using squat capitals (e.g. Fig. 60). Thirdly 'early imperial', using shaded capitals, common in Rome itself under Augustus but percolating more slowly to outlying regions in Italy and to the provinces (see Fig. 4). Finally 'late imperial', where letters may include some which resemble the more flowing forms derived from writing with a pen or brush, and including quite elaborate serifs (above, p. 18). Such lettering is particularly associated with the third century and after, but it can be seen on much earlier monuments (Fig. 10). These categories may be useful as a preliminary guide to dating, but they are not clear cut and must not be thought of as constituting a definitive scheme.

Examination of the way some individual letters are carved can also offer clues to dating, though once again caution is advised. The use of a long I, or the presence or absence of the *apex* accent (see p. 21), has been remarked upon. The use of an 'unclosed' P (deriving from the Greek pi) has sometimes been considered as offering a terminus ante quem of (about) the end of the Julio-Claudian period, but it can continue to be 'open' until much later (Figs. 4, 16). It is more useful, when dating a particular text, to study it in the context of other inscriptions from the same locality or general geographical area, rather than in isolation, or by reference only to (say) inscriptions from Rome itself.

10 Statue base in honour of L. Saevinius Proculus, who governed a succession of provinces in the later second century AD. (AE 1969–70, 601). Ankara, Turkey.

The emperor Claudius, a respected scholar and historian, ordered three new letters to be added to the existing 23 of the Latin alphabet, to represent sounds which he felt were not already catered for.[6] These were Ⅎ to serve as a short 'u' (in place of 'y') in words of Greek origin (such as *Aegyptus*, Egypt); a reversed and upside-down F to serve as the consonantal V (the Greek digamma); and Ↄ to serve as PS or BS (the Greek psi). Suetonius notes that these new letters 'were still to be found in lots of books, in the daily gazette and on monumental inscriptions'.[7] The first two letters are indeed found on surviving inscriptions of Claudius' time, and so permit the texts to be closely dated;[8] but the new letter-forms never became universal, even within Claudius' reign, and were soon dropped. We must applaud Claudius' desire to fill gaps in the alphabet, though the signs themselves now strike us as strange.

The spelling of individual words can be a guide to dating, for example 'archaic' spellings and case endings which had gone out of use by the time of the rich flowering of Latin literature from the first century BC onwards.[9] In the ensuing centuries of the Roman Empire, we see the growing influence of Late Latin forms also manifesting itself on inscribed texts.[10]

It may seem obvious that inscriptions could also be datable by consideration of the architectural and sculptural style and ornament of the building they once adorned or still adorn. Often this approach can offer valuable clues, but again caution is advisable. The Pantheon bears a famous inscription recording its construction by Marcus Agrippa (see Fig. 6 and above, p. 24); but the building itself was wholly reconstructed under Hadrian, and it seems probable that the text was recut then.[11] The eastern architrave of the Parthenon in Athens bore a Greek inscription in honour of Nero. No one would suppose that it was built in his reign![12] Alexander the Great offered funds to the people of Ephesus to complete the construction of the gigantic Temple to Artemis (Diana), if his name could be inscribed on the buildings; but the Ephesians refused.[13]

Therefore it must be admitted that many Latin inscriptions cannot be accurately dated. Sometimes we can say no more than that a particular text should belong, for example, in the first or second centuries AD, or in the third or fourth centuries AD. If the inscription has been recovered during an excavation, the archaeological context may serve to date the inscription, rather than (as often averred) vice versa.

5

THE SURVIVAL OF ROMAN INSCRIPTIONS

Well before the end of antiquity, it is clear, many inscribed stones had been taken down or reused; many were probably destroyed when the buildings which they had commemorated and adorned became disused or dangerous and had to be demolished, or when they were destroyed by fire or other disaster: sack, earthquake or flood. Some altars in the provinces had but a short lifespan: those to Jupiter erected by a military unit might be replaced after a single year, and buried. Inscriptions on wood or other non-durable materials would be easily lost; those on bronze would be particularly liable to be melted down in times of crisis.

Inscribed stone slabs could be reused, with a second text superimposed on the first, or placed on what had been the rear face. A good example of such economy is that milestones often bear a second inscription testifying to later repairs to the road; or they might even be up-ended with an inscription set on the portion which had formerly been hidden in the ground.[1]

The progressive deterioration of monuments, especially tombs, was something already remarked upon in antiquity. Cicero mentions that when *quaestor* in charge of the financial management of the Roman province of Sicily in 75 BC, he went in search of the grave at Syracuse of the famous mathematician Archimedes who had been killed there in 212 BC.[2] The tomb had been forgotten and neglected, almost hidden by undergrowth. Cicero had the brushwood cleared away, and was able to read about half the inscription, the rest being 'eaten away'. Ausonius in a fourth-century poem writes: 'Are we to be surprised that men are forgotten? The stones decay, and death comes to the stones and the names on them'.[3]

REUSE OF INSCRIBED STONES IN ANTIQUITY

Sometimes inscribed stones were reused as building material without any concern shown for the fact that they represented formal mementoes of past labours. Inscribed slabs could be cut up to suit a new employment: some gravestones at Ostia found a new use as toilet seats.[4] At Caesarea a dedicatory slab erected by Pontius Pilate for a *Tiberieum*, or Tiberius-cult centre, was reused face down in a fourth century reconstruction of the theatre (below, p. 76). On Hadrian's Wall two large panels recording reconstruction of Birdoswald under Severus and Caracalla (AD 205–6) and Diocletian and Maximian (c. 297) were both reused, one of them face downwards, as flooring of a barrack block when it was rebuilt for the final time in or soon after AD 367 (Fig. 11).[5]

From the early third century AD onwards the onset of troubled times meant that townspeople turned their thoughts to the provision of defensive town-walls where none had existed before or were long disused. As cemeteries lay immediately beyond the town limits, monuments and grave slabs formed a ready source of raw material for the construction work that had urgently to be taken in hand.[6] For example, at Chester nearly a hundred tombstones of soldiers of the legions II *Adiutrix* (the garrison in AD 77–86) and XX *Valeria* (the garrison from 86 onwards into the fourth century), as well as of auxiliary soldiers and some civilians, who had been buried outside the fortress ramparts to the north, were incorporated, along with other material, into a reconstruction of the walls in the later third century.[7] Similarly, at Apamea in Syria, grave slabs of legion II *Parthica* erected in the early third century AD were re-employed a few generations later in walls constructed against the invading Persians.[8] The deconsecrated church of Notre Dame de Lamourguier at Narbonne now houses over 1300 inscribed and sculptured Roman panels, most of which had been reused in the medieval walls of the town, which were dismantled in the nineteenth century.

In London, the substantial monument commemorating the procurator Julius Classicianus, which belongs in the mid first century AD, was broken up to provide building material for a fourth-century bastion; presumably it had formerly stood fairly close by (below, p. 77). Other bastions in London incorporated reused stonework, and in 1975 parts of a third century monumental archway were found built into the fourth-century riverside wall of the city.[9]

Monuments themselves acquired a new role: tombs and other large structures were sometimes made into fortresses (below, p. 32). Augustus' mausoleum at Rome served, at various times, as a fortress, an amphitheatre used for bull-fighting and a concert hall, into the twentieth century. Temples might have a new lifespan as Christian churches (below, p. 91–2), though the dedicatory inscriptions may have been erased or covered over.

The reuse of gravestones may seem to us deplorable, but despite laws, pleas and curses against disturbance of graves (below, p. 108–9), the practice was evidently widespread. In our own stable society graveyards can be swept away within a generation or two of use. A newspaper report in the 1970s spoke of gravestones of British soldiers on the North-West frontier being reused as house-building material in Afghanistan.

Throughout the Middle Ages and beyond,

Roman inscribed stones formed a valuable source of building material, along with the mass of squared stonework from now disused and abandoned buildings. A gravestone at Mainz, which incorporates a familiar scene of an auxiliary cavalryman riding down a barbarian opponent (see below, p. 82) was hollowed out in Frankish times to serve as a sarcophagus. Another gravestone depicting a legionary in full armour served as its lid.[10] The twelfth-century bell-tower of the cathedral at Gaeta near Formia (southern Lazio) is a hotchpotch of reused stonework, which derives from nearby tombs, like that of Lucius Sempronius

11 *Late fourth-century barracks at Birdoswald fort, Hadrian's Wall, during excavation, 1929. The photograph shows a group of archaeologists and visitors to the site, in a mock-sacrifice at an 'altar'. Reused in the paving below their feet are RIB 1909 and 1912, which commemorated earlier phases of construction work. Left to right: Mr J.Charlton; Prof. Eric Birley; Mr R.Turner; Mr F.G.Simpson; Mr H.S.Addison; Dr K.Stade; Prof. S.Applebaum; Prof. R.G.Collingwood. (I.A.Richmond, reproduced by courtesy of Durham University Journal.)*

12 Inscribed and sculptured stones employed in the construction of the cathedral bell-tower (left) and the Rocca dei Rettori (right), Benevento, Italy.

Atratinus (consul 34 BC), the foundations of whose circular tomb are still visible. On the hill above the town a similar monument to Lucius Munatius Plancus (consul 42 BC) and his family survives more or less intact, through serving as a medieval fortress and, more recently, as a naval semaphore station from 1885 onwards. It was bombed as a strongpoint during the Second World War.[11]

Several tombstones, inscriptions and an unpublished relief showing military decorations can be espied high up in the thirteenth-century bell tower of the cathedral at Benevento (Fig. 12), which (unlike most of the cathedral itself) survived wartime bombing in 1943; similarly, the Rocca dei Rettori, overlying one of the town's Roman gates, is a mass of Roman stonework, evidently available in bulk from adjacent cemeteries when the tower was built in 1321. Many other examples could be adduced of this common practice. For the builders such stonework was raw material to be utilized as required.

In some cases rather more deliberate reuse of Roman stonework can be identified: at Trieste, an upright gravestone to the Barbius family was sawn vertically into two parts, and used as the two orthostats on either side of the main (west) door of the fourteenth-century cathedral of S. Giusto (Fig. 13).[12] The two halves of the slab were 'swopped' over to give a neatly dressed edge against which the doors could be hung. As seen now there appear to be three busts ranged vertically to either side, but closer scrutiny and a reading of the accompanying Latin texts show that the sawing process has all but

removed a third (central) bust in each register. One female head (bottom right on Fig. 13) had been refashioned as a military saint, presumably S. Giusto (St Just) himself, holding the halberd symbol of Trieste and with divine fire issuing from his head.

INSCRIPTIONS AS 'CURIOSITIES'

From the Middle Ages onwards slabs were built into later constructions, to their ornament and decoration, either quite intentionally enhancing the appeal of the new structure, or as a deliberate act to ensure their preservation.[13] Stones became the subject of legend, and a source of pride. Beside the west door of the crusader church at Abu Ghosh in Palestine, on the Jerusalem–Jaffa road, is a rectangular slab mentioning building work by the legion X *Fretensis*; it should testify to a military post nearby.[14] Stones discovered on the land of a rural estate frequently found their way to the country house at its centre. Rather later, owners deliberately sought out and collected stones as evidence of their own antiquarian interests. For example, at Sir Walter Scott's house at Abbotsford, stone reliefs from Penrith and an inscription

13 Graveslab cut in half vertically, now flanking the west door of the cathedral, Trieste, Italy. Early Empire. (Dr R.A.Knox.)

possibly from the Antonine Wall are incorporated into the walled garden.[15] The collection itself includes a small altar, perhaps from Italy; it is seemingly unpublished. These often substantial private assemblages form the basis of many modern museum collections. Indeed the practice of acquiring and displaying stonework of Roman, medieval or later ages still flourishes. With the rediscovery of classical antiquities at the Renaissance, inscriptions, altars and tombs were included in paintings, prints and other works of art. This awakening of interest, however, encouraged forgeries (below, p. 133).

INSCRIPTIONS LOST AND FOUND

The total number of inscriptions surviving today may be reckoned at over 300,000. Publication (see below, p. 36ff.) often lags behind discovery. There are few Italian museums where the informed visitor may not chance upon unreported material. The number of stones which are newly dug up, noticed or reported on each year must be in excess of 1000. Yet there is an opposite process too. The editors of the great *Corpus of Latin Inscriptions* in the later nineteenth century (below, p. 36) could not locate all the stones to which earlier antiquarians and clerics had referred. Some had disappeared from view. Similarly, not all the stones reported in the *Corpus* can be found now. Some have simply changed location and may yet survive, but we have to take into account accidental or even deliberate destruction over the generations down to the Second World War and indeed to the present day. As an example of the loss of material in the present century, some part of the collection housed in the Landesmuseum Mainz was reduced to fragments by wartime bombing, even though protected by sand.

It is difficult to estimate what proportion the surviving collections represent of all those originally erected. One study has suggested that we have available about 5 per cent of dedications to provincial priests in North Africa, erected between the later first and mid third centuries AD.[16] It is unlikely that this percentage offers a general guide to survival rates elsewhere, where different social and economic pressures applied and the practice of erecting inscribed stones was less well entrenched for so long. More than likely 5 per cent is a higher

than average survival rate. If it were applied to the Roman world as a whole, the total volume of those originally erected would be about 6,000,000!

It is clear that survival rates must differ enormously according to region and province, the circumstances of erection and reuse of the stones, and the alertness of local antiquarians over many centuries. On the Antonine Wall, perhaps one third of all the commemorative distance slabs erected to mark its construction have survived, largely because at the close of the brief history of the Wall's use, they were seemingly taken down and deliberately buried, to be found again during ploughing in much more recent times. Thus they were denied to those who would have destroyed, damaged or re-utilized them over the centuries. On Hadrian's Wall, it is assumed that the building of each of the 46 stone milecastles was commemorated under Hadrian by two inscribed stones, one erected over each gateway. Of these, six at most have survived.[17]

At Šempeter in Slovenia (Yugoslavia) elaborate tomb-monuments, erected beside the road from Ljubljana (Emona) to Celje (Celeia) in the mid second century AD, fell into the stream bed of the nearby River Sava as its banks eroded in the mid third century, and were covered by silt and sand until rediscovered in 1952–56.[18] They have now been re-erected nearby (Fig. 14). Further east along the same road, similar monuments remained safe from the waters, but were robbed at the end of antiquity; only their foundations now survive.

After the bell-tower of St Mark's, Venice, collapsed on the morning of 11 July, 1902, a funerary inscription in honour of the military tribune Lucius Ancharius was found amid stonework in its base. The stone must have come from a nearby town, probably Este or Padua, before the eleventh century. After the bell-tower was rebuilt, the slab was taken for safety to the nearby cloister of S. Apollonia, where it is now displayed.[19]

In Britain too stones have been walled up or used as building material. A stone naming legion XX was recently discovered built into Gloucester Cathedral; presumably it had been there since the fifteenth century.[20] Similarly in Carlisle a large altar, erected in the early third century by a tribune of legion XX, was seen during a recent survey of the stonework of Carlisle Castle.[21]

An altar to Silvanus, god of the woodland, reported in about 1620 to the antiquarian William Camden as being walled up, or perhaps displayed at, Kilsyth Castle (in central Scotland) disappeared from view when the Castle was blown up by Cromwellian troops in 1650. Much later the lower half was found again during excavation of the castle in 1976.[22]

From the city of Rome over 40,000 inscriptions are known. Among other major collections are those at Ostia (over 10,000), Salona (about 7000), Ephesus and Aquileia. There are other important Italian collections at Naples, Capua, Verona and Padua; and in the provinces at Mainz, Cologne, Narbonne, Vienna and Carnuntum. In Britain there are substantial collections at Newcastle and Chester. Smaller assemblages are to be found elsewhere, for instance, at Bath, Carlisle, Maryport (Cumbria), Glasgow, Edinburgh and in the British Museum, London. Some stones have migrated to the Americas, and Australasia, far from their original sitings.[23] There are many medium-sized museum collections, but some institutions have but a single stone, or none at all.

14 Re-erected tomb monuments, Šempeter, Yugoslavia. Second century AD.

6

RECORDING AND PUBLICATION

Inscriptions began to be catalogued by scholars in the High Middle Ages and, after a gap, from the fourteenth century onwards. Poggio Bracciolini (died 1459) compiled lists of the texts which he had personally seen in Rome. Cyriacus of Ancona (died *c.* 1450) compiled three volumes of inscriptions in manuscript. In 1492 Giovanni Pontano at Naples erected a memorial chapel in classical style to his recently deceased wife; in it he also placed his own collection of Greek and Latin inscribed texts.[1]

In late September 1464 the humanist Felice Feliciano of Verona went with a group of antiquarians to the shore of nearby Lake Garda.[2] They noted down dedications to several Roman emperors in the churches of Toscolano, on the western shores of the lake. After crowning themselves with garlands of ivy and myrtle in imitation of their classical forebears, they visited a ruined temple of Diana. The day continued with a sail on the lake to the sound of the lyre, and concluded with a visit to the church of S.Maria Maggiore at Garda, where they gave thanks to God for a well-spent day. This is perhaps the earliest recorded archaeological field excursion, by a fifteenth-century predecessor of today's learned societies. The sixteenth century saw the publication of collections in printed book form, beginning with Mazochi's *Epigrammata Antiquae Urbis* (Roma, 1521).

In the later sixteenth century scholars from the Prussian Academy at Berlin, at the instigation of Joseph Scaliger (1540–1609), travelled in Europe to collect texts, and make them more widely available. Scaliger also encouraged Johann Gruter (1560–1627) of Antwerp to compile a corpus of inscriptions, which was published in 1602. Important collections were made available to scholars, such as that assembled and judiciously published by Scipione Maffei (1675–1755) at Verona. Texts of selected inscriptions began to become a regular feature of local histories. Major surveys of particular categories of inscriptions were attempted on the basis of personal knowledge and extensive travels by such scholars as Ludovico Antonio Muratori (1672–1750) and (more successfully) by Bartholomeo Borghesi (1781–1860).

THE CORPUS OF LATIN INSCRIPTIONS

In 1847 a committee was formed in Berlin to organize and carry through a far-reaching and comprehensive publication of the original Latin texts from all parts of the Roman world. This was entitled the *Corpus Inscriptionum Latinarum* (*Corpus of Latin Inscriptions*; more commonly referred to as *CIL*). The driving force behind the project was Theodor Mommsen, then 30 years old. Mommsen himself undertook to compile several of the volumes on Italy. The work involved personal inspection of the stones where they survived, together with a survey of earlier literature, references and publications, to determine the findspots and confirm the texts. Where the stone was lost, the editor endeavoured to establish the true reading from a combination of antiquarian sources, not always with total success.[3]

The survey was geographically based, covering Italy and the provinces. Fifteen volumes were envisaged to provide the geographical coverage; three more volumes have dealt with, or are to deal with, particular categories of text (see Appendix 4). The volumes began appearing in 1862–63. Mommsen himself was particularly diligent; his volumes on southern and central Italy served as models for the series. Latin, the then universal language of scholarship, was used for the commentaries throughout; it is still used, even in the most recent fascicules. Each volume opened with a list of earlier antiquarians and a general discussion of their reliability. There followed next a list of *falsae vel alienae* (inscriptions which seemed unreliably reported, or were manifestly forgeries, and those which belonged outside the geographical location being investigated). All genuine inscriptions were grouped under the town where, or in whose territory, they had come to light. Inscriptions on every sort of material were included, though texts on clay, glass, brick and the like (the so-called *instrumentum domesticum*) were gathered at the end of each volume (except for Rome where the material was large enough for a separate volume, *CIL* XV). The section on each town was prefaced by an often still valuable account of the history of the town and the contributions that inscriptions had made towards an understanding of its civic life.

The format (39 × 29cm (16 × 12in.), a paper size known as 'folio') is large by today's standards. Some fifteen or more inscriptions could be described on a single page, usually in up to three columns. The texts were presented in majuscule type (i.e. capitals), with the original line and word distribution maintained. But there were no line-drawings of individual stones. A few photographic plates accompanied some later volumes. Only occasionally was reference made to sculptural ornament and other decoration. Only a few of the more recent volumes provide the dimensions of the stones. Numerous supplements have appeared to the original volumes, in the same format, and others are described as being 'in preparation'.

It would be hard to describe *CIL* volumes as easy to use. A knowledge of Latin is all but essential. Most of the volumes have extensive indices, a valuable and important feature, which tabulated the data the volumes contained; but the searching out of a particular stone may still prove a ponderous task.

Because the stones are grouped under the town-name, it could be tempting to suppose that it constituted the stone's findspot. But the town could house a major private collection, with stones lacking a secure provenance in fact deriving from a wider geographical area. Moreover, it will always be worth checking whether the stone was in fact recovered at the town-site (or the cemeteries around it) or from somewhere in its territory, perhaps at a dependent village, or from a farmstead.

The geographical spread of the volumes reflected known or suspected concentrations of material; eight volumes were envisaged for Italy itself and two for Rome. A single volume was considered sufficient by itself to cover all the Alpine lands, the Balkans, Asia Minor, the Near East, Egypt and part of North Africa.

The mass of material available for study encouraged Hermann Dessau to edit a selection of some 9000 texts, named *Inscriptiones Latinae Selectae* (*ILS*), arranged in categories according to subject matter, with brief commentary to assist scholars in identifying important source material on a variety of subjects (Berlin 1892–1916). Here, too, the pace of discovery was such that this selection required a supplement to take account of material which had come to light during its preparation.[4]

HANDBOOKS

Handbooks designed to provide the student with background information appeared as long ago as the eighteenth century. A fully comprehensive guide first became available in 1886 with the publication of René Cagnat's *Cours élémentaire d'épigraphie latine* (later editions down to 1914), which can still be regarded as the classic work though obviously somewhat out of date. In English there is J.E.Sandys, *Latin Epigraphy* (2nd ed. 1927), a treasure-house of detail.

Among more recent handbooks, reference should be made to Ida Calabi Limentani, *Epigrafia latina* (2nd ed. 1968), and to judicious but brief surveys by H.Meyer, *Einführung in die lateinische Epigraphik* (1973) and G.Susini, *Epigrafia latina* (1982). Both can be warmly recommended to readers with the necessary linguistic facility. In English, the past decade has seen the publication of Arthur Gordon's *Illustrated Introduction to Latin Epigraphy* (1983), an invaluable survey which represents the culmination of a lifetime's close study of the material. The bibliography at p. 148 lists other recent handbooks.

MODERN SELECTIONS

Scholars have also assembled collections of important inscriptions for use in undergraduate teaching, drawing on *CIL* and also more recent, and sometimes rare or often inaccessible publications in which important discoveries may easily languish unnoticed. For the Roman Republic there is the collection by Attilio Degrassi, with a photographic record, in larger format, published in 1965; for the reigns of Augustus and Tiberius there is a volume by Victor Ehrenberg and A.H.M.Jones; for Gaius, Claudius and Nero, one by Mary Smallwood; for the Flavian emperors one by Michael McCrum and A.G.Woodhead, and for Nerva, Trajan and Hadrian, another by Mary Smallwood. (For full details see bibliography at p. 149.) It is to be hoped that scholars and publishers can be found to continue the sequence at least till the Severan age, and into the later Empire. These collections have generally grouped inscriptions into categories such as 'historical events', 'senators', 'equestrians', 'cities of the Empire' 'administration of the Empire', 'the army and navy' and so on. They are of considerable value to students of Roman history, though they may cast unmerited shade on inscriptions not so selected. Selections have also been made by scholars in other European languages.

Potentially invaluable (but disappointingly incomplete and over-optimistic in its original concept) is the *Dizionario Epigraphico di Antichità Romane*, devised by E.de Ruggiero; after more than a century publication has reached only to the beginning of the letter M. A selection of inscriptions in Greek relevant to the Roman world is collected in the compilation *Inscriptiones Graecae ad res Romanas pertinentes* (*IGRR*), published in 1906–27, and now out of date.

NEW MATERIAL

From 1888 the French periodical *Revue Archéologique* began to include a supplement entitled '*L'Année Épigraphique*' (the Epigraphical Year). This continues to appear, now quite independently of its parent volume; it is now running about three years in arrears. The latest issue to appear (at the time of writing) is the volume for 1987, which has 1132 entries marshalled geographically. The texts are briefly presented, in italics, without line-drawings or photographs. Usefully, some relevant texts in Greek as well as Latin are included. Reference should always be made to the source cited by *AE*, in the search for further details.

A number of specialist journals report work in progress, and announce new discoveries. The foremost among them is the Italian journal *Epigraphica* (1939 onwards).[5] Most learned journals on Roman history and archaeology contain the occasional article on epigraphic matters or accounts of important discoveries. Quinquennial epigraphic congresses report recent work and discoveries, and suggest timetables for progress on the major corpora.

The Association Internationale d'Épigraphie Grecque et Latine (AIEGL) organizes conferences on specific themes. More accessible to the general reader is a sequence of papers reviewing epigraphic discoveries and research, from the viewpoint of the Roman historian, which has appeared at regular intervals since 1960 in the *Journal of Roman Studies* (see bibliography at p. 150 for details).

Today we can look back on a flood of publications, some updating and expanding on the work of *CIL* volumes, others detailing the contents of museum collections; many are essays on individual stones. Numerous regional or national corpora have appeared, and continue to do so. For Britain, we have volume I of the *Roman Inscriptions of Britain*, by R.G.Collingwood and R.P.Wright, published in 1965, but including material known to the editors only up to 1954. Other volumes have been promised: *RIB* II is to contain some 5000 examples of *instrumentum domesticum*, with a cut-off date in the mid 1980s; its first fascicules have recently appeared. A third volume (*RIB* III) will contain more recent material on stone. Discoveries in Britain have been included annually in the

Journal of Roman Studies (from 1921 to 1969), and in *Britannia* (1970 onwards). Among important national or provincial corpora are those produced in recent years for Yugoslavia, Hungary, Romania, Bulgaria, Spain, Turkey, Libya, Tunisia, Algeria, Morocco, Syria, France, Belgium and Switzerland. There have also been volumes for many individual cities and towns of the Roman world (see bibliography).

Some progress has been made in the computerization of parts of *CIL*. The earliest such project, at the University of Western Australia, involved entering on magnetic tape the texts of inscriptions from the city of Rome published in *CIL* VI. The end result was a massive seven-volume index, enormously valuable in the consultation of the 30,000 or more texts contained therein.[6]

More recently has come news of a project directed by Professor Geza Alföldy at Heidelberg, and financed by the German Government. This consists of plans to computerize the complete series of *CIL* volumes, and to generate indexes for them all. A beginning has been made on a comprehensive index for *Année Épigraphique* (*AE*), which should become available for scholars before too long. A number of other projects have been announced in several countries.[7]

PUBLICATION

As has already been made clear, inscriptions continue to be discovered. Some are first noticed built into standing structures; others can be found in museums where they have lain unregarded and unpublished sometimes for many years. Inscriptions are also found during ploughing, road building, pipelaying, housebuilding and other activities, or during excavation or field survey. When found during an excavation or as part of a survey project, they are likely to be 'written up' as part of a larger report.

'Publication' today usually means the description and discussion of the stone and the text inscribed on it, sometimes accompanied by one or more photographs, or a line drawing. Those compiling a catalogue or corpus of stones from a particular town or region are required, by the mass of evidence to be presented, to be brief; many of the stones will already have been published elsewhere. But initial publication of a newly discovered text may require lengthy discussion, especially where the inscription is fragmentary or the information contained in it particularly complex.

An account of any inscription should begin with a description of the item: the type of stone, its dimensions (width, height and thickness), the findspot and context, and a description of any decorative features. The dimensions of the letters should be given, with some indication of their style. The text itself may be written out in capitals, as it appears on the stone, followed by a transcription in italics with each word written out in full. A standard notation has been devised to identify abbreviations, missing letters, punctuation and so on (see Appendix 5 for a list of these epigraphic 'conventions'). There should also be a translation of the inscription.

Next should come a discussion of the content, and an estimate of the date. The present location of the stone should also be given, and a bibliography of previous publications, if any.

The publication of each stone may be accompanied by a good black-and-white photograph. A photograph allows the reader to check the information presented against the item itself. Here lighting is crucial. If artificial lighting is used, it should be directed not full-face on to the stone, but from one side, or both sides. Carefully positioned raking light accentuates the incised lettering. A scale should be included.

In *The Roman Inscriptions of Britain* (vol. I) description and discussion are accompanied by a line-illustration. Most other catalogues prefer to use photographs alone. A line illustration has its drawbacks: the subjective judgement of the draughtsman is interposed between the stone and its reader. But a line illustration is often much clearer than a photograph if the stone is dark, stained or weathered, the lighting unhelpful and the text damaged.

Ideally, if space and money allow, both a drawing and a photograph can be provided. A line drawing will feature the front face of the stone, at an appropriate scale, which will depend on its size. The drawing is likely to be reduced on publication to $\frac{1}{8}$ or $\frac{1}{12}$ of the actual size. The drawing should highlight the lettering, and give some idea of the character of the stone, with suitable shading.

SQUEEZES AND REPLICAS

It is of course easiest to follow these procedures where the stone has been taken after discovery to a museum or conservation laboratory, where suitable facilities may be at hand. But some inscriptions may have to be studied and recorded *in situ* – for example if they are on a rock face, or otherwise immovable because of size. Where inscriptions have been noted abroad, it will almost certainly be necessary to record the inscription on the spot. To cater for this eventuality, scholars long ago devised a method of obtaining an impression of the front or other faces of the stone and its inscription, by making a 'squeeze'.[8] One of the several techniques for this involves the use of filter paper which is wetted, and placed on or against the stone (which should first be cleaned of moss, soil and dirt) and beaten on to its surface by means of a stiff brush. The sheet or sheets of filter paper should be large enough to allow a reasonable amount to be folded over the sides of the stone. If the paper proves liable to disintegration, pressing it on with the fingers may be enough. When the paper dries it can be peeled away. Sometimes if a stone is worn or discoloured by iron staining, or chemicals, the photograph of a squeeze may be more useful than a photograph of the stone itself, at least for the decipherment of the text. At times it can be hard to tell at first glance whether the photograph is of the stone itself or of a squeeze. One can always look for joins in the paper!

It is possible to prepare a squeeze with less than perfect, but nevertheless adequate, materials. Blotting paper or even newspaper will do, with the aid of a suitable hardening agent, for example a raw egg; but the squeeze will be difficult to read. 'Rubbing' an inscription, like a brass effigy in a church, is not a recommended method, except by those expert in doing so, unless the surface of the stone is very hard and firm.

Other methods of preparing a likeness of the stone, or indeed a complete replica, have been developed over the years. Making a cast in plaster is a long-established method. More recently moulds have been prepared from latex rubber which forms a translucent skin that can be peeled away. Care has to be taken that the surface of the stone is sufficiently durable or compacted, and will not itself peel off when the mould is removed.

Powdering the surface of the stone with French chalk may reduce the risk of damage.

The three altars at the Temple of Mithras at Carrawburgh (below, p. 97 and Fig. 59) are a good example of replicas in concrete, virtually indistinguishable from the originals. In 1937 plaster replicas of inscribed slabs together with models of famous monuments throughout the Roman world were assembled at Rome for a special exhibition to commemorate the bimillennium of the birth of the emperor Augustus. The exhibition was later expanded and made permanent, constituting the *Museo della Civiltà Romana*, with 60 rooms, in the city's EUR suburb. As such it provided scholars with an invaluable, all-embracing assemblage of material housed within a single building. However, in recent years, difficulties with roofing, and vermin attacking the wooden supports of the individual replicas, have resulted in the Museum being closed.

Many inscribed stones have stood in museums for centuries, or in their outside courtyards, acquiring soot, grime, paint and dirt. Cleaning should be attempted with care, and only after expert advice.[9]

METHODS OF DISPLAY

A traditional method of displaying inscribed stones in museums has been to embed them in the walls, perhaps in several rows, one above the other, like paintings in art galleries of the eighteenth and nineteenth centuries. Only the front face of the stones will be visible. In the Church of Notre Dame de Lamourguier at Narbonne (above, p. 41), inscribed stones and sculptured panels are piled in rows four high, like goods in a supermarket. Scholars can, however, learn much from the sides and back of a stone block, so ideally it should be fully accessible.

More recently, it has been the custom to leave stones free-standing or to construct individual plinths. Stones can also be mounted on metal supports, or tracks, as (most successfully but expensively) in the Lateran Galleries at the Vatican Museums.

It is a frequent practice in museums to paint in the letters of an inscription to enhance their appearance and make the text more legible. This practice has its adherents and its opponents.

Certainly, painting over the letters can make them more visible for visitors; but it may perpetuate errors of reading. Such painting needs to be done carefully and the paint used should be water soluble. Carefully positioned lighting, directed from the side or from above, may achieve a suitable degree of visibility without resorting to other methods.

THE WORDS AND THE STONES

It should be emphasized again that autopsy, that is seeing the stone, or a photograph of it, for oneself, is the best guarantee of the correct reading (Fig. 15). Mistakes can arise in the transmission of texts. What may have been a serious lapse was recently brought to light by Philip Bartholomew, formerly of the Ashmolean Library, Oxford.[10] A well-known inscription found at Konya (Iconium) in Turkey reported (or seemed to report) a procurator, Marcus Arruntius Frugi, sent to Britain to conduct a census, apparently in the mid second century. Scholars nowadays refer to Dessau's *ILS* for the text reporting that appointment.[11] However, a check by Mr Bartholomew back to the initial publication[12] showed that a complete line had been added in the Dessau volume, including the reference to an appointment in Britain. As the stone is apparently now lost, scholars have to decide whether Dessau himself received additional information about its text, or the line was added in error, perhaps by duplication from another text.[13] We cannot now be certain that the man had ever served in Britain at all!

Close scrutiny of even familiar texts can bring its rewards. A most salutary lesson was brought home to British scholars by Professor Jules Bogaers of Nijmegen, who re-examined the slab at Chichester reporting a temple dedicated to Neptune and Minerva on the authority of Tiberius Claudius Cogidubnus, client king in Britain in the early decades of the Roman conquest. Cogidubnus was long credited, on the basis of this text, with the anomalous title *legatus Augusti in Britannia* ('the emperor's legate in Britain'), implying that he had an official position and title conferred by the emperor. Now the text has been read as reporting instead the title *rex magnus Britanniae* ('great king of Britain'), allowing a fresh flood of discussion.[14]

15 Gravestones being examined by visiting scholars, Klosterneuburg, Austria, 1986.

7

THE EMPEROR

Rome had, in its earliest days, been ruled by kings, but after a 'revolution' in about 509 BC, the state was ruled by annually elected magistrates, of which the most senior were the consuls. This system of government lasted nearly five centuries. However, the series of civil wars in the first century BC, which culminated in the victory of Octavian over Antony and Cleopatra in 31 BC, ushered in a long era during which control was exercised by a single man. He was called not 'king' but *princeps* – the 'leading citizen' of the state. In 27 BC Octavian took the title *Augustus* (the revered one) by which he was afterwards known. Rule by emperors, who succeeded mostly by virtue of family relationships, though also by adoption or military coup, lasted until the fall of the Roman Empire in the west in AD 476. Although the emperor had supplanted the consuls as the leading power in the state, they and other magistrates continued to be elected annually by the Senate, and aided the emperor in the running of state affairs.

THE TITLES OF THE EMPEROR

The names and titles of the Roman emperors are frequently met with on Roman inscriptions from the late first century BC onwards, often in abbreviated form, and it behoves the reader to become familiar with them, especially as such inscriptions are by definition often closely datable (above, p. 25f). The sequence of titles followed a fairly standard pattern, into which the personal names of the current incumbent would be inserted.[1] Put rather differently, the imperial nomenclature developed round the names of the first holders of the position, and then became increasingly standardized.

Not every inscription will include every element in the titulature. A likely sequence is as follows: first comes the title *imperator*, originally a title awarded under the Roman Republic to a magistrate in the field, by spontaneous acclamation of the troops present, to mark a victory in battle. Julius Caesar adopted it as part of his permanent titulature, and placed it in front of his own name in place of a *praenomen*. Augustus employed it too, and although some of his successors disclaimed the title (note its absence on Fig. 19), it soon came into general use. For an emperor, the acclamation as *imperator* signified his accession to power. The emperor put the title at the head of his nomenclature as an indicator of continuing military power and supremacy.

Frequently the name *Caesar* comes next, originally of course a surname of the Julian family, particularly associated today with Julius Caesar, consul and dictator. His heir Augustus gained the name *Caesar* by testamentary adoption; in due course it came to be thought of as a title. The name has continued to be associated with kingship in both Germany (*Kaiser*) and Russia (*Czar*). The Persian *Shah*, though it might seem superficially similar, has a different linguistic origin.

Next come the personal names of the current emperor (for instance, Titus Flavius Vespasianus – Vespasian), followed by the title *Augustus*, itself originally awarded to a particular individual (the young Octavian) in 27 BC (above, p. 42), but conferred on or assumed in turn by the successors of the original Augustus. Both *Caesar* and *Augustus* served to link a new emperor with his predecessor(s) and helped to legitimize his rule. Thus the appearance in an inscription of the words *Caesar* or *Augustus* should not be assumed to refer to those particular individuals. (Similarly when a senator reports himself as *legatus Augusti*, this does not mean that he had served as legate of Augustus himself, merely of 'the emperor'.) Younger male members of the Julio-Claudian household also had the family name *Caesar*. It was given to younger members of later imperial families to designate the heir to the ruling emperor.

It was normal for an emperor to adopt some of the family names of his predecessor, when he had been formally adopted. Thus inscriptions honouring Hadrian, who was the adopted son of Trajan, refer to him as *Traianus Hadrianus*, those of Antoninus, who was the adopted son of Hadrian, as *Hadrianus Antoninus*, and so on. The sequence of names and titles needs to be read through slowly and carefully, before the reader can safely conclude which emperor is being honoured (see Appendix 1). After their deaths some emperors were deified, and were accorded the title *divus*. If the incumbent was the son of an emperor who had been deified, he could be termed *divi filius*. An emperor such as Marcus Aurelius (himself to be deified in due course) could present himself as great-great-grandson of the deified Nerva (*divi Nervae abnepos*), great-grandson of the deified Trajan (*divi Traiani pronepos*), grandson of the deified Hadrian (*divi Hadriani nepos*) and son of the deified Antoninus (*divi Antonini filius*). The wife of an emperor was regularly given the title *Augusta*, and the title could be awarded to other female members of his family. The first *Augusta* was Livia, who was given this title after her husband Augustus' death in AD 14.

The use of a predecessor's personal names also helped to reinforce the impression of legitimate succession when this was rather dubious. Severus referred to himself as the son of Marcus Aurelius

16 *Statue base from Ostia, Italy, in honour of the emperor Septimius Severus, AD 196. (Now in the Cortile della Pigna, Vatican Museums.)*

and so brother of Commodus, the much despised incumbent murdered at the end of AD 192. Severus was not related in any way to Marcus or Commodus, but the nomenclature suggested continuity, especially with Commodus' more reputable predecessors. A statue base from Ostia (Fig. 16), now in the Vatican Museums, reads:

Imp(eratori) Caes(ari) divi | M(arci) Antonini Pii | Germanici Sarmatici fili(o) divi | Commodi fratri | divi Antonini Pii nepoti | divi Hadriani pronepoti | divi Traiani Part(h)ici abnepoti | divi Nerv(a)e adnepoti | L(ucio) Septimio | Severo Pio | Pertinaci Aug(usto) Arab(ico) | Adiabenico p(ontifici) m(aximo) trib(unicia) pot(es-

tate) IIII | imp(eratori) VIII co(n)s(uli) II p(atri) p(atriae).[2] 'To the emperor Caesar, son of the deified Marcus Antoninus Pius, victor over the Germans and the Sarmatians, brother of the deified Commodus, grandson of the deified Antoninus Pius, great-grandson of the deified Hadrian, great-great-grandson of the deified Trajan, victor over the Parthians, great-great-great-grandson of the deified Nerva, Lucius Septimius Severus Pius Pertinax Augustus, victor over the Arabs and the Mesopotamians, chief priest, holder of the tribunician power four times, saluted *imperator* eight times, consul twice, father of his country.'

(For the meanings of the various extra titles employed, see below.) Note how elements important to Severus – his links to his predecessors, Commodus and Marcus – are emphasized.

Severus also gave his son Bassianus, better known to us by a nickname, Caracalla, the names *Marcus Aurelius Antoninus Pius*, to highlight the link with popular emperors of the past. Needless to say, such nomenclature forms a ready source of confusion and error for the modern reader.

THE TERMINOLOGY OF VICTORY AND POWER

The emperor might also accumulate and employ a growing sequence of honorary titles that commemorated victories won or provinces or peoples added to the Empire. Similar titles had been taken under the Republic by victorious generals, such as (from a much earlier time) Coriolanus, the conqueror of the small town of Corioli. But under the Empire, such titles became the preserve of the emperor's family. Augustus' stepson Drusus posthumously gained the title *Germanicus*, victor over the Germans, which was inherited by his sons, including the future emperor Claudius, and grandson Caligula.[3]

Claudius himself was offered the title *Britannicus*, to mark his successes in AD 43, but he apparently declined it, though the title was borne by his infant son.[4] Domitian was proclaimed *Germanicus* in AD 83–84. Trajan became not only *Germanicus*, but also *Dacicus* (victor over the Dacians) and *Parthicus* (victor over the Parthians).

This latter title, as many others, was adopted somewhat prematurely. As time passed, such titulature became more prolific and perhaps less meaningful. It began to occupy an increasing percentage of the available space on an inscription, squeezing out other details (below, p. 125). Some honorary titles were more general in tone – Trajan became *Optimus*, 'best' of emperors, Antoninus became *Pius*, the 'dutiful'. The adjective *Felix*, 'lucky' or 'fortunate', was increasingly adopted from the later second century onwards.

These names and epithets are regularly followed by a sequence of titles listing posts and positions held by the incumbent emperor. First is often the title *pontifex maximus*, chief priest of the Roman state. Under the Roman Republic this priesthood was an elective magistracy held for life. Caesar became *pontifex maximus* in 63 BC. Augustus acquired the office long after becoming emperor (on the death of the previous holder) in 12 BC; it was conferred on each of his successors in turn. This is still the formal title employed today by the Pope as head of the Roman Catholic Church.

Next may come a statement of the number of times the emperor had held the power of a tribune (*tribunicia potestas*). The tribunate was an old office of the Roman Republic, whose holders had the particular remit of defending the common people against the excesses of aristocratic magistrates. In 23 BC Augustus assumed the power of a tribune (but not the actual office, which continued in existence), to symbolize his care and concern for the ordinary citizen. Subsequent emperors followed his example. Though the power was normally held for life, it was formally renewed annually; thus it served to indicate the number of years the emperor had been in power. In this way a reference to the holding of tribunician power for (say) the tenth time often provides a fairly exact date.

It will be remembered that the emperor on his accession was saluted as *imperator*, a title which often headed his list of titles, and which had originated as an award to generals in the field to mark a great victory. The Roman emperors continued to accept such acclamations from their soldiers or the Senate, *after* their accession, when military success warranted it. Thus an inscription may repeat the title *imperator* later in the text, followed by a number indicating how many times it had been gained. The victories could be won by the emperor himself at the head of an army, or by legates in his provinces operating under his auspices. The first success in each reign to be so commemorated would produce the title *imperator II* (i.e. it was the second, in addition to the initial acclamation), normally shortened to IMP *II*; and so on. Claudius was saluted 27 times, and Domitian 22 times. Hadrian took only a single additional salutation, on the successful conclusion of the Jewish War in AD 135. Antoninus took his second salutation to mark his victories in north Britain in AD 142–3. A multiplicity of salutations should be indicative of extensive fighting by the Roman army, and their absence a time of general peace; but some emperors, we may suspect, took salutations more readily than others.

The inscription may also record the number of times the emperor had held the supreme republican magistracy, the consulship. On an inscription this is usually abbreviated to COS, for *cosol*, an early spelling of the word. Some emperors also record their holding of the old Republican office of *censor*, and from the early second century we find use of the title *proconsul* to signify military command and governorship of provinces.[5]

The sequence of titles is likely to end with the designation *pater patriae*, Father of the Fatherland, or Father of the Nation, a title originally given personally to Augustus in 2 BC, and usually awarded to each successor.

The text of a dedication, even to a Roman emperor, did not have to be in Latin. Texts from the Greek-speaking eastern half of the Empire employed Greek translations of Latin titles, or their equivalents (see Fig. 42). In Egypt the emperor can be shown in the guise and dress of a pharaoh, whose role he continued, with suitable inscriptions in the traditional hieroglyphics.

THE ARCH OF TITUS

One of the most familiar of all Latin inscriptions adorns the south-east side of the Arch of Titus in the Roman Forum (Fig. 17), which sits on a conspicuous summit on the line of the *Via Sacra*. The inscription is brief, easy to read and the words are hardly abbreviated at all. It reads: *Senatus*/ *Populusque Romanus | divo Tito divi Vespasiani*

f(ilio) | Vespasiano Augusto.[6] 'The Senate and People of Rome to the deified Titus Vespasianus Augustus, son of the deified Vespasian'. The arch was thus erected at some date after the death of Titus in AD 81, astride the route used by generals and emperors celebrating a Triumph; scenes carved inside the arch show Titus celebrating his Triumph (in AD 71), and depicting the spoils from the Temple Mount in Jerusalem, including the seven-branched candlestick. The arch is built of marble with the inscribed text originally inset with bronze letters, now lost. Seeing the arch today, the viewer may easily forget that in the Middle Ages it formed part of a palace of the Frangipani family and was attached to other buildings. Restoration work was carried out in 1821–23; the inscription on the north-west face (i.e. towards the Capitoline

17 Arch of Titus, The Forum, Rome. Late first century AD.

45

Hill) commemorates the restoration under the auspices of Pope Pius VII. It presumably replaced an original Latin text.[7]

THE ARCH OF CLAUDIUS

The sequence of an emperor's titles is so stereotyped that restorations of a fragmentary text honouring a particular emperor can often be attempted with some confidence. A good example is the inscription which, when complete, was once placed above an arch of the *Aqua Virgo* in Rome, to commemorate Claudius' British conquests.[8] The arch does not survive as a standing monument, but recent investigations have gone some way towards reconstructing its sculptural decoration which included scenes of fighting and of soldiers on parade.[9] The arch stood astride the *Via Lata*, now the Via del Corso, near the Piazza Venezia and carried the *Aqua Virgo* across this important boulevard; the aqueduct itself was restored by Claudius. The inscription, which has itself recently undergone fresh scrutiny,[10] is among the most valuable epigraphic records we have for the early history of Roman Britain. The letters were of bronze – holes for their attachment are clearly visible – and were arranged over a series of three or four marble panels. The largest and most valuable fragment, found in 1641, can now be seen set into a courtyard wall of the Palazzo dei Conservatori on the Capitoline Hill (Fig. 18). Other small fragments, recovered at the same time, are apparently now lost. The large fragment preserves the left-hand edge of each of the nine lines of the inscription. What survives is enough to establish the gist of the subject matter, and to allow the various smaller fragments to be inserted in appropriate places. But it should be remembered that these fragments could derive from two identical versions of the text, set on either face of the archway.

The subject of the Latin text (for the complete version, see p. 47) comes in line 5: *Senatus Populusque Romanus* (the Senate and the People of Rome). The first four lines are taken up with the names and titles of an emperor, whom we can easily identify as Claudius (Tiberius Claudius, son of Drusus, Caesar Augustus Germanicus), in whose honour the arch was inscribed. The more or less

18 Inscribed panel from the Arch of Claudius, Rome. AD 51–52.

standardized order in which the information is generally presented in imperial titles, and our knowledge of those actually held by Claudius himself, allow the following lines to be reconstructed without undue difficulty. The main fragment reports him as *pontifex maximus*; this would be followed normally by the tribunician power and a numeral for the number of times he had held it. A separate fragment provides the necessary details, and the numerals XI. Claudius held the tribunician power for the eleventh time between January 51 and January 52 AD. Next there is a reference to the fact that he had been consul five times, and

19 Restored text on the Arch of Claudius. (After Castagnoli and Gatti.)

had been acclaimed *imperator* on a number of occasions. From our knowledge of Claudius' titulature we can expect a reference to the fact that he was *censor* and *pater patriae*. Here the same secondary fragment fixes the layout. Doubt remains only over the number of imperial salutations. Space allows the insertion of the Roman numerals for 22 salutations, but a higher figure might be possible.

In the second half of the text the restorations are less certain, but the overall meaning is not in doubt. There is a reference to kings of Britain (*reges Britannorum* or *reges Britanniae*), the achievement of some success without any loss of manpower (*sine ulla iactura*), a mention of tribes (*gentes*) and the fact that Claudius had been the first (*primus*) to bring them under Roman control. A small fragment preserves the numerals XI, which could be the number of kings defeated. The text, as thus restored (Fig. 19), reads:

Ti(berio) Clau[dio Drusi f(ilio) Cai]sari |
Augu[sto Germani]co | pontific[i maxim(o)
trib(unicia potes]tat(e) $\overline{XI}$ | co(n)s(uli) $\overline{V}$
im[p(eratori) $\overline{XXII}$ cens(ori) patri pa]triai |

senatus Po[pulusque] Ro[manus q]uod | reges Brit[annorum] XI d[evictos sine] | ulla iactur[a in deditionem acceperit] | gentesque b[arbaras trans Oceanum] | primus in dici[onem populi Romani redegerit]. 'For Tiberius Claudius, son of Drusus, Caesar Augustus, victor over the Germans, chief priest, holder of the tribunician power eleven times, consul five times, saluted *imperator* 22(?) times, *censor*, father of his country, The Senate and the People of Rome, because he brought eleven kings of Britain, defeated without any loss, to a surrender, and was the first to bring barbarian tribes on the far side of Ocean into the sway of the Roman people.'

The archaic spelling of *patriae* and (as restored) of *Caesari* may reflect Claudius' antiquarian leanings (above p. 29).

The inscription commemorates the successful Roman invasion of Britain, which took place in AD 43, but the text is dated to AD 52. We could suspect that the erection of the arch was linked to the display to the Roman people in AD 51 of King Caratacus, an event which kept the military victories in Britain in the forefront of public attention.

20 *Restored text of commemorative slab, York,* AD *107–108. (After Richmond.)*

THE NINTH LEGION AT YORK

Our knowledge of imperial titles can be similarly put to work when dealing with a fragmentary slab from York that records building work on the legionary fortress during the reign of Trajan, one of the epigraphically best-documented emperors. The fragment was found in 1854, close to the site of one of the fortress-gateways. Only the central part survives, but as five out of the six lines of text are devoted to Trajan's names and titles, restorations can be attempted with some confidence. These suggest that the slab, when it fell (or was removed) from its position above the gate, could have been broken into three almost equal parts. The exceptionally high standard of carving and the spelling out of many of the phrases make this stone valuable for instructional purposes. The wording of the second line cannot be disputed, and assuming that the first line is 'centred', we can fix the overall length of the lines with some confidence (Fig. 20). From what survives, the text can be restored to read:

[Im]p(erator) Caesar | [divi N]ervae fil(ius Ne[rva | Trai]anus Aug(ustus) Ger[m(anicus)

Dac | icus po]ntifex maximu[s tribu | niciae po]testatis XII imp(erator) V[I co(n)s(ul) V p(ater) p(atriae) | portam] per leg(ionem) VIIII Hi[sp(anam) fecit].[11] 'The emperor Caesar, son of the deified emperor Nerva, Nerva Traianus Augustus, victor over the Germans, victor over the Dacians, chief priest of the state, holder of the tribunician power twelve times, saluted *imperator (at least)* six times, consul five times, father of his country, *(constructed ? a gate)*, through the legion VIIII *Hispana*.'

Given the standardization of titles, only two points can remain in doubt, the number of times he had been saluted *imperator* when this stone was erected (at least five times, given the survival of part of the letter V), and the number of times he had been consul. Trajan held the tribunician power for the twelfth time from 10 December 107 until 9 December 108.[12] He was consul for the fifth time in 103 and for the sixth time in 112; so COS *V* is required here. Trajan became IMP *VI* at the close of his Second Dacian War in 106, and did not take a further salutation as IMP *VII* before the onset of the Parthian War in 114; so IMP *VI* is the correct reading.[13] On these restorations the slab was erected sometime during a twelve-month period beginning in December 107. Here again it is open to the reader to juggle with the text to see if other restorations would be possible. The final line has its own interest. The central surviving portion reports that the building work, whatever it was, was carried out 'through the agency of the legion VIIII *Hispana* (*per legionem VIIII Hispanam*). It was common to have no specific word to say exactly what was being commemorated or had been built, as the inscribed stone was meant to be set into the building concerned. Here, however, it is possible that one or more words were inserted before and after the surviving portion. At the end might come a verb, almost certainly *fecit*, that is 'he (the

21 *Arch of Severus, The Forum, Rome, south-east side, AD 203.*

22 Arch of Severus, The Forum, Rome. Close up of inscription, north-west side of arch, showing evidence for alteration in line 4.

emperor) built (it)'. At the beginning of the line could be a description of what was constructed. The word *portam* (a gate) is highly probable, given the findspot.

Not only does this inscription provide an exact date for the reconstruction of at least part of the fortress in stone, marking the acceptance that it was to be a long-term military base, but it also constitutes the latest securely datable evidence for the presence of the Ninth Legion as part of the Roman garrison in Britain. It used to be thought that the legion was destroyed in some catastrophe in northern England, even in Scotland, and this view formed the basis of Rosemary Sutcliff's famous novel, *The Eagle of the Ninth* (1954). Now it is generally believed that the legion was in fact transferred to one of Rome's provinces on the Continent. We still do not know what its eventual fate was.

THE ARCH OF SEVERUS

The Arch of Septimius Severus in the Forum at Rome (Fig. 21) bears on both sides identical inscriptions in honour of the emperor and his sons Caracalla and Geta, and is dated to AD 203. All the letters were of bronze and the text, as originally inscribed, read:

Imp(eratori) Caes(ari) Lucio Septimio M(arci) fil(io) Severo Pio Pertinaci Aug(usto) patri patriae Parthico Arabico et | Parthico Adiabenico pontific(i) maximo tribunic(ia) potest(ate) XĪ imp(eratori) XĪ co(n)s(uli) ĪĪĪ proco(n)s(uli) et | imp(eratori) Caes(ari) M(arco) Aurelio L(uci) fil(io) Antonino Aug(usto) Pio Felici tribunic(ia) potest(ate) VĪ co(n)s(uli) proco(n)s(uli) et | P(ublio) Septimio L(uci) fil(io) Getae nobiliss(imo) Caesari | ob rem publicam restitutam imperiumque populi Romani propaga-

tum | insignibus virtutibus eorum domi forisque S(enatus) P(opulus)q(ue) R(omanus).[14] 'For the emperor Caesar Lucius Septimius, son of Marcus, Severus Pius Pertinax Augustus, father of his country, victor over the Parthians of Arabia and of Adiabene, chief priest, holder of tribunician power eleven times, acclaimed *imperator* eleven times, consul three times, proconsul, and Marcus Aurelius, son of Lucius, Antoninus Augustus Pius Felix, holder of the tribunician power six times, consul, proconsul, and Publius Septimius, son of Lucius, Geta, most noble Caesar; because of the restoration of the state and the extension of the empire of the Roman people by their distinguished abilities at home and abroad, the Senate and the People of Rome (*erected this arch*).'

Here the emperor Severus himself (who has taken the name of a short-lived predecessor Pertinax; cf. above, Fig. 16) is given two lines of the text; his elder son (and joint emperor) Caracalla has one line. As first inscribed, the fourth line honoured the younger son, P.Septimius Geta as *nobilissimus Caesar*, most noble Caesar. However, in AD 212 (the year after the death of Severus himself), Caracalla had his younger brother murdered. The fourth lines of the texts on either side of the Arch were altered to read OPTIMIS FORTISSIMISQVE PRINCIPIBVS ('best and bravest of emperors'), referring to Severus and Caracalla alone. A new set of bronze letters was affixed in the fourth line on both sides, so concealing the original text.[15] The effects of chiselling the front of the marble blocks to remove traces of the original letter-outlines are clearly visible and examination of the layout of the surplus holes allows the original Latin wording to be restored (Fig. 22).

8

LOCAL GOVERNMENT
AND SOCIETY

When the Romans subjugated lands around the eastern Mediterranean, they found many areas already urbanized, with numerous small city-states ornamented with substantial public buildings. In many parts of the western empire, however, the Romans themselves brought urbanization and town life, where for the most part, except along the Mediterranean coastline in areas colonized by the Greeks or Phoenicians, little had existed before.

In the ancient world the town was the main market centre for the surrounding countryside, a place where the rural population sold their agricultural produce and obtained goods they could not produce themselves. Administratively the town and the surrounding countryside formed a single unit, the land constituting the *territorium* of the town. Thus a corpus of inscriptions from a town and its territory can provide the beginnings of a commentary on local politics, preoccupations and interests. Marriage and dynastic links within the élite may become evident, important in the local or even the national scene. Who some of the chief local families were in a town can soon be established from inscriptions, from their tenure of magistracies and priesthoods and from benefactions to the town and its citizens. The tombs of such families, where they survive, occupy the prime locations outside its gates (below, p. 100). Almost all that we are likely to know about the local government in any particular town derives from epigraphic evidence. Each town that had been formally constituted by the Romans as a colony or *municipium* (see below), had a constitution, embodied in a *lex coloniae* or *lex municipii*. Frequently copies of this law were erected in bronze in the forum of the town or in some other public place for all to see. Parts of a few such charters survive, providing specific details on such features as the powers of magistrates, the holding of magistracies, the procedures for meetings of town councils and the assembly of citizens for elections, the duties of public slaves, even regulations on burial.[1] A recent important addition to our knowledge has been the partially preserved charter of a previously unknown town called Irni (or Irnium) near Seville.[2]

THE MAGISTRATES OF A TOWN

Towns with Roman-inspired constitutions were governed by magistrates elected annually. Colonies were usually governed by two *duoviri*, assisted by two *aediles*; municipalities often by two *quattuorviri iure dicundo* assisted by two *quattuorviri aedilicia potestate*. The senior magistrates of each group, that is the *duoviri* (in a colony) or the *quattuorviri i.d.* (in a *municipium*) dispensed justice. The junior officials (*aediles*) had responsibility for religious buildings, roads and drainage, the public baths, markets and for ensuring the continuity of the food supply. Often added to each group of magistrates were two *quaestores*, responsible for the financial affairs of the town. There was also a town council, the *ordo decurionum*, some-times of substantial size. These *decuriones* (to be distinguished from military *decuriones*, who were junior officers of cavalry) had to possess a certain amount of property and own a house of reasonable size in the town (Fig. 23).

Every five years, the two chief magistrates of the town assumed an extra role as censors (they were known as *duoviri quinquennales* or *quattuorviri quinquennales*) and were charged with revising the census roll of citizens and of the town council. It was common practice for men who had held a magistracy in the previous five years to be invited to join the *ordo*, if they were not already among its members. The minimum age for the decurionate was 30, but exceptions could be made; young children of influential families are found holding office well before the legal age (below, Fig. 58).

Details of elections are usually hidden from us, though information on the procedures involved may survive on some charters. At Pompeii, we are fortunate in having knowledge, from the survival of notices painted on the walls of buildings along the main streets of the town, of the names of candidates for office in the final years of its existence. These notices (Fig. 24), like election

23 Seating in the Large Theatre, Pompeii, with an inscription (once with bronze lettering) honouring Marcus Holconius Rufus, magistrate and benefactor during the reign of Augustus. (Seen from above.) Between the two halves of the text there may once have stood a bronze chair for a distinguished visitor or presiding magistrate.
(CIL X 838.)

*24 Election 'notice', Pompeii, Italy (CIL IV 7868).
Lollius stood for election as aedile in AD 78.*

posters or placards today, urged the passerby to vote for a particular candidate and might name some of his supporters or sponsors. We could suppose that, after each election, the old notices would be plastered over; but by their very mass they must belong to a period of several years.[3] For the posts of *duovir* at Pompeii it is likely that there were never more than two candidates each year for the two available posts.

At Varia (now Vicovaro) near Tivoli, Marcus Helvius Rufus Civica erected baths for his fellow citizens and visitors to the town, as a plain rectangular slab still preserved in the town proclaims.[4] There might seem no particular reason to single out this man, were it not for the fact that he is mentioned by the historian Tacitus. In AD 20 during the native revolt in north Africa led by Tacfarinas, a detachment of reservists, left as garrison for Thala near the legionary fortress at Ammaedara (Haïdra), fended off an attack by superior rebel forces. During the battle, a certain Marcus Helvius Rufus saved the life of a fellow soldier. Tiberius awarded him the *corona civica* (civic crown), the traditional award for such a deed, and the nearest Roman equivalent to the Victoria Cross.[5] The inscription at Varia shows him in later life, as a retired chief centurion, a big fish in a small pool, having adopted *Civica* as an extra surname, and benefactor of his home town.

BENEFACTIONS AND CIVIC PRIDE

Magistrates frequently marked their year of office by some act of liberality, by sponsoring games or an athletic contest, or by building some public edifice, an aqueduct or fountains, re-paving. or improving the streets or providing sets of weights and measures (below, p. 110).[6] The new building or facilities could bear the name of the magistrate forget the outpourings of wealth, the games and the entertainment offered by magistrates and leading families of a town. In the temple-precinct of Apollo at Pompeii stands a pillar with a panel (Fig. 25) inscribed as follows:

L(ucius) Sepunius (Luci) f(ilius) | Sandilianus | M(arcus) Herennius A(uli) f(ilius) | Epidianus | duovir(i) i(ure) d(icundo) | d(e) s(ua) p(ecunia) f(aciundum) c(uraverunt).[7] 'Lucius Sepunius Sandilianus, son of Lucius, (and) Marcus Herennius Epidianus, son of Aulus, joint magistrates with power to dispense justice, had (*this*) made at their own expense.'

Sometimes an archway could be erected in a town, or on a road leading away from one of its gates, with the principal aim of commemorating the family who had paid for its erection. (Such arches are often called triumphal arches, but strictly speaking this epithet is only true for a small group in Rome itself, built along the route used by generals and emperors celebrating a Triumph and perhaps a few others at other towns where celebration of an imperial victory was intended.) Good examples of such commemoration are at Verona (the Arch of the Gavii, re-erected from fragments, and not *in situ*)[8] and at Pula in Yugoslavia (the Arch of the Sergii).[9] The latter is thought to commemorate two of the founding colonists of the town, and the son and wife of one of them. It was erected by the wife in honour of the others, all of them evidently already dead (Fig. 26). Almost certainly this arch and others were topped by statues of the family. A few arches commemorate a particular act, for instance that put up by Trajan at the establishment of his colony of Timgad, in North Africa, to commemorate its foundation,[10] and by communities of Lusitanians on a bridge over the Tagus at Alcantara, on which they record how much money they had all contributed to the cost of its construction.[11]

Adjacent to the so-called Library of Celsus at Ephesus (below, p. 73f.) stands a newly re-erected double arch leading to the Lower Agora (Fig. 27). The flat surfaces are inscribed with numerous texts, and across the attic storeys are the names of the two rich freedmen who had it constructed in 4–3 BC, in honour of Augustus, his wife Livia, his daughter Julia and her (deceased) husband Marcus

25 Pillar in the temple-precinct of Apollo, Pompeii, Italy, with names of the two magistrates who had it erected. Late first century BC. The pillar could have supported a sundial.

(or magistrates if they acted as a pair) and, prominently set into one wall, an inscription acted as a permanent record of an individual's generosity. It was not intended that the populace should

26 Arch of the Sergii, Pula, Yugoslavia. Late first century BC. *(From an early nineteenth-century print.)*

27 Arch of Mazaeus and Mithridates, Ephesus, Turkey, 4–3 BC.

28 Slab advertising baths owned by Marcus Crassus Frugi, Pompeii, Italy, c. AD 50. (Museo Archeologico, Naples.)

Agrippa.[12] Statues of those honoured, whom the two dedicators laud as their patrons, originally stood atop the arch.

At Pompeii two of the earliest *duoviri* of the colony established there in 80 BC paid for the erection of an amphitheatre and for a covered theatre.[13] At Paestum, two *duoviri* provided a network of fountains and the piping to supply them.[14] At Luceria (Lucera) in south-eastern Italy, a former military tribune in a legion, who became *duovir* of the colony, built an 'amphitheatre on his own private property with a boundary wall round it, in honour of the emperor Caesar Augustus and of the Colony'.[15] Some reflected glory doubtless accrued to the tribune and his family. At Terracina in southern Italy, the man who paid for the paving of its forum had his name spelled out in huge bronze letters in due sequence on the paving slabs, where they can still be seen.[16]

Today we can see all over a modern town inscriptions naming public buildings, offices and services, doctors' surgeries and so on. Such inscriptions survive much more rarely from Roman times, largely, it may be, because they were not always inscribed on stone, but rather painted on wall plaster which has long faded or disintegrated. From Pompeii (Fig. 28) comes an advertisement for public baths on a stone tablet: *Thermae | M(arci) Crassi Frugi | aqua marina et baln(eum) | aqua dulci Ianuarius l(ibertus).*[17] 'The hot baths of Marcus Crassus Frugi; sea water available and a bath with fresh water. The freedman Januarius.'

Frequently, as we shall see (below, p. 73ff), the Town Council erected a statue or monument in honour of an illustrious magistrate or a native son who had prospered on the national scene or in the service of the emperor. If a prominent public figure had agreed to be the town's patron, this might be commemorated. In the provinces the incumbent governor or a local military commander could be so honoured. The link of patronage might continue over future generations.

The prominent local families had the most opportunity, reason and funds to ensure that their names received permanent commemoration. The visitor to an ancient town could quickly learn who the important families were. The Elder Pliny deprecates the widespread habit of erecting statues to adorn the public places of a town and inscribing on them the records of a lifetime's service to the community.[18] At Pompeii the sides of the forum were adorned with a line of statues in bronze or marble. A monument honouring Lucius Virtius Ceraunus, magistrate at nearby Nuceria (now Nocera), had one side decorated with a laudatory inscription, itself flanked by representations of the magistrate's chair from which Virtius had been entitled to dispense justice in the town, and figures of his ceremonial attendants, the lictors.[19] He or his heirs were concerned to stress that his service to the community was what was worth commemorating about his life.

Freedmen, excluded from magistracies, could hold office as *seviri Augustales* ('members of a

29 *Dedication slab at the shrine of the* Augustales, *Herculaneum, Italy. Shortly before* AD 14.

board of six priests of Augustus'). These were priesthoods initially of the living then dead Augustus, and then of subsequent emperors too. They might advertise their generosity, as for example at Falerii in Etruria where, in honour of Augustus, the *magistri Augustales* ('chief officers of the Augustales') 'paved the Augustan Way with limestone from the *Via Annia*, beyond the gate as far as the temple of Ceres, at their own expense, in place of games'.[20] Excavation of the shrine of the *Augustales* at Herculaneum produced the following text (Fig. 29):

Augusto sacr(um) A(ulus) A(ulus) Lucii A(uli) filii Men(enia tribu) | Proculus et Iulianus | p(ecunia) s(ua) | dedicatione decurionibus et | Augustalibus cenam dederunt.[21] 'Sacred to Augustus. Aulus Lucius Proculus and Aulus Lucius Julianus, sons of Aulus, of the voting-tribe *Menenia*, at their own expense. To mark the dedication they gave a meal for the town councillors and the *Augustales*.'

(Notice how the two *praenomina* are placed together in the inscription.)

The actual workings of the town council are occasionally reported. At Pisa in AD 2 and again in AD 4 the council despatched deputations to Rome, to express to Augustus their grief at the deaths of his beloved grandsons, first Lucius and then Gaius Caesar: altars were to be erected in the town, side by side, where offerings could be made on the anniversaries of their deaths, and an arch was constructed.[22]

In general any link that was forged with an emperor would be the occasion for enthusiastic local commemoration. Copies of the emperor's decrees would be conspicuously displayed (see below, p. 127). Local pride, inter-town rivalries and the quest for the emperor's favour were important. If a petition to a governor or the emperor went in its favour, the community was of course quick to celebrate, and might inscribe the text of the reply on stone or bronze, and have it publicly displayed.[23] At Aphrodisias in Caria, Greek texts of letters to the town from emperors from Augustus onwards down to the mid third century AD were inscribed on a wall of the town's theatre.[24] Municipal calendars in stone or bronze listed local feast-days, national holidays, anniversaries of deaths of certain members of imperial families, military victories or sometimes disasters. Lists of *duoviri* or *quattuorviri* in due sequence of office-holding formed part of the formal record of the town's history. There must of course have been a myriad of other events, functions and announcements painted up on the walls. The surviving notices at Pompeii give some idea of the range.

In Italy such records of municipal benefaction, construction, rivalry and success are commonplace. For some provinces, such as those in France, Spain, Greece, Turkey and North Africa, we sometimes have more evidence than for parts of Italy itself. In the poorer or more remote provinces the evidence may be sparse; any individual inscriptions that survive can be extremely valuable in determining the civic status of a community and highlighting any events in its history.

In Britain little is known about local government, with only a few inscriptions recording magistrates or *decuriones*; these come principally from the colonies.[25] At Wroxeter (Viroconium), the *civitas Cornoviorum* (tribal-state of the Cornovii) marked the completion of a new forum and basilica by erecting, probably on an archway through which the visitor reached the new complex, a massive inscription, among the largest from Roman Britain.[26] In 1955 some fragments of a large commemorative panel were found together at St Albans (Verulamium), dating from the early months of the reign of the emperor Titus in AD 79.[27] Quite clearly the text reported large-scale construction work carried out during the governorship of Gnaeus Julius Agricola, the first, and so far the only, record on stone of his presence in Britain, and handy confirmation of Tacitus' report that he encouraged Romanization and building in the British towns early in his governorship.[28]

LIFE IN THE COUNTRYSIDE

Not all inscriptions derive from towns; many of a town's citizens, in some areas probably a majority, lived in the *territorium*, up to a day's journey or more from the civic centre. For them security of land tenure was a prime concern. Inscribed pillars or panels can mark the boundary between one town or tribe and another, or the adjudication of disputes.[29] If a colony was established, its land was normally surveyed for allocation and details of the resulting survey inscribed on bronze panels and publicly displayed in the town. At Arausio (Orange) in southern France, which was made a colony in 35 BC, substantial fragments of marble panels have survived which detail landholdings set against a large-scale map of the *territorium*. Most of the fragments were found in 1949–54 during the digging of a strongroom for the local branch of the Société Marseillaise de Crédit.[30]

When a grid had been marked out on the *territorium* of a town, the corners of the square plots, often of 200 Roman acres (*iugera*), were marked by terminal stones (*cippi* or *termini*), often bearing an abbreviated coding of the location of that particular stone in the overall grid system. Several stones survive in southern Italy, which testify to the activities of land commissioners acting under the legislation of Tiberius Gracchus in 132–130 BC, when land was distributed not in colonies but individually to poor Romans. The stones provide useful confirmation of the Commission's long-term activities, which were not terminated by the violent death of Gracchus himself in 132.[31]

Details of landholding in Italy also emerge from documents such as the 'Alimentary Tables' from Ligures Baebiani (near Campobasso) and Velleia (near Parma). These take the form of inscribed sheets of bronze, which detail financial awards made by the emperor Trajan in the early second century AD to individual landowners in these places; the landowners were to pay a certain amount by way of interest on the loans towards the welfare of local children. Such schemes were widespread in Italy. The Tables form a useful guide to the ownership of land and the size of individual estates in those areas at the end of the first century AD. Many farms had evidently been amalgamated into larger units over previous generations.[32]

9

THE ROADS
THAT LED TO ROME

'All roads lead to Rome' is a familiar phrase. Surprisingly, it seems not to be a direct quotation from a Latin or Greek author of antiquity, but has a medieval origin, referring to pilgrims journeying on foot to the shrine of St Peter. In ancient Roman times all roads led to Rome as the centre of a Mediterranean-wide empire. Perhaps more correctly we should say that all roads led *from* Rome, linking the capital to the regions of Italy and then to the provinces. In 20 BC the emperor Augustus erected a 'golden milestone' (*milliarium aureum*) in the Forum behind the speakers' platform (or *rostra*). This was a stone pillar ornamented with gilt bronze sheets on which were inscribed the distances from Rome to various important cities of the Empire;[1] fragments of the podium can still be seen. At much the same time, Augustus' lieutenant Agrippa had a large map prepared on stone panels which showed the provinces and the road system. Unfortunately it has not survived.

The earliest roads went only as far as adjacent towns or to territory under direct Roman control (Fig. 30). Often they must have replaced existing tracks. As Rome expanded and established colonies in ever more distant parts of peninsular Italy, the need arose to establish and maintain means of quick communication between them and Rome itself. Chief among the Roman roads of Italy were the *Via Appia* (The Appian Way), from Rome to Campania, later extended to Brundisium; and the *Via Flaminia* (The Flaminian Way), which led across the Apennines to the Adriatic coast, thence to Ariminum (Rimini), the gateway to the Po Valley. Roads were named after the magistrate, usually a *censor*, who had been responsible for the placing of the contract to build each one.

REPAIRS TO THE ROAD SYSTEM

Today we are familiar with neatly paved roads beautifully cambered. But the earliest roads, including the *Via Appia*, were merely of gravel or of rough stones topped by gravel. Many major roads did not achieve their final, familiar form until the Empire. The process of refurbishment and renewal was never-ending. Augustus undertook a major upgrading of the *Via Appia*, *Via Flaminia* and other roads.[2] Numerous bridges had to be rebuilt. To commemorate the completion of work on the *Via Flaminia* in 27 BC, arches were built at its two termini, on the Milvian Bridge at Rome and at Rimini, where the arch was inserted into the town's south gateway and topped by statues of Augustus and his family. An inscription on the arch reads: 'The Senate and the People of Rome, to the emperor Caesar Augustus . . . to mark the repair of the *Via Flaminia* and the rest of the trunk roads of Italy at his instigation and expense.'[3] The original course of the *Via Appia* at Terracina brought the road up a steep slope to the temple of Jupiter Anxur on its magnificent headland. In AD 110 Trajan opened up a route round the sea-front by cutting back the side of a rock-pillar now called the Pesco Montano, to a height of 37m (120ft). The side of the rock face was inscribed at 3-m. (10-ft) intervals with the distances from the peak as a record of the work.[4]

In southern Italy, Trajan upgraded an older road from Beneventum to Brundisium, as an alternative to the *Via Appia*. It was known as the *Via Traiana* and completed in AD 109.[5] To commemorate the work an arch was erected in his honour in Beneventum at the starting point of the upgraded road (Fig. 31) (see also below, p. 66). The sculptured panels are decorated with themes of imperial propaganda in Italy and beyond; the inscription makes no reference to road-building.[6]

Bridge-building was an essential concomitant to road construction. Many bridges in Italy and the

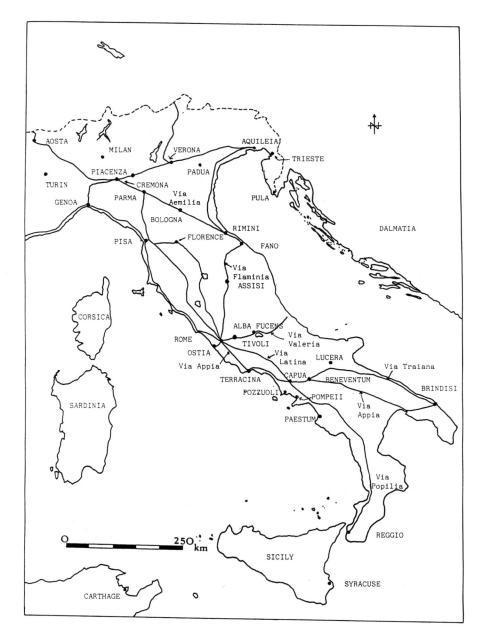

30 Map of Italy showing the road system.

provinces survive, and are still in use, though several in Italy suffered serious damage during the Second World War when they were blown up by retreating armies. A particularly fine example of an (intact) Roman bridge in Rimini carries the *Via Aemilia* out of the town to the north across the River Marecchia. It was begun by Augustus and completed by Tiberius in AD 22.[7] Originally,

31 Arch of Trajan, Benevento, Italy, at the starting point of the Via Traiana, *AD 114.*

32 Pons Fabricius, *over the Tiber, Rome, 62 BC.*

arches stood at either end and statues were placed in niches along its sides. The surviving *Pons Fabricius* at Rome, across the Tiber, bears a total of six inscriptions recording its construction in 62 BC, together with others reporting repairs (Fig. 32). The main texts read:

> *L(ucius) Fabricius C(ai) f(ilius) cur(ator) viar(um) | faciundum coeravit.*[8] 'Lucius Fabricius, son of Gaius, curator of roads, saw to (*its*) construction.'

An almost perfectly preserved bridge in a spectacular setting spans the ancient River Chabana, now the Cendere Çay, in Commagene (south-eastern Turkey). Set into the balustrade are three columns with texts in honour of Septimius Severus, his wife Julia Domna and his elder son Caracalla.[9] Doubtless there was once a fourth column honouring Geta, murdered in AD 212 (above, p. 50). The bridge, perhaps originally of Flavian (late first century) date, was remodelled in AD 200 (Fig. 33).

THE RISKS OF TRAVEL

Travel in the ancient world was a dangerous business. The traveller might be attacked by dogs or wolves, or by bandits and disappear without trace.[10] Nowadays we tend to assume that we will reach our destination and return safely. In the Roman world it was common to dedicate an altar (or promise to erect one) to an appropriate god, perhaps Mercury, god of trade and travel, or Neptune, god of the sea, in the hope of a safe journey; if all went well, the traveller at the end of his journey could erect the altar at his destination or on his safe return home. (Today travel insurance is an essential element in any traveller's plans.) Travel by sea in ancient times was also dangerous, if not more so, as – for example – St Paul discovered, though if the weather was kind, a much smoother and quicker journey over long distances was certainly possible. Along the roads were wayside shrines, as in many countries today, sometimes at road junctions. Here the traveller could placate the spirits of the road. At the summit

33 Bridge over the Cendere Çay, Turkey, with commemorative pillars in honour of the emperor Septimius Severus and his family, AD 200.

of the Great St Bernard Pass was a shrine to *Jupiter Poeninus*, protecting deity of the Poenine Alps. Many offerings and dedications are known, for example a small bronze plaque that was once attached to something, possibly a statuette (Fig. 34). The text reads:

Poenino | pro itu et reditu | C(aius) Iulius Primus | v(otum) s(olvit) l(ibens) m(erito).[11] 'To Poeninus, for a (*safe*) going and a (*safe*) coming back, Gaius Julius Primus willingly and deservedly fulfilled his vow.'

34 Bronze plaque once attached to an offering left at a shrine to the god Poeninus. 10.6 × 5.5cm (4 × 2in.) (Musée de l'Hospice du Grand St Bernard). Notice how it has been broken on the left, with a new hole cut to aid attachment.

The offering must have been left by the traveller on the second leg of his journey, when he could be reasonably sure of reaching home safely.

Along the roads were posting stations and inns, offering various facilities. Official travellers on state business carried an authorization document (a *diploma*); others had to pay. Some travellers were on mules or horseback or in carriages or carts, but many had to walk. A graveslab from Aesernia (Isernia) in southern Italy commemorates L.Calidius Eroticus and his wife Fannia Voluptas, who ran an inn.[12] The inscription continues with an imaginary conversation between Calidius and a departing traveller, as the bill is being totalled up. 'Inn-keeper, let us work on the bill. You had a pint of wine; one *as* was the cost of the bread, 2 *asses* for the pillow; agreed. Eight for the girl – agreed too. And two asses for the mule's hay. That mule will be the death of me'. The names of Calidius and his wife are surely nicknames, in part at least. Below is a sculptured scene, showing the cloaked traveller on the point of departure, with his mule, doing his arithmetic on his fingers.

MILESTONES

When the road-builders had completed each section of their work, they erected a stone pillar (a *milliarium*) at every Roman mile of 1000 paces (hence the name), that is 1481m (4920ft). These milestones not only measured the distance along the road from its starting-point, they also reported construction work and who had been responsible for it. Distances were recorded in one direction only. In Italy the distances usually became greater as the traveller journeyed away from Rome. For example, the traveller from Rome to (say) Brundisium would find the recorded distances getting bigger as his journey progressed. Conversely those travelling towards Rome would find the distance reducing. Quintilian remarks on the soothing effect on weary legs of the ever-reducing tally on milestones as the long-suffering traveller passed them.[13] In all, over 4000 milestones are known. Milestones used to be published in individual volumes of *CIL*, as appropriate. More recently, volume XVII of *CIL* is being devoted to them; but only one fascicule has been published.

Some milestones still stand *in situ*, or lie recumbent close to the road they commemorated; thus

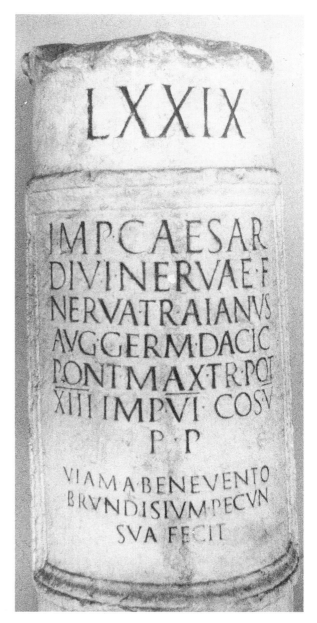

35 *Milestone from the* Via Traiana, *Italy,* AD *108–109. (Cast in Museo della Civiltà Romana, Rome.)*

they remain at risk of damage or destruction. Many have fortunately been transferred to museums or civic centres. Through the efforts of *l'Association 'Via Domitia'*, some facsimiles of milestones have been erected beside tracts of that road (below,

p. 67) in the Languedoc-Rousillon region of southern France.

The majority of surviving milestones date from the time of the Empire and give the name of the emperor who paid for the roads to be built or repaired. His name also served as a guarantee of the genuineness of the distance. A good example comes from the *Via Traiana* east of Beneventum. It marked the 79th mile from Beneventum in the direction of Brundisium (Fig. 35). The text reads:

LXXIX | Imp(erator) Caesar | divi Nervae f(ilius) | Nerva Traianus | Aug(ustus) Germ(a-nicus) Dacic(us) | pont(ifex) max(imus) tr(ibu-nicia) pot(estate) | $\overline{XIII}$ imp(erator) $\overline{VI}$ co(n)s(ul) $\overline{V}$ | p(ater) p(atriae) | viam a Benevento | Brundisium pecun(ia) | sua fecit.[14]

'79. The emperor Caesar, son of the deified Nerva, Nerva Trajanus Augustus, victor over the Germans and the Dacians, chief priest, holder of the tribunician power thirteen times, saluted *imperator* six times, consul five times, father of his country, made the road from Beneventum to Brundisium at his own expense'.

Milestones, if they were first recorded *in situ*, provide a guide to the location and course of a road, where its route is uncertain or already worn or ploughed away. They may form a guide to the frequency (or otherwise) of repairs. Sometimes several milestones erected side by side can reflect a sequence of repairs, each separately commemorated; or one milestone can bear more than a single inscription. In some cases the pillar has been

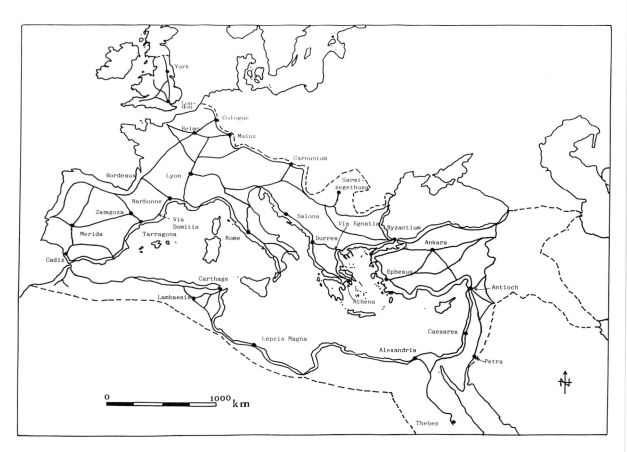

36 Map of the Roman Empire, at its greatest extent, AD 117, showing the road system.

37 Towpath at the Iron Gates, Yugoslavia, as widened by Trajan. (S.S. Frere.)

upended, with the lower part providing a fresh surface to inscribe (above, p. 30). Not all roads were constructed at public expense; some were built by landowners. An inscribed plaque or pillar would tell the traveller when he was intruding on private property.[15]

THE SPREAD OF THE ROAD SYSTEM

The Romans did not build roads in Italy alone. Routes were planned to and in the various provinces from the mid second century BC onwards: the *Via Egnatia*, from Dyrrhachium (Durrës in Albania) across the mountains of northern Greece to Thessaloniki, was built in 148, in the aftermath of Roman conquest; and the *Via Domitia* linking Italy to Spain via southern France was laid out in 118 BC. Under the Empire, road-building in the provinces continued apace: for example, Agrippa

built many roads in Gaul, Tiberius in Spain, Claudius in the Alpine passes and Trajan in the East. The road system, designed in the first instance for military and administrative convenience, also provided easy routes for the passage of Roman-made goods to the frontiers of the Empire (Fig. 36). By the time of Diocletian there were 272 trunk roads in the Roman Empire, covering a total of some 53,000 miles.

Some of these roads were major feats of civil engineering. For example, Tiberius built a road along the southern shore of the Danube, to help river traffic negotiate the treacherous Iron Gates at Orşova.[16] Here the river was flanked by sheer cliffs (Fig. 37). Tiberius had a narrow tow-path cut into the cliffside a few metres above the flowing torrent, and with the aid of timber supports this could be broadened into a usable trackway. The chock-

38 Milestone in situ, *near Petra, Jordan, recording the conversion of Arabia into a province and the construction of the* Via Traiana; *it marked the 54th mile along the road. (P.W.Freeman.)*

holes for the timber underpinning survive, although all is now submerged below the waters of a dam at Djerdap. Trajan had the footpath widened, an achievement commemorated by an inscription: 'The emperor Caesar, son of the deified Nerva, Nerva Trajanus Augustus, victor over the Germans, chief priest, holder of the tribunician power for the fourth time, father of his country, consul three times, having cut out the mountain-cliffs and inserted angled supports below, repaired the road.'[17] Before the original roadway was submerged by the waters of the dam, the panel was moved to a new, higher location. More recently an inscription has been found recording the excavation of a canal nearby.[18] It reads 'Because of the danger of the cataracts,

Trajan diverted the river, and thus made the Danube safe for shipping.'

Much of the road-building work in the provinces was done by the army, none too willingly at times.[19] Soldiers complained at the utilization of their energies as labourers, just as their successors have done down to modern times. A unique insight into the building of one road constructed on Trajan's orders in the new province of Arabia in 106 is provided by a papyrus letter from Egypt, in which a soldier reports to his father how he had avoided the hard labour of road-building in the hot sun by obtaining a posting to legion headquarters as a clerk.[20] He can have been none too popular with his less astute comrades. Milestones on the line of this road (Fig. 38) record more prosaically how Trajan, 'having reduced Arabia to the status of a province, opened up and paved a new road, through the agency of the emperor's legate C.Claudius Severus, from the boundaries of Syria as far as the Red Sea.'[21]

Britain, a late-comer to the Roman Empire, soon acquired a network of roads, fanning out from London, indicative of routes used by the army in the decades immediately after the Claudian invasion. There were at least 6000 miles of Roman road in Britain, a network not equalled till the eighteenth century. Some 100 milestones are known; the earliest to survive, dating from the reign of Hadrian, was found at Llanfairfechan, and marked the fifth mile along a road to Caernarfon from the fort at Caerhun. It is now in the British Museum.[22]

Of all the contributions made by the Romans to the landscape of Europe and the Mediterranean lands, probably none has been so familiar or enduring as the system of roads which joined the capital to the far corners of the imperial provinces. They continued in use through the Middle Ages and the network in western Europe has only recently been supplanted by motorways which often seek to bypass towns rather than unite them.

10

ADMINISTRATION OF AN EMPIRE

For the period of the Roman Republic, that is down to 31 BC, much of our evidence for the way in which the Romans controlled their growing domains derives from literary sources. But inscriptions do provide valuable details, for example on treaties between Rome and her allies and other kingdoms, on city constitutions and on construction work by Roman magistrates in their provinces.[1] The *fasti consulares* and *fasti triumphales* inscribed at Rome and elsewhere provide, where they survive, a good framework for observing the continued success of Roman armies under the Republic and who commanded them.

Epitaphs of individuals are rare before the first century BC. Texts from the Tomb of the Scipios at Rome report the careers of several members of that famous family between the fourth and first centuries BC.[2] One of the best known texts is the inscription on the side of the sarcophagus which held the remains of L.Cornelius Scipio Barbatus; it is now in the Vatican Museums. The text recounts that he had been 'consul [298 BC] censor, aedile, had captured Taurasia, Cisauna in Samnium and subjugated all of Lucania, taking hostages'.[3] There survives from Delphi the base of a monument erected by Lucius Aemilius Paullus in 168 BC, which commemorated his defeat of the Macedonians.[4] Augustus erected commemorative plaques (called *elogia*) in his Forum at Rome, to famous men of past ages, summarizing their careers. Some other towns did the same. These documents are not contemporary with the lifetimes of those commemorated, as a study of the lettering makes clear.[5]

From the later first century BC onwards, inscriptions bring before us much more detail on the government of the Empire and its provinces, in particular the careers of governors or procurators and their staffs. From these the sequence of office holding and the relative seniority of posts can be established with some certainty. Some understanding of the system is necessary if the reader is to appreciate the contribution of epigraphy to our knowledge of it.

When Rome felt the need, or saw an opportunity, to intervene in an area under the Republic, the Senate despatched a magistrate to campaign there, as his *provincia* (i.e. a sphere of command; the later meaning, of a precise geographical region, developed from it). If full annexation was decided upon, the area was assigned on a regular basis. At first, magistrates were despatched to a province during their year of office at Rome as consul or praetor. These commands could if necessary be extended beyond the year of office holding at Rome, and the holder designated *pro-consul* or *pro-praetor*, having the same authority as if they were still in office at Rome. By the 80s BC, magistrates were only very rarely sent during their year of office, partly because of the distances involved, but could hope for appointment as a provincial governor, with the title *proconsul* or *propraetor*, after the year of office at Rome had expired. Where governors had to rule a sizeable geographical area, they were authorized to appoint legates to assist them, to whom they 'delegated' part of their military or juridical responsibilities.

From 27 BC onwards, when Augustus regularized his position as head of state on what proved to be a permanent basis, he had himself allotted a large 'province' that comprised Gaul, Spain and Syria. These were the areas where the bulk of the Roman legions was then stationed. Augustus did not plan to spend much of his time in these provinces, but appointed legates who would govern the areas on his behalf and command the armies stationed in them. Legates who were in effect the governors of each province were entitled

legatus Augusti pro praetore (legate of the emperor with the powers of a praetor) and legates who held command of a legion were entitled *legatus legionis* (legate of a legion). All held their authority from Augustus himself, though on the spot the *legatus Augusti pro praetore* had authority over the legionary legates. Most legates could expect to hold office for about three years, but some were left in post for longer periods. Egypt and a few smaller provinces or military districts were also taken by the emperor, and assigned by him to equestrians with the title *praefectus*. Egypt had become a province on the defeat of Antony and Cleopatra in 31–30 BC, and was kept within the emperor's sphere of command. Though legions were stationed there, it was not allocated to a senatorial legate, but to an

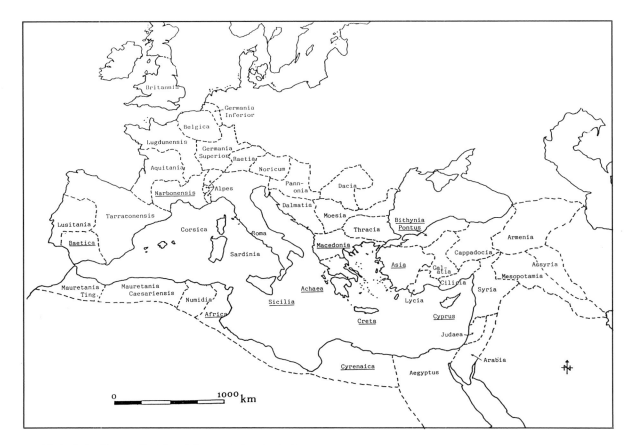

39 *Map of the Roman Empire at its greatest extent, AD 117, showing imperial and (underlined) senatorial provinces.*

equestrian prefect. Egypt was felt too crucial to the Empire to be in the hands of senators, who were not permitted to visit it without prior imperial approval, lest they foment revolt.

Those provinces not taken into his sphere of command by the emperor were left for the Senate to assign to its members under the old system (Fig. 39), and were allocated by lot. All the governors despatched, of whatever rank and status, had the title *proconsul* and they governed normally for one year only. In theory the senatorial provinces and their governors were independent of the emperor, but in practice he could influence the selection of proconsuls, give them written instructions and intervene in their provinces. As the Empire continued to expand, more provinces were created; usually, as these were likely to contain substantial military forces, they were taken by the emperor.

Financial affairs in each imperial province were assigned to equestrians with the title *procurator* (lit., one who takes care on someone else's behalf), who were responsible to the emperor, and arranged for the payment of the troops stationed there. In senatorial provinces finance was in the hands of a *quaestor*, holder of the old Republican magistracy. Men who took charge of the administration of the emperor's own property could be found in all provinces; some were his freedmen. They too had the title *procurator*. In Claudius' reign prefects of small imperial provinces (see above) had their titles changed to *procurator*, simplifying the nomenclature. Egypt however remained under a *praefectus*.

THE HIERARCHY OF COMMAND

Gradually there developed a hierarchy of posts, positions and appointments through which a man could rise. For a senator, these were interspersed with tenure of the old Republican magistracies at Rome. When a man had reached the praetorship at Rome, he could look for the command of a legion and next of a small province with one legion; if he had become consul, he might then be given command of a province with a larger garrison (up to three or four legions in the Early Empire) or of a substantial geographical area. One route of promotion and advancement was marked out for senators, and another (quite separate) for equestrians. However, the sons of successful equestrians

might be admitted to the senatorial career. Moreover, it became possible for especially favoured or successful equestrians to transfer in mid life to the higher career-track. This might be the result of patronage or a reward for the adherents of the successful aspirant in a civil war, or even the result of exceptional abilities, especially from the second century AD onwards, when talent, particularly military talent, became as important to the survival of the Empire and its frontiers as social class.

AULUS PLATORIUS NEPOS

Rather than digress at length on the intricacies of the system, it may be better to look at some specific careers. A good example, relevant to the student of Roman Britain, is the career of Aulus Platorius Nepos, governor of Britain in AD 122–24, the man who was given the responsibility for building Hadrian's Wall and whose name appears on several inscriptions found along its length (above, Fig. 9, below, p. 90). His career is recorded on a splendid statue base (Fig. 40 and the front cover) at Aquileia in north-east Italy.[6] He had been appointed 'patron' there, and the town councillors happily marked the event. The text reads:

A(ulo) Platorio A(uli) f(ilio) | Serg(ia tribu) Nepoti | Aponio Italico | Maniliano | C(aio) Licinio Pollioni | co(n)s(uli) auguri legat(o) Aug(usti) | pro praet(ore) provinc(iae) Bri | tanniae leg(ato) pro pr(aetore) pro | vinc(iae) German(iae) Inferior(is) | leg(ato) pro pr(aetore) provinc(iae) Thrac(iae) | leg(ato) legion(is) Ī Adiutricis | quaest(ori) provinc(iae) Maced(oniae) | curat(ori) viarum Cassiae | Clodiae Ciminiae Novae | Traianae candidato divi | Traiani trib(uno) mil(itum) leg(ionis) XXII | Primigen(iae) p(iae) f(idelis) praet(ori) trib(uno) | pleb(is) ĪĪĪ vir(o) capitali | patrono | d(ecreto) d(ecurionum). 'To Aulus Platorius, son of Aulus, of the voting tribe *Sergia*, Nepos Aponius Italicus Manilianus Gaius Licinius Pollio, consul, augur; legate of the emperor with praetorian powers of the province of Britain, legate with praetorian powers of the province of Lower Germany, legate with praetorian powers of the province of Thrace, legate of the legion I *Adiutrix*, quaestor of the province of Macedonia, curator of the

Cassian, Clodian, Ciminian and New Trajanic Roads, a candidate nominated by the emperor Trajan, military tribune of the legion XXII *Primigenia Pia Fidelis*, praetor, tribune of the plebs, one of the Board of Three in charge of capital sentences, Patron. By decree of the councillors.'

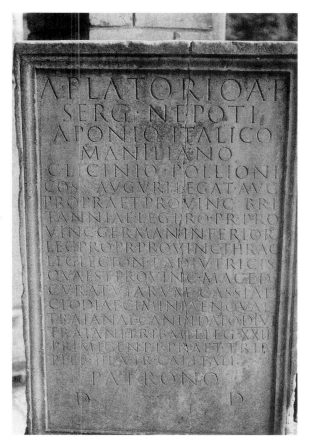

40 Statue base reporting the career of Aulus Platorius Nepos, Aquileia, Italy c. AD 125. (Museo Archeologico, Aquileia.)

The posts are recorded, as the discerning reader may already have divined, in a descending order, that is with the most important mentioned first; this is a sort of *Who's Who* entry in reverse. There are two important exceptions to the sequence – two posts, those of *consul*, the supreme magistracy at Rome, and the religious post of *augur* (held at Rome), have been taken out of sequence, and noted

first. There is also a very serious disordering of the posts Nepos held in the earlier part of his career.[7]

Platorius Nepos bears the long string of personal names typical of a time when adoptions, inheritances and legacies carried with them a legal obligation to assume the benefactor's name(s) (see above, p. 19). Nepos may have been born Gaius Licinius Pollio and was later adopted by an Aulus Platorius Nepos whose string of names he places first. His career began, probably about AD 95, with a post in Rome, with responsibility for overseeing the carrying out of executions of those condemned in the courts. This was followed by a post as military tribune in a legion in Upper Germany. Next he was elected quaestor and was sent in that capacity to the senatorial province of Macedonia, to handle its finances under the proconsul; then he was Tribune of the People in Rome, then praetor (an office which marked the moment when he was qualified for more responsible posts); he then held a curatorship of a number of roads in southern Etruria, not far from Rome. For one or more of these posts in Rome he had been specially singled out by the emperor Trajan as a candidate whom he supported (*candidatus*); Nepos was thus all but assured of election. Next he commanded a legion in Pannonia, and subsequently became legate of nearby Thrace, a province without a legionary garrison. He was consul in AD 119. Afterwards he was despatched to Lower Germany as provincial governor, based at Cologne; the province had two legions. Lastly, he was sent to Britain, a province with three legions.

Without this inscription we should know almost nothing about his career. Nepos is reported as the builder of Hadrian's Wall by a late biographer of the emperor Hadrian, who also says that he subsequently lost the confidence of the emperor, and retired from public life.[8] The inscription is a record of the posts held; no mention here, for example, of the Wall for which he may now be remembered.

CELSUS AND HIS LIBRARY

The inscription to Platorius Nepos can be paralleled by many hundreds of career texts, often reporting individuals not of course so successful. Similar inscriptions from the eastern provinces are very often in Greek. One example is from Ephesus

41 *Library of Celsus (reconstructed), Ephesus, Turkey,*
AD 110.

where the reconstructed façade of the Library of
Celsus at Ephesus must rank as one of the most
eye-catching sights for the present-day visitor to
an ancient city (Fig. 41). The building was
presented to Ephesus by Ti. Julius Aquila, consul
in AD 110, in memory of his father, Ti. Julius
Celsus Polemaeanus, consul in 92, and later
proconsul of the province of Asia; Celsus was a
native of Ephesus. The reconstructed façade
incorporates many inscriptions in their original
setting. To either side of the main steps are the
plinths for equestrian statues (Fig. 42), which bear
the names and detail the career of Celsus in Latin
and in Greek.[9] He had been 'consul, proconsul of
Asia, tribune of the legion III *Cyrenaica*, promoted into the Senate with the status of aedile by

the deified emperor Vespasian [whom he had very
probably supported in the civil war of AD 69],
praetor of the Roman People, legate of the deified
emperors Vespasian and Titus [for legal affairs] in
the provinces of Cappadocia, Galatia, Pontus,
Pisidia, Paphlagonia and Lesser Armenia, legate of
the deified Titus of the legion IIII *Scythica* [in
Syria], proconsul of the provinces of Pontus and
Bithynia, prefect of the military treasury [at
Rome], legate of the emperor with praetorian
powers of the province of Cilicia.' Again his most
senior appointments are given first: he was consul
in AD 92 and proconsul of Asia, his home province,
in 106. The name Ti. Julius Celsus should indicate
a local family of considerable influence, most
probably given Roman citizenship by the emperor

42 Statue-bases flanking steps to the Library of Celsus, recording the career of Celsus in Latin and Greek.

Tiberius, which then reached equestrian status by Nero's reign at latest, and achieved entry to the Senate under Vespasian. Within the Library itself is a sarcophagus which still contains the body of Celsus.

AN EQUESTRIAN OFFICER

From Aquileia has come a valuable inscription recording the career of an equestrian officer, which can serve as an example of his class.[10] 'To Gaius Minicius Italus, son of Gaius, of the voting-tribe *Velina*, *IIIIvir* [joint mayor of Aquileia] with juridical powers, prefect of the 5th Cohort of Gauls with cavalry attachment, prefect of the 1st Cohort of Breucians with cavalry attachment, Roman citizens; prefect of the 2nd Cohort of Varcaeans with cavalry attachment; military tribune of the legion VI *Victrix*, cavalry prefect of the First Wing of *Singulares*, Roman citizens; decorated by the deified emperor Vespasian with a golden crown and silver-topped spear; procurator of the province of Hellespont, procurator of the province of Asia, the governorship of which he took over, on the emperor's instructions, at the death of the proconsul; procurator of the provinces of Lugdunensis and Aquitania (including the tribal state of Lactora); prefect of the Corn Supply, prefect of Egypt; priest of the deified emperor Claudius. By decree of the town councillors.'

The inscription adorns the front of a marble statue base. On one of its sides, at great length, the councillors explain the circumstances of the statue's erection and their great pride in the exceptional achievements of their native son, and the benefits he had obtained for the community from

43 *Slab reporting the dedication of a* Tiberieum *by the prefect of Judaea, Pontius Pilatus, AD 26–36. Caesarea, Israel. (Cast on site; original in Israel Museum, Jerusalem.)*

the emperor Trajan. The statue was evidently in bronze, and was set up in AD 105. The voting-tribe *Velina* confirms him as a native of Aquileia itself, as does the fulsome praise accorded by the councillors. His career probably began with the post of *IIIIvir* of the town. Thereafter he was launched into what had become the standard equestrian career in the service of the emperor. Italus' career began under Vespasian, with three posts as prefect of auxiliary regiments, followed by the tribunate of a legion based in Germany, and the prefecture of a cavalry regiment again in Germany.

At some point during this early phase of his military career he received military decorations. Subsequently he was procurator of a small province in the Dardanelles; then he looked after imperial property in the important senatorial province of Asia (Western Turkey) in which he was made acting governor for a time, when the incumbent proconsul (whom we can identify as C.Vettulenus Civica Cerealis) was executed in AD 89.[11] Next he was transferred to the west, to be procurator of a group of imperial provinces in Gaul. Afterwards he rose to the highest ranking positions, as prefect of the Corn Supply at Rome, and prefect of Egypt, the most senior appointment (as judged in the Flavian period and later) which any equestrian could hold with the exception of the prefecture of the Praetorian Guard at Rome.

PONTIUS PILATE

A particularly intriguing text, already referred to (above, p. 30), from Caesarea in the Roman province of Judaea names Pontius Pilatus. The text reads:

> ---s *Tiberieum* | ---*Pon]tius Pilatus* | ---*prae-f]ectus Iudae* | ----[12] 'In honour of ....?, ... Pontius Pilate, ... prefect of Judaea (*dedicated*) a Tiberius-cult building.'

The wording in line 3 disposes finally of the uncertainty over Pilate's title which Tacitus reports (anachronistically) as *procurator*.[13] Caesarea was the residence of the Roman governor of Judaea. As governor of a small province on the fringes of the Roman world the title *praefectus* is entirely appropriate to time and place. On the slab found at Caesarea (Fig. 43) Pilate demonstrates his loyalty to the emperor. Nothing is known about

44 Tomb of the procurator Julius Classicianus, London (British Museum), soon after AD 61. (After a British Museum drawing, with additions.)

Pilate's career, apart from his tenure of this post which can be dated to AD 26–36; presumably he had held other posts before being sent to Judaea. He could have been a tribune in a legion, or a prefect of a regiment of auxiliaries, or both; he may even formerly have been a centurion. After ten years in Judaea he was relieved of his command for brutality in suppressing civil unrest, and sent to Rome to answer to Tiberius.

JULIUS CLASSICIANUS

Standing in a corner of the Roman Room at the British Museum is a substantial tomb monument in the form of a giant altar commemorating Julius Classicianus (Fig. 44), mentioned by Tacitus as despatched to Britain in the aftermath of the Boudican rebellion in AD 61 to be procurator of the province. (For its discovery, see above, p. 31.) The monument is only partially preserved, but the reconstruction is familiar to all students of Roman Britain.[14] The text is restored to read:

Dis | [M]anibus | [C(ai) Iul(i) C(ai f(ili) F]ab(ia tribu) Alpini Classiciani | (two lines) | proc(uratoris) provinc(iae) Brit[anniae] | Iulia Indi filia Pacata I[.......] | uxor [f(ecit)]. 'To the spirit of the departed Gaius Julius, son of Gaius, of the Fabian voting-tribe, Alpinus Classicianus........... procurator of the province of Britain. Julia Pacata, daughter of Indus, I......., his wife, set this up.'

The procurator's full name is revealed here: Gaius

45 Restored text recording the construction of an amphitheatre at Alba Fucens, Italy, according to instructions left in the will of Q.Sutorius Macro. c. AD 40. Replaced in original position.

Julius Alpinus (or is it Alpinius?) Classicianus. As reconstructed, there is a gap for posts held before his appointment to Britain. Most probably he had already been a tribune in a legion, or prefect of auxiliary infantry, or both, and perhaps procurator of a small province. The inscription ends with the name of his wife, Julia Pacata, daughter of Indus. She can reasonably be identified as a daughter of Julius Indus, a nobleman among the Treveri of eastern Gaul, who raised a cavalry regiment, subsequently called the *Ala Indiana*, in the Roman interest at the time of a serious Gallic revolt under Tiberius. The daughter's surname (*Pacata*) might indicate that she was born soon after the revolt was put down. The final word of line 5 is restored to read *Indiana* (an extra surname, derived from her father's name, Indus) or *infelix* (unfortunate), an adjective to be taken with *uxor*, wife.[15] His own names reveal Classicianus as a Gaul, presumably of a tribal aristocracy, and well connected by marriage into the top echelons of the Gallic nobility.

SUTORIUS MACER

The careers of those intimately involved in political events at Rome itself are also reported. A sequence of excavations at the town of Alba Fucens near Avezzano in central Italy in 1957 cleared among other buildings the town's amphitheatre. Set above both sides of one of the two gateways into the arena were identical inscriptions recording the circumstances of its construction (Fig. 45). Each of the inscriptions reads:

Q(uintus) Naevius Q(uinti) f(ilius) Fab(ia tribu) Cordus Sutorius Macro | praefectus Vigilum praefectus praetori | Ti(beri) Caesaris Augusti testamento dedit.[16] 'Quintus Naevius, son of Quintus, of the Fabian voting-tribe, Cordus Sutorius Macro, prefect of the *Vigiles*, prefect of the Praetorian Guard of Tiberius Caesar Augustus, gave (*it*) in his will.'

The man responsible, probably a native of Alba Fucens, is the Macro familiar perhaps from the pages of Tacitus and *I Claudius*, who assisted Tiberius in the overthrow of the Praetorian prefect Sejanus in AD 31. It will be remembered that Tiberius, then resident on the island of Capri, summoned Macro, a former commander of the *Vigiles* (the Rome fire-watch), gave him a commission to succeed Sejanus, and despatched him back to Rome with a lengthy letter to be read out to the Senate, which was to meet in the Temple of Apollo on the Palatine Hill. While Sejanus was listening to its wordy contents, Macro dismissed the detachment of the Praetorian Guard routinely on duty outside, and substituted a group of the paramilitary *Vigiles*, to whom he was a familiar figure of authority. Macro proceeded to the Praetorian Camp, on the outskirts of Rome, to cement their loyalty to Tiberius, in his capacity as their new prefect. Tiberius' letter ended by denouncing Sejanus and demanding his punishment by the Senate. When Sejanus emerged from the meeting, he found the commander of the *Vigiles* waiting to arrest him; he was executed the same evening. Macro helped Caligula become emperor on the death of Tiberius in AD 37. According to popular rumour, he hastened the latter's demise with the aid of a smothering pillow. He was then offered the prefecture of Egypt but never took it up, for he was forced to commit suicide in AD 38. The inscription shows him as a generous benefactor of his home town; no hint here of momentous events or eventual downfall.

HELVIUS PERTINAX

A good example of the promotion available to a man with military abilities is Publius Helvius Pertinax, briefly emperor in AD 193. His early career has been highlighted by an inscribed statue-base found in 1959 near Cologne, hollowed out probably in the later third century AD for secondary use as part of a sarcophagus.[17] A biography written long after his death claims that he was son of a freedman and began adult life as a schoolteacher; but finding his chosen profession ill-paid, he tried to obtain a post in the army as a centurion.[18] None of this is confirmed by the inscription which reports his first post as prefect of an infantry regiment of auxiliaries in Syria. Thereafter he was military tribune of legion VI *Victrix* in Britain and then held a second post there, probably as prefect of a cohort of infantry, this time a larger unit, 1000 men strong; next he commanded a cavalry *ala* in Moesia. The rest of his career has to

be pieced together from the references in the biography. Proceeding to a junior appointment as a procurator, he next commanded the Roman fleet on the Rhine, based at Köln-Alteburg, a posting which probably was the occasion for, or later prompted, the erection of the statue at Cologne. He then went on to hold the procuratorship of Dacia.

Soon he was promoted into the Senate, with praetorian rank, held a legionary command as legate, then a consulship in absence, and was governor of five important imperial provinces in quick succession. The biographer makes a telling comment that he only entered the Senate House in Rome after being governor of four provinces, testimony to the overriding importance of jobs to be done in the field; the consulship had become the necessary qualification for important posts, and no longer in itself a pinnacle. After a period of enforced retirement, Pertinax became governor of Britain in 185, was proconsul of Africa, then prefect of the city of Rome and consul for a second time with the emperor Commodus at the beginning of AD 192. All in all, he was well placed to be acclaimed emperor himself after Commodus was murdered on the last day of the year. If we are to believe the biography, Pertinax achieved the amazing transition from humble birth to equestrian rank, and then to the Senate, and finally, if only briefly, to the imperial purple, in the course of a lifetime.

Inscriptions thus show the creation of posts, the development of the hierarchy, and the ease of transfer from one part of the Empire to another. It will be remembered that such inscriptions commemorate only the most successful, not a community's less resplendent sons who left to join the army and were not heard of again, or exited from the imperial service under a cloud. Similarly we rarely hear of petitions or applications which were unsuccessful. Occasionally it may prove possible to identify a gap in a career, and we may suspect periods of disfavour or illness, but more often such changes of fortune lie concealed in the bare intimation of offices held.

11

THE ARMY
AND THE FRONTIERS

The Roman state always possessed an army, comprising men selected from among its citizens. Military service was both a duty and a privilege, and was initially unpaid. Soldiers served mostly for short periods, but as the Roman domains grew they were retained longer under arms. The norm in the Late Republic was six years continuous service. No epitaphs appear to survive of men who specifically describe themselves as soldiers, before the mid first century BC. In part the reason must be that reference to military service, in an age when most adult males had served in some capacity for a few years, was not considered essential information. After the end of the civil wars which marred the final generation of the Late Republic, the army became a professional long-service force, based in increasingly permanent stations in the frontier provinces, and most of it soon along the outermost limits of those provinces.

The legions were the backbone of the imperial army. There were some 30 in permanent commission, each of about 5000 men, and bearing numerals and titles which reflected battle-honours and past service, or were taken from an emperor who had founded or reconstituted the legion. For example, Legion II *Augusta*, The Augustan; IV *Macedonica*, The Macedonian; VI *Victrix*, The Victorious. The legion was divided into 10 cohorts usually of 480 men, and each cohort into six centuries of 80 men. The legionaries were Roman citizens. They were supported in battle and on garrison duty by auxiliary regiments of between 500 and 1000 men, usually recruited from non-citizen communities. The auxiliary infantry were organized in *cohortes* and the cavalry in *alae* (wings). An infantry cohort might have a small cavalry force attached to it; in which case it was entitled a *cohors equitata*.

The legions comprised a substantial concentration of Roman citizens based for long periods in specific localities. We can expect the legionaries to erect inscriptions and be commemorated after their death. Most auxiliaries, on the other hand, being often recruited from recently conquered districts, were initially less epigraphically conscious. Inscriptions complement literary sources in providing the names and titles of legions and regiments of auxiliaries, so enabling an 'army list' to be drawn up. Two small pillars found long ago in Rome each give a list of legions, in a clockwise geographical order round the Empire, compiled in about AD 165, with later additions.[1] As an institution the army was concerned with proper forms and traditions, and the commemoration of comrades who died on service was an important factor in the maintenance of morale. It has been so down to modern times. In the more remote provinces it is noticeable how the incidence of inscriptions corresponds to centres of military activity.

SOLDIERS' EPITAPHS
The most frequently surviving category of military

inscriptions is of gravestones from the now permanent or semi-permanent bases of the legions. The tombstones were largely of men of the resident garrisons who died in harness. A legionary of the Augustan age whose cremated remains were interred at his home town of Cremona in northern Italy had his military decorations buried next to the ashes.[2]

Casualties suffered on the battlefield were cremated.[3] (The opening sequence of the film *Cleopatra* (1963) shows huge pyres for the dead constructed in the aftermath of the battle at Pharsalus.) Occasionally an individual might be given a special monument, as Caesar's centurion Crastinus at Pharsalus; Appian reports that Caesar erected a separate tomb for him 'near the common one for the mass of soldiers'.[4] From Xanten on the Lower Rhine has come a fine panel which was once part of a cenotaph of the centurion Marcus Caelius who 'fell in the Varian War' (of AD 9) and whose bones, if found, were to be placed inside the monument; but it may be doubted if they ever were.[5] When the army of Germanicus visited the scene of the disaster in AD 15 they collected and buried their comrades' bones under a large mound;[6] funeral pyres were unnecessary, as the bones were already stripped bare of flesh.

The order of information provided on the gravestone of a soldier or veteran follows a reasonably regular sequence: name, father's name and tribe (as on a civilian tombstone), followed by place of origin, military rank, the name of the legion or other military unit in which the deceased had served, and the number of years spent under arms. Sometimes the soldier may name the centurion in whose century he served. Only rarely is a date given for the year of enlistment and of discharge (or death).[7]

The reader needs to be familiar with the range of military ranks and how they are abbreviated. The most common are *mil(es)*, a soldier, and *vet(eranus)*, a retired soldier. The use of the sign 7 (for the word 'centurion' or 'century') is frequently employed. There is some uncertainty over the origin of the sign, though its meaning is clear.

The epitaphs were erected sometimes by a brother also serving, or by a fellow soldier designated as heir. Officially soldiers could not marry during service, before the end of the second century AD; but wives or concubines are reported.[8] It seems that there was a burial club to which soldiers contributed to make certain of proper commemoration as the need arose. Soldiers shared a common purpose and experience; most died away from home, to be commemorated by their comrades.

In the early first century AD it became fashionable for the epitaph itself to be accompanied by a full-length representation of the deceased in uniform, seen as he wished to be remembered by his comrades and future generations. Such depictions are important to our understanding of the development of equipment and weaponry. Many such graveslabs have survived from the Rhineland where the practice was particularly in vogue. There are a few such tombstones from Britain. A particularly fine example comes from Colchester, which shows Marcus Favonius Facilis in his uniform, with elaborately decorated belt, holding his sword (*gladius*) by its pommel and a vine stick (*vitis*), the symbol of his rank as centurion, standing within an arched niche decorated with floral designs (Fig. 46). Almost certainly the stone dates from the early years of the Roman occupation, while the legion XX was still in garrison at Colchester itself. Traces of paint were observed in the niche and on the lettering. The inscription gives the name of the deceased in the nominative case, but abbreviated.

M(arcus) Favoni(us) M(arci) f(ilius) Pol(lia) Faci | lis 7 leg(ionis) XX Verecund | us et Novicius lib(erti) posu | erunt h(ic) s(itus) e(st).[9] 'Marcus Favonius Facilis, son of Marcus, of the voting-tribe Pollia, centurion of legion XX. The freedmen Verecundus and Novicius erected (*it*). He lies here.'

The lettering, which is not well arranged on the stone, is consistent with a date of about 40–70 AD. No place of origin is given, but several north Italian towns were registered in the voting-tribe *Pollia*, which might suggest he came from that area. The legion lacks any distinguishing titles; it had probably not yet received the epithets *Valeria Victrix*. The two freedmen were formerly slaves of Facilis, and on manumission must have become M.Favonius Verecundus and M.Favonius Novicius. The slave names, translated literally, mean

46 Gravestone of Marcus Favonius Facilis, centurion of the Twentieth Legion, Colchester, England. Mid first century AD *(Colchester and Essex Museum).*

'Modest' and 'New-boy' (above, p. 20). The stone was found lying on its front face; it could even have been pushed over by the Boudican rebels in AD 60–61. In the ground nearby was a lead canister containing ashes. Similar is the graveslab of Caecilius Avitus, commemorated at Chester. The inscription reads:

> *D(is) M(anibus) | Caecilius Avit | us Emer(ita) Aug(usta) | optio leg(ionis) XX | V(aleriae) V(ictricis) st(i)p(endiorum) XV vix(it) | an(nos) XXXIIII | h(eres) f(aciendum) c(uravit).*[10] 'To the spirits of the departed. Caecilius Avitus, from Emerita Augusta (*now Mérida in Spain*), *optio* of the Twentieth Legion, Valiant and Victorious, of 15 years' service, lived 34 years. His heir had (*this*) done.'

In a legion, the *optio* was second in command of a century.

Auxiliary cavalrymen are also shown in sculptured reliefs (Fig. 47). Often the deceased is portrayed, with spear raised, on horseback, in the moment of triumph over a barbarian warrior, a scene which also symbolized the victory of life over death. Auxiliary infantrymen were seldom depicted, this is perhaps because of cost: cavalrymen always received higher pay.

THE ROMAN ARMY MACHINE

This mass of data provides valuable information on a number of important aspects of the Roman military machine. First is an enhancement of our knowledge of the internal organization of individual army units and the posts and ranks that a soldier could hold. Many ranks are known only from the epigraphic record. Such details, which we could not expect to recover from literary sources, have been the subject of close and sustained study. Centurions often list a succession of legions in which they served and their epitaphs reveal a system of transfers throughout the Empire – a mobility not accorded to the individual ranker, who was likely to serve throughout his career in one legion. Details of the higher command structure can be pieced together from the career inscriptions of legates, tribunes and prefects, as recorded in their home towns or from their garrison postings.

A second benefit is that military tombstones,

47 Tomb monument of Longinus Biarta, Thracian cavalryman in the Ala Sulpicia, *Cologne, Germany. In the upper panel the deceased reclines in a funeral banquet scene. In the lower, his horse, weapons and servant are depicted. Römisch-Germanisches Museum, Köln. CIL XIII 8312. (Rheinisches Bildarchiv.)*

together with altars erected by units and their commanders, allow scholars to identify the garrison of a fort or fortress at any particular time. An examination of the mass of such details allows a picture to be built up of the movement of regiments between postings. Such is the volume of material, especially for legions stationed on the Rhine and Danube, that their movements and transfers can be closely dated. But on some frontiers, for instance in Britain and the East, the evidence remains deficient.

Thirdly, inscriptions tell much about the ori-

gins, lifespan and service careers of individual soldiers, allowing tentative conclusions on survival rates and on casualties suffered on particular frontiers.[11] Where soldiers died away from home (and most would), the tombstones regularly specify the town of origin, allowing a picture to be built up of the changing recruitment patterns of the units. Scrutiny of these statistics indicates how rapidly the percentage of Italians in the legions fell away during the first century, so that by the time of Hadrian they had practically ceased to serve. The bulk of a legion's manpower was now drawn from the provinces, especially those near to which, or within which, the legion itself was based. The transfer of a legion from one province to another might result in recruitment from different geographical areas, which may be documented in the epigraphic record. Normally such conclusions will rest on the accumulated data from a mass of individual gravestones. However, a substantial statue base, in honour of Antoninus Pius, found in 1939 at the legionary fortress of Nicopolis west of Alexandria in Egypt, names no fewer than 136 veterans of the legion II *Traiana* who had been released in AD 157.[12] The soldiers are individually named, with their towns of origin. Only a minority (25) came from the eastern provinces – most (89) came from Africa and the Danube lands; 15 are from Italy, and of these three came from Rome itself. The overall pattern contrasts sharply with other evidence emphasizing increasingly localized recruitment. In fact the date of release offers a clue to this anomaly: the soldiers had been recruited in 132–33, at the time of the outbreak of the Second Jewish Revolt, in the suppression of which we know II *Traiana* took part. The emergency led to conscription of troops from sources not normally tapped, including Italy itself, which seems now to have been drawn upon only when new legions were being raised.

THE AUXILIARIES AND THEIR DIPLOMAS

Inscriptions are equally valuable in the study of auxiliaries, though surviving stones are much less numerous. Here the inscriptions give the names of a regiment (a *cohors* or *ala*), and thus sometimes identify the place where they were stationed. Often a centurion or prefect will erect an altar on the regiment's behalf. A useful bonus to any study of auxiliary garrisons of a province comes from what are usually termed military diplomas. These consist of pairs of hinged folding bronze tablets, often measuring about 16 by 12cm (6½ by 5in.) when folded, which were presented to, or obtained by, individual auxiliaries at the end of 25 years' service. They were a formal proof of the chief rewards of that service: the grant of citizenship and regularization of an existing marriage, so that any children would be citizens also.[13] The exact date of issue is given, with the names of the consuls of the year, useful information for historians. The possession of the document could be particularly important to the retired auxiliary as proof of the enhanced status of himself and his family in whatever community he might chose to settle. Inscribed on the tablets (twice, inside as well as outside, to deter forgery and impersonation) was a copy of the text as preserved at Rome, including a list of all those regiments of a province which had veterans so honoured on the same day, followed by specification of the unit in which the particular individual had served, his commanding officer, his own name, and members of his family as appropriate. Finally came a list of those who had witnessed the issue of the document.

Diplomas are, when studied with care, probably the single most important source of information on the strength and make up of a province's auxiliary garrison at known dates. Occasionally diplomas reveal specific incidents of war. Here is the text of a diploma found at Cluj in Romania in 1939:[14] 'The emperor Caesar, son of deified Nerva, Nerva Trajanus Augustus Germanicus Dacicus, chief priest, holder of tribunician power 14 times, saluted *imperator* 6 times, consul 5 times, father of his country, to the infantry and cavalry who are serving in the First Cohort of *Brittones*, 1000 strong, surnamed *Ulpia Torquata*, Loyal and Faithful, Roman Citizens, which is in Dacia under Decimus Terentius Scaurianus, whose names are listed below, who served loyally and faithfully in the Dacian Expedition, [he] gives Roman Citizenship before the completion of their due service. On the third day before the Ides of August, at Darnithithi, in the consulship of Lucius Minicius Natalis and Quintus Silvanus Granianus [AD 106]. To the infantryman M.Ulpius Novantico from Leicester, son of Adcobrovatus.' It refers back to an award, made on the battlefield at a place called Darnithithi, of Roman citizenship 'before the completion of their due service' (i.e. the full 25 years), to members of an infantry regiment of *Brittones*. Subsequently (as was normal in such circumstances), the cohort kept the letters C.R. (*civium Romanorum*) as a permanent part of the unit's titulature. Though the date of the award was AD 106, the diploma itself was not issued until 110, presumably when the time came for Novantico to be released. He must therefore have enlisted in AD

85, presumably in Britain, and his unit was later to serve in the Dacian war. Novantico has taken the emperor's names, to become Marcus Ulpius Novantico.

WAR AND ITS COMMEMORATION

Though epitaphs of soldiers usually specify which legion or regiment they served in, and may report how many years they had been under arms, they rarely mention the locality of service, or the wars in which they had taken part. One exception is where a soldier was killed in combat,[15] or more positively where he had acquired military decorations for valour. Several veterans who were settled in northern Italy after the defeat of Antony and Cleopatra at Actium in 31 BC adopted, or were awarded, the title *Actiacus* (Actium-fighter) as a surname.[16] The most frequent types of military decorations were *torques* (necklets of bronze), *armillae* (arm-bangles) and *phalerae* (embossed metal discs). There was a hierarchy of award, according to rank. Sometimes these decorations are shown in relief on the stone itself, or the soldier is depicted wearing them.[17]

A gravestone found in 1965 near Kavalla, in the territory of the town of Philippi, in north-eastern Greece, records in detail the military career of Ti.Claudius Maximus, a legionary by origin, but who transferred on promotion to a regiment of auxiliary cavalry.[18] He fought in Trajan's Dacian War from AD 101 onwards, gaining further promotion and exceptional military decorations in AD 106 'because he captured Decebalus and brought his head to him [i.e. to Trajan] at Ranisstorum'. Above the inscription is carved a scene showing Maximus in the act of capturing the body of Decebalus, the Dacian king, who has committed suicide only moments earlier; shown below are two *torques* (torcs) and two *armillae* (bracelets), which were among the decorations he received.[19]

Octavian established a city at Actium to mark the site of his victory over Antony and Cleopatra, called *Nicopolis*, 'victory-city'.[20] A focal point was a substantial podium, marking the site where Octavian's tent had been pitched. It was decorated with ships' prows and bore an inscription recording a dedication to Mars and Neptune. The inscription, in a single line, was 55m (180ft) long! Recent excavations have yielded important details about its decorative elements.[21]

Towns did not have war memorials as such where the dead in a particular war or campaign were remembered. Victories in Roman times were marked by the erection on the battlefield of a trophy of captured arms and equipment, often suspended from a tree. Such scenes, which may include bound captives, are frequently represented on coin issues. In AD 16 'Germanicus built a pile of weaponry, with a proud inscription attached, reading: "The army of Tiberius Caesar, after subduing the nations between the Rhine and the Elbe, dedicated these offerings to Mars, Jupiter and Augustus"'.[22] At Adamklissi in the Romanian Dobrudja, close to the mouth of the Danube on its southern bank, a group of monuments was erected early in the second century to commemorate wars fought along the river against the Dacians. They mark in part the final victory, but also earlier defeats. One of the monuments, a huge altar, lists individually by name some 3800 soldiers who had fallen 'for the state'.[23]

Augustus marked the completion of his conquest of the Maritime Alps by erecting a monument at a spot henceforth known as *Tropaeum Augusti* (Augustus' Trophy, now La Turbie) near Monte Carlo. The Elder Pliny reports the inscription, and surviving fragments have been set into the partly reconstructed monument.[24]

SOLDIERS AT ROME

No legions were normally stationed in Italy itself before the beginning of the third century AD when Severus constructed a fortress for the legion II *Parthica* at Albano in the hills south of Rome. But many military inscriptions have been found at Rome, in particular of the cohorts of the Praetorian Guard, which grew out of Augustus' wartime bodyguard and was retained by successive emperors to protect their position in Rome. Most probably the Guard under the Julio-Claudians numbered about 5000 men, in 9 (later 12) cohorts; under the Flavians and after there were 10 cohorts, each probably of 1000 men, equivalent to two legions. From Tiberius' reign onwards they were based in a brick-built fortress on the edge of Rome, called the *Castra Praetoria*.

Cemeteries around Rome have yielded numerous epitaphs of the Praetorians, who in the Early

48 *Gravestones of soldiers of the German Bodyguard* (corporis custodes) *of the Julio-Claudian emperors. Mid first century* AD. *(Museo Nazionale, Rome.)*

Empire were mostly Italians recruited directly from civilian life. From the beginning of the third century they were drawn from experienced legionaries of the frontier garrisons. There were also three (later four) *cohortes Urbanae* (Urban Cohorts), the Rome police force; and seven *cohortes Vigilum* (cohorts of watchmen), a paramilitary fire-brigade. In the Julio-Claudian period, the emperors maintained a personal bodyguard of Germans and Batavians, chiefly or perhaps wholly cavalry (Fig. 48). In the later first century AD, a cavalry regiment, the *Equites Singulares Augusti*, was formed from selected auxiliaries of the provincial garrisons. In addition, inscriptions reveal numerous soldiers of provincial armies seconded for service in the capital, or dying while on special missions there.

A panel (Fig. 49) from a statue-base at Turin (*Augusta* of the Taurini) is inscribed:

C(aio) Gavio L(uci) f(ilio) | [S]tel(latina tribu) Silvano | [pr]imipilari leg(ionis) VIII Aug(ustae) | [t]ribuno coh(ortis) II Vigilum | [t]ribuno coh(ortis) XIII Vrban(ae) | [tr]ibuno coh(ortis) XII praetor(iae) | [d]onis donato a divo Claud(io) | bello Britannico | [to]rquibus armillis phaleris | corona aurea | [p]atrono colon(iae) | d(ecreto) [d(ecurionum)].[25] 'To

Gaius Gavius Silvanus, son of Lucius, of the voting-tribe *Stellatina*, chief centurion of legion VIII *Augusta*, tribune of the second cohort of *Vigiles*, tribune of the 13th Urban Cohort, tribune of the 12th Praetorian Cohort, decorated by the deified Claudius in the British War, with torcs, bracelets, medals, (*and*) a gold crown; patron of the colony, by decree of the town councillors.'

A local man from Turin (as the tribe *Stellatina* indicates), Silvanus' early military service is omitted in favour of higher appointments. Very probably he enlisted as a soldier in the Guard, and came to notice during the invasion of Britain in AD 43 when he received military decorations. Later he was a centurion and later still chief centurion in a legion, VIII *Augusta* in Moesia. Next he was posted to Rome itself where he was tribune (i.e. cohort commander) successively in the *Vigiles*, Urban Cohorts and Praetorians – the standard sequence of office holding. At some point, probably during tenure of this last post, he was made patron of his home town – the councillors having identified a local boy made good, who might be able to represent them at Rome. We happen to know a little more about the last days of Silvanus' life, not reported on in this source: in AD 65, as a

49 Panel from the statue base honouring Gaius Gavius Silvanus, decorated for military service in Britain under Claudius, c. AD 65. (Museo Archeologico, Turin.)

praetorian officer with access to Nero, he joined the Pisonian Conspiracy to murder the emperor. When the conspiracy (which was unsuccessful) began to fall apart, Nero despatched Silvanus (of whose complicity in it he was as yet unaware) to enforce the suicide of Nero's former tutor, the philosopher Seneca.[26] Silvanus carried out this assignment without revealing his own feelings. A little later he was implicated, but Nero (oddly enough) forgave him. Soon after, Gavius Silvanus, doubtless ashamed at his by no means glorious part in this whole episode, committed suicide.

THE FLEET

Inscriptions also provide a picture of the organization of the imperial fleets.

The two major bases were at Misenum (on the Bay of Naples) and Ravenna (near the head of the Adriatic). Gravestones survive in substantial numbers from both localities which name individual sailors and their families, the names of the ships in which they served, and much of what we know about the internal organization and hierarchy of command. Smaller squadrons, which unfortunately are epigraphically less well attested, cruised on the Rhine and Danube, in the Black Sea, in the English Channel (the *classis Britannica*) and on the Nile.

LIFE IN THE ARMY

It needs to be remembered that for a great part of a soldier's service he would not be fighting. Through the centuries, commanders of regiments, and of armies, have faced the problem of maintaining a state of readiness among a large group of highly trained, but potentially under-employed men, and putting their energies to good use.

A visit by the emperor Hadrian in AD 128 to legion III *Augusta* and auxiliary regiments stationed at or near Lambaesis in North Africa is remembered to this day, from the survival on stone of the text of the speech he made to the troops when he had watched them exercising and practising camp-building, encouraging them to new efforts.[27]

The army was frequently used in construction projects for civilian communities. One unusual case, from the reign of Antoninus Pius, is reported from Saldae in Mauretania where the citizens, while constructing an aqueduct, had attempted to dig a tunnel through a mountain starting from both sides.[28] Unfortunately they or their architects had made a poor job of calculating the angles, and the two tunnels did not meet. The procurator of Mauretania then petitioned the legate of Numidia for help. Nonius Datus, a former soldier of the nearby legion, III *Augusta*, who during his military service had supervised the initial stages of the original project, was despatched from Lambaesis. After being mugged en route, he arrived at Saldae (now Bejaïa in Algeria), re-surveyed the angles, and got the two tunnels to meet. On his return to Lambaesis, he erected a commemorative pillar with a wordy text detailing these events, and honoured various personifications, including Patience, Virtue and Hope.

At Caesarea in Palestine the legions of the garrisons of Syria and Judaea built an aqueduct (attached to an existing aqueduct built in the reign of King Herod) in the aftermath of the Second Jewish Revolt (AD 135). Set into the side of the aqueduct is a series of inscribed tablets which report their work; many other such slabs doubtless remain hidden beneath the wind-blown sand which still covers part of the monument.[29]

On stones commemorating such work it was normal for army units to give the name of the emperor for whom the task was undertaken, that of the commander and perhaps of a centurion, often coupled with the regimental emblems. The wild boar of the 20th legion must have been as familiar in some areas of northern Britain as the HD symbol put down as a marker of its presence and progress by the 51st Highland Division, which earned for itself during the Second World War the nickname of 'Highway Decorators'. Soldiers left graffiti in quarries opened up to provide raw material for constructional projects; a favourite deity to be named was *Hercules Saxanus* (i.e. Hercules, god of the stones).[30] The army established its own stores depots and manufactured tiles and bricks, suitably marked with the unit's name; regiments also manufactured and stamped their own pottery. Catapults bore the units' names (Fig. 50), as did lead slingbolts.[31] Soldiers, as in all ages, put their names on their equipment, which they would have to replace, if lost.[32] A fine shield boss (Fig. 51) found in the River Tyne in 1867, bears the name of the legion VIII *Augusta* and (vertically on the left border) of its owner. The Latin inscriptions read:

Leg(ionis VIII Aug(ustae). 7 Iul(i) Magni Iuni Dubitati.[33] 'Belonging to Legion VIII *Augusta*; century of Julius Magnus; Junius Dubitatus.'

Soldiers scratched their names on walls, wherever they passed by.[34] Some of the military standards of the legions and other regiments might bear inscriptions naming the unit or the emperor (Fig. 57); but the legionary eagles themselves did not.

The army had a strong sense of loyalty to the emperor, his family and the state religion. The *Feriale Duranum* (the Dura Festival List), dating to the reign of the emperor Severus Alexander (AD 222–35), is part of a calendar of the army's religious year, preserved as a papyrus roll, at Dura Europus, a city in northern Mesopotamia.[35] It lists festivals and feast days in honour of the gods, of present and past (deified) emperors, and in commemoration of victories or other successes.

In the winter of 179–80 AD a detachment of legionaries from the garrison of Pannonia wintered at Trenčin (in modern Slovakia) some 120km (72 miles) north of the frontier in an area which the emperor Marcus Aurelius hoped to turn into a new

50 Bronze catapult plate, belonging to the Fourth Legion Macedonica, *from the battlefield at Cremona, AD 69. Emblems of the legion are shown and the consular date of construction, AD 45. (Museo Civico, Cremona, Italy. Photo: D.Baatz.)*

51 *Bronze shield boss, with enamelling, showing emblems and standards of the Eighth Legion* Augusta. *Mid second century–early third century* AD. *Found in the River Tyne, 1867 (British Museum. Photo of facsimile: Museum of Antiquities, Newcastle.)*

province, and left an inscription carved high up on a rock face (Fig. 52) where it can be seen today.[36] The most easterly Roman inscription known is of military origin; it comes from the mountain of Beiouk-Dagh in the Baku area on the west side of the Caspian Sea. It records the presence there in the reign of the 'emperor Domitianus Caesar Augustus Germanicus' of Julius Maximus, centurion of the legion XII *Fulminata*.[37]

A soldier of the legion I *Minervia* set up an altar at Cologne to his favourite local mother-goddesses the *Matronae Aufanae*, on return from a 2000 mile journey with a detachment of his legion when it travelled from Bonn to fight with the emperor Lucius Verus in the East in AD 162–66. The soldier, Julius Mansuetus, states on the altar that he had been 'at the river Alutus beyond the Caucasus mountain'.[38]

There are tales of sadness too – men killed on garrison duty, in accidents, by drowning and by brigands.[39] A much decorated centurion, 'after an upright life of 49 years, close to the day when he was actually to take up an appointment as chief centurion, paid his debt to nature'.[40]

THE ARMY AND THE FRONTIERS

The army was often engaged on the building of frontier works which, from the later first century and especially from Hadrian's reign onwards, were constructed along the outer limits of outlying provinces as a formal marker of where the Empire ended and the barbarian world began. Hadrian's

52 *Dedication to* Victoria Augustorum *(The Victory of the Emperors), on a rock-face at Trenčín, Czechoslovakia,* AD *179–80.*

Wall and the Antonine Wall may be most familiar but similar, if less substantial, barriers were built across Hessen, the Palatinate, Baden-Württemberg and Bavaria; in modern Romania, Tunisia and Algeria. Inscriptions give invaluable aid towards an understanding of their constructional and occupational histories. On Hadrian's Wall records survive reporting the construction or reconstruction of forts, the building of milecastles and of the curtain wall itself. The work of specific centuries and cohorts is noted on roughly inscribed 'centurial' stones set into the wall-structure.[41] On the Antonine Wall, a series of richly ornamented 'distance slabs' details the precise lengths of the *opus valli* (the work of the rampart) completed by each of the contributing legions.[42]

Often soldiers remained after service in the areas they had come to know well after half a lifetime in the army. Standing 14.6m (48ft) high, in a custom-built gallery at the Römisch-Germanisches Museum, Cologne, is the tomb monument of Lucius Poblicius and his family (Fig. 53). Poblicius was a veteran of the legion *V Alaudae*, who retired from the army in the mid first century AD.[43] The monument, reconstructed from over 100 fragments, is eloquent testimony to the wealth that a retired soldier could accumulate in provincial society.

The discovery over several years at Vindolanda fort (just to the rear of Hadrian's Wall) of a large number of wooden writing tablets inscribed in ink has provided an unexpected but most welcome insight into the life-style of both the ordinary soldiers and of the officers on the northern frontier in Britain at the beginning of the second century AD. They give details of foodstuffs ordered and delivered, and letters addressed chiefly to one of the prefects and his wife. Those published recently include an invitation to a birthday party, a complaint about the deficiencies of British recruits to the Roman army, and a comment on the poor state of the roads connecting the frontier forts to supply bases in the south. Further revelations can be confidently expected.[44]

53 Monument to Lucius Poblicius, veteran of the Fifth Legion Alaudae, *as reconstructed from fragments in the Römisch-Germanisches Museum, Cologne, Germany. (Rheinisches Bildarchiv, Köln.)*

12

TEMPLES AND ALTARS TO THE GODS

Like other peoples of antiquity the Romans were strongly religious, venerating a variety of gods and goddesses, many deriving from the natural forces important in a primarily agricultural economy. Under the influence of the Greeks these coalesced into a 'divine family' and acquired human characteristics. As Roman domains expanded, these deities were exported to conquered lands, and conversely other gods were added to the Roman experience. Expansion eastwards brought them into contact with the deities of Asia Minor, Syria, and Egypt; often these were matched with Roman or Greek equivalents. Similarly in the west, Roman deities were worshipped alongside Celtic divinities of the mountain and the stream. In general, local deities and religious practices were tolerated or ignored. More forceful action was taken only if they constituted or seemed to constitute an alternative focus to loyalty and a threat to the stability of the Empire and its administration.

A substantial amount of the detailed evidence for Roman state religion and local cults throughout the Empire derives from inscriptions. These document the construction of temples and shrines where worship was concentrated, or of the altars which might be placed in and around the shrines over many hundreds of years.

THE ROMAN TEMPLE

The most obvious focus of worship was the temple. Early Roman temples might be timber-built, with a decorative skin of terracotta plaques and pedimental sculpture likewise in terracotta. Gradually such buildings were replaced in stone and raised on a substantial podium with steps leading up to a façade of columns. Temples often occupied central positions on one side of the market place of the town. Needless to say, many of the largest and most elaborate temples in the Roman world were to be found in Rome itself. Atop the Capitol was a huge temple to Jupiter Capitolinus, frequently rebuilt after destructive fires.

Across the façade above the columns would normally be an inscription naming the deity commemorated and sometimes also the benefactor who had paid for the building's construction as evidence of his piety. The letters of the inscription were frequently in bronze (above, p. 15). A small number of temples survives more or less intact, so that the dedications can be studied *in situ*: for example, the temple to Roma and Augustus at Pula (Fig. 54),[1] and a temple in honour of Augustus' grandsons at Nîmes (the so-called Maison Carrée).[2]

The survival of such structures has often resulted from their continued use as Christian churches up to the present day. For example, the temple of Minerva at Assisi is now the church of S. Maria sopra Minerva (St Mary above Minerva).[3] In the Forum at Rome the temple of the deified Antoninus Pius and his empress Faustina (Fig. 55) was converted in the eleventh century into the

54 Temple of Roma and Augustus, Pula, Yugoslavia. Early first century AD.

whose 'house' it was, as well as an array of dedications and offerings of varying sizes, much like many modern churches. Worshippers could donate a statuette, or the like, suitably inscribed on its base as a record of the gift. People restored to health after prayers to a god might leave an image of the affected part of the anatomy, in terracotta or a precious metal.

Temples were erected by communities or by individuals at their own expense. Outside, in front of the temple and at the foot of the steps leading to its interior, would be a substantial altar, where offerings were made and prayers spoken. On the larger altars a fire was lit, and offerings (foodstuffs, or the entrails of animals) were consumed in the

55 Temple of Antoninus and Faustina, The Forum, Rome. Built AD 141 on death of Faustina. The inscription was emended on death of Antoninus, AD 161.

church of S. Lorenzo in Miranda, the raised floor level being an eloquent testimony to the then ground surface in the Forum. In 1602 it was rebuilt in baroque style. The text of the inscription reads:

Divo Antonino et | divae Faustinae ex s(enatus) c(onsulto).[4] 'To the deified Antoninus and to the deified Faustina, according to a decree of the Senate.'

The temple was erected in AD 141 on the death of Faustina. The extra line in honour of Antoninus must have been added later, on his death in AD 161.

Where the original columns of a temple have not survived rebuilding work through the centuries, the temple-podium may yet form the floor of a present-day church. At Pozzuoli a temple on the hilltop promontory had been refashioned over the years into the cathedral church of S. Nicola. A serious fire in 1964, which was followed by an earthquake, led to the demolition of the cathedral, revealing the walls of the temple and columns enclosed in the later masonry.[5]

A temple contained statues to the god or goddess

flames, with the smoke and vapours ascending to heaven; milk, wine or olive oil were poured on top by the dedicator or an officiating priest. Animals might be killed, and their blood poured on top, but their carcasses were cooked separately and eaten by the worshippers. For the population, a festival was literally a 'feast' day, when the local aristocracy paid for a meal for their less well-off fellow citizens. There were no professional full-time priests in Roman state religion, but inscriptions from many towns reveal local worthies and magistrates elected as priests who would officiate at sacrifices on feast-days in the presence of the townspeople.

ALTARS

Individuals could, and often did, erect their own altars to the gods, to be placed either in the temple precinct, or on their own land. Such private altars have a distinctive shape: in essence they are squared-off, miniature columns, usually demarcated into capital, shaft and base (see Fig. 59). On the capital, which was regularly flanked by bolsters, was a saucer-shaped depression generally called a *focus* (literally, a fireplace), where offerings could be placed.[6]

The altars erected by individuals vary greatly in size. Some might approximate to the temple-altars, on which a fire could indeed be lit, but most were quite small, perhaps no more than 1m (3¼ft) high. Whether a fire could actually be kindled on some small altars may be doubted; more probably offerings would be piled on top and liquid poured on. Some altars were very small, hardly more than 30cm (1ft) high. These must often have belonged in household shrines. The size and decoration of the altar could depend on the dedicator's ability or willingness to pay, or his assessment of the value of his debt to the deity. Sometimes, when the altar is apparently uninscribed, the text was probably painted on in red letters. Roman literature speaks frequently of altars erected in the countryside from piled blocks of turf, sufficient for an open-air dedication; these leave no epigraphic testimony.[7]

PRAYERS AND VOWS

The construction of a temple or the erection of an altar frequently represented a personal statement of hope or gratitude on the part of the dedicator. The erection of an altar was one element in a contract between the worshipper and the god. In some cases, an altar could be erected in advance of an event, and the offering made on it represented a prayer for future assistance. In other cases the erection of the altar came as a climax: the dedicator had promised an altar or a gift if events turned out according to his prayers. If the god or goddess had obliged, the dedicator arranged for an altar to be prepared in fulfilment of the promise, and he offered a sacrifice according to his means. In theory the altar might be used just once, and then forgotten, the contract having been fulfilled. But others must have been repeatedly used.

Inscriptions on altars often follow a fairly standard form. First comes the name of the god or goddess to whom the altar was dedicated, in the dative case, indicating that the altar was offered *to* the god. Next came the name or names of the dedicator(s); finally, if the altar was erected in fulfilment of a vow made earlier, there came a formula which emphasized that element: VOTVM SOLVIT LAETVS LIBENS MERITO ('fulfilled his vow gladly willingly and deservedly'). The gratitude of the dedicator was there for all to see; both sides of the bargain had been kept. The final phrase was normally abbreviated to the initial letters V S L L M, and the very appearance of this formula on a stone can identify it as an altar. The same formula can also appear on plaques marking other offerings left at a temple (see Fig. 34).

A good example of the fulfilment of a promise comes from Bordeaux. In 1921 an altar was found built into the late Roman wall of the town (Fig. 56). The inscription reads:

Deae Tutel(a)e Bou(r)dig(alensi) | M(arcus) Aur(elius) Lunaris IIIIII | vir Aug(ustalis) col(oniae) Ebor(acensis) et | Lind(ensis) prov(inciae) Brit(anniae) Inf(erioris) | aram quam vover(at) | ab Eboraci evect(us) | v(otum) s(olvit) l(ibens) m(erito) | Perpetuo et Corne-(liano consulibus).[8] 'To the tutelary goddess Bourdiga (*protecting goddess of Bordeaux*), Marcus Aurelius Lunaris, *sevir Augustalis* at the colonies of Lincoln and York in the province of Lower Britain, gladly and willingly fulfilled a vow he made on leaving York, by the erection of this altar, in the consulship of Perpetuus and Cornelianus.'

The date is AD 237. Lunaris, priest of the imperial cult (below, p. 95) at two important cities in Britain, had just completed a sea voyage from York

56 Altar erected to the protecting goddess of Bordeaux by Marcus Aurelius Lunaris, AD 237. (Photo: J.M.Arnaud, Musée d'Aquitaine.)

to Bordeaux, sailing down the east coast of Britain and across the Channel, perhaps for reasons of trade, and was expressing his thanks to the tutelary goddess of the city of Bordeaux, for a journey safely completed.[9] Notice the frequent ligaturing of letters, here to save space (above, p. 20) Above the inscribed panel is a badly battered scene which may show the oriental goddess Cybele in the partial guise of a mother goddess. The left side of the altar bears the figure of a reclining river god with an anchor (presumably the Garonne on which Bordeaux stands) and on the right-hand side is a boar standard, evidently symbolizing York itself.

RELIGION AND THE ARMY

The Roman army's religious observances were strictly organized (see above, p. 88). It has frequently been so down to modern times. Before a battle, a general or his soldiers might seek the approval of the gods, especially Mars, for the forthcoming fight. On the sculptured side-panel of a slab of Antonine date, from Bridgeness, West Lothian, a group of officers from the legion II *Augusta* looks on while their commander pours a liquid offering from a saucer on to the *focus* of a small altar (Fig. 57). In front three animals are led forward for sacrifice. The ceremony is a *suovetaurilia*, which required the ritual killing of a boar (*sus*), a ram (*ovis*) and a bull (*taurus*), and sought the favour of the gods for the fighting to come.[10]

Auxiliary regiments stationed at the forts of a frontier garrison might erect altars communally to important deities, especially Jupiter, with the prefect or a centurion seeing to the preparation and erection of the stone. On the third of January each year the regiment renewed its vows to the emperor and the gods; a fresh altar or group of altars would be erected, and the old ones removed and perhaps buried.[11] Dedications could be made to the *genius loci*, the 'presiding spirit of the place' where the regiment was stationed, and to the *genius* of the regiment itself. The 'birthday' of the regiment was commemorated, and its standards venerated, as were the birthdays and accession days of the present, and some previous, emperor(s). Outside the fort at Osterburken on the Outer German *limes* was a shrine favoured by officials (*beneficiarii*) from the provincial governor's military headquarters, who were attached to the local garrison for short tours of about six months each. On departure each *beneficiarius* erected an altar in commemoration of the successful completion of his stint. Over 30 altars, arranged in neat rows, were found during rescue excavation in 1982 and 1983.[12]

WORSHIPPING THE EMPEROR

The worship of the emperor himself was immensely important as a focus of loyalty in the Roman world. Ruler-cults were normal in Hellenistic times. From Augustus' reign onwards temples were erected to the emperor; or to the emperor and to the goddess Roma jointly, in Italy and in the provinces where they served to unify the popula-

57 Officers and soldiers of the Second Legion Augusta, *sacrificing at an altar, on a 'distance slab' from Bridgeness, West Lothian, Scotland, AD 142. (National Museums of Scotland, Edinburgh.)*

tions in loyalty to Rome. After their deaths many emperors were deified (above, p. 43). The emperor could be associated with traditional deities in the same temple: at Ephesus, Hadrian was associated with an existing temple to Artemis, protectress of the city.[13] An inscription honouring him was placed on the façade. Later, other emperors were similarly linked to Artemis and their statues placed in front (below, p. 127). The name of the emperor was associated also with various personifications, e.g. *Pax Augusta* (Imperial Peace) and *Liberalitas Augusta* (Imperial Liberality).

A special priesthood, whose members were the *Augustales*, was created to minister to (and pay for) a cult to the dead (and subsequently deified) emperor Augustus, first in Rome, then in the provinces (above, p. 57). They served other deified emperors in due course. Often freedmen, who were excluded from local magistracies, served as priests; it was a means of stimulating their civic pride.

In Britain the Claudian conquest was soon followed by the establishment at Colchester of a cult for the living emperor Claudius. A large temple was constructed and festivals inaugurated, which the local nobility of the Trinovantes was expected to finance and support by acting as its priests. The temple was to be a focus of loyalty for the whole province; it also commemorated Claudius' own triumphal entry into the capital of Cunobelinus and Caratacus. Colchester became a colony for veterans of the legions stationed in the province. The cost of the cult was a factor in encouraging disaffection at the time of the Boudican rebellion in AD 60, when Colchester was attacked and destroyed. The surviving defenders made a last stand inside the temple.[14]

THE MYSTERY RELIGIONS

Roman expansion east of the Aegean brought her world into contact with the mystery religions of Anatolia, the Near East and Egypt, such as those of Cybele, Atthis, Serapis and Isis. Sometimes these figures were honoured together with Graeco-Roman deities; more often they attained prominence wholly on their own account. There was a temple of Isis at Pompeii by the beginning of the first century BC (Fig. 58). An inscription above the entrance to the temple-precinct records that it was repaired after suffering earthquake damage in AD 62. The text reads:

N(umerius) Popidius N(umeri) f(ilius) Celsinus | aedem Isidis terrae motu conlapsam | a fundamento p(ecunia) s(ua) restituit. Hunc decuriones ob liberalitatem | cum esset annorum sexs ordini suo gratis adlegerunt.[15] 'Numerius Popidius Celsinus, son of Numerius, restored the temple of Isis from its foundation at his own expense, after it had collapsed in an earthquake. The town councillors co-opted him, though aged only six, on to the Council without having to pay a fee, because of his generosity.'

Family wealth and influence lay behind this special honour.

58 Doorway to the Temple of Isis, Pompeii, Italy. AD *62–79. The inscription records repairs to the temple after earthquake damage.*

59 Replica altars to Mithras, in situ *at a Mithraeum beside Carrawburgh fort, Hadrian's Wall. Early third* century AD. *The original altars are in the Museum of Antiquities, Newcastle.*

Mithras, a Persian god of truth and light, gained adherents throughout the Empire from the later first century AD onwards, including many in the army. Some have viewed the cult as a rival to Christianity. Dedications and shrines to Mithras are widespread; among the better known are those below the Church of S. Clemente at Rome, at Capua in central Italy, at Dura Europus on the Euphrates and in London. Often the dedication is to DEO INVICTO MITHRAE ('To the Invincible God Mithras').

One *Mithraeum* built immediately south of the fort at Carrawburgh on Hadrian's Wall was found during excavation in 1949.[16] At the far end of the oblong building was a sculptured relief showing Mithras slaying a bull; below stood a group of three altars, erected by prefects of the resident garrison, the First Cohort of Batavians, in the early years of the third century AD.[17] Exact replicas can be seen *in situ* today (Fig. 59). The altar on the left incorporates a representation of Mithras' head, with the stone hollowed out behind and partially perforated to simulate the rays of the sun emerging from the god's head. A lamp would be placed behind the altar to illuminate the rays in the darkened interior of the building. The altar on the right has a particular interest: erected like the others *Deo Invicto Mithrae*, it names as *praef(ectus) coh(ortis) I Batavorum*, Aulus Cluentius Habitus, a man whose nomenclature exactly matches that of a worthy of the town of Larinum in southern Italy (now Larino), defended by Cicero in a notorious court-case in 66 BC. We appear to have here a member of the same family or household, commanding a regiment on the far north-west frontier of the Roman Empire some 250 years later. The connection is confirmed by a reference (spread over three lines) to the prefect's home town as *colon(ia) Sept(imia) Aur(elia) L(arinum)*. The actual name of the town is abbreviated to a single letter. While it must be rather unlikely that readers of this inscription at Carrawburgh would make any connection between the prefect's name and the south Italian town, the prefect himself doubtless decided on the text; the link was obviously clear enough to him.

13

GRAVESTONES AND TOMB MONUMENTS

The Romans, like most other societies in ancient and modern times, were much concerned with the permanent recording of the life and achievements of an individual on his death. When a person died the family, heirs or freedmen arranged for disposal of the body. Sometimes a tomb or tomb monument had been prepared in advance (below, p. 107) during the individual's lifetime. During the Late Republic and Early Empire cremation on a funeral pyre was preferred. Funeral processions are frequently recorded in Latin literature. At Pollentia in northern Italy townspeople in Tiberius' reign halted the funeral procession of an ex-centurion, until his heirs agreed to pay them to go away; such was his reputed wealth.[1] From Rome comes an interesting slab (Fig. 60) with an unusually specific text:

Sex(tus) Aemilius Sex(ti) l(ibertus) | Baro | frumentar(ius) | in ignem inlatus est | prid(ie) Non(as) Quinct(iles) | Cn(aeo) Pompeio co(n)- s(ule) tert(ium?) 'Sextus Aemilius Baro, freedman of Sextus, a corn merchant, was brought to the pyre, on the day before the Nones of *Quinctilis*, in the third consulship of Gnaeus Pompeius' (*i.e. 6 July, 52* BC).[2]

The ashes from a cremation were gathered and placed in a small stone chest, an urn or other container. The day of interment might be marked by a meal at the tomb, as was the end of the nine days' formal mourning. At Pompeii a group of mourners paying their last respects retired into a tomb for safety against the falling pumice, and were themselves entombed there in August AD 79.[3] Sculptured reliefs frequently show the deceased on a couch with a food-laden table in front. The dead man was envisaged as participating in the funeral banquet and in meals to celebrate anniversaries of his death (see Fig. 47).

The form and type of tombstones vary quite markedly. Some were upright slabs of the type predominating in most cemeteries today (see Fig. 48). Others, however, took the form of altars (see Figs 5, 44) – it was in any case customary for the family or heirs to make offerings at the grave on anniversaries of the death.

Many tombs stood within a carefully defined plot, demarcated at the edges by a low wall, or at the very least with the corners marked by four stone pillars. The pillars at each corner proclaimed the size of the plot, according to the following formula: IN FRONTE PEDES XII, IN AGRO PEDES X ('across the front, 12 feet; back from the road, 10 feet'). The words are often abbreviated to: IN FR P XII IN AG P X, or the like. If the central monument did not occupy all the available ground-space, smaller memorials to slaves and freedmen may be found, in a variety of forms, within the same enclosure. At Aquileia near Trieste the modern visitor can see a reconstructed sequence of tomb enclosures along a road leading westwards from the town (Fig. 61).

*60 Slab from the tomb of
Sextus Aemilius Baro,
Rome, 52 BC.*

SEX·AEMILIVS·SEX·L
BARO
FRVMENTAR
INIGNEM·INLATVS·EST
PRID·NON·QVINCT
CN·POMPEIO·COS·TERT

*61 Burial plots at
Aquileia, Italy.*

Tombstones yield a very significant percentage of all known inscriptions. Mostly they derive from the cemeteries outside the walls of a town, especially along the roads leading out into its *territorium*. A cemetery was meant to be a public place, deliberately in full view, not hidden away. Contrary to normal practice in Britain today, burial inside a town's limits was prohibited by law, and there was as yet no link between temples and shrines in a town and the burial of worshippers. At Rome itself the cemeteries of the Republican period began outside the old Servian Wall, stretching away along the major roads. However, as the city outgrew its early limits, many of the monuments must have disappeared below the new suburbs; some remain to be seen today, well within the third century Aurelianic walls of the city. But at the time of construction they lay beyond the built-up area.

More substantial monuments could be erected, if the money was forthcoming. Some early Roman tombs followed a habit, widespread in the Mediterranean world and favoured by the Etruscans, of excavating tombs underground or in rock, and designing the layout to resemble the houses of the living. At Rome this style was exemplified by the Tomb of the Scipios, which first came into use by 300 BC, and continued for at least a century and a half.[4]

It was common for people to oversee the construction of their own tombs before death. In Petronius' *Satyricon*, the host Trimalchio turns to his old friend Habinnas the stonemason, with specific instructions:[5] 'I strongly beseech you to put my puppy dog round the feet of my statue and some wreaths and perfume jars and all the fights of [the gladiator] Petraites so that by your skill I shall live on after death. I want the monument to have a frontage of 100 feet and a depth of 200 feet. For I should like to have all kinds of fruit growing round my ashes and a profusion of vines. Most of all I want it stated that "This monument is not to descend to my heir". It will certainly be my concern in my will to provide against any injury being done to me when I am dead. I am making one of my freedmen guardian of the tomb to prevent folk running up and shitting on it. I beg you to put ships too, in full sail, on the monument, and me sitting in my official robes on the official seat, wearing five gold rings and distributing money to the populace from a little purse. For, as you know, I gave them a meal costing two denarii each.' Concern for a lasting memorial which will present the deceased's achievements in a good light is paralleled on surviving epigraphic texts.

The exterior surfaces of a tomb and the uninscribed areas of a tombstone were frequently sculpted with scenes, motifs or symbols recalling the activities or work of the person whose remains lay within. Former soldiers might have tombs ornamented with distinctive weaponry, standards or military decorations, or be shown standing full-length on upright graveslabs (above, p. 81). Craftsmen could be depicted with the tools of their trade; domestic items and weaving apparatus are shown on the gravestones of women. Office-holders might have their magistrate's chair, even attendant lictors (above, p. 57). When Nero, during the traumatic last months of his reign, was returning to Rome from his tour of Greece, he passed a monument showing a Roman cavalryman defeating a Gaul, and took it as an excellent omen in his fight against Vindex, the rebel governor of central Gaul.[6] Civilians too could be shown full-length in toga or tunic, or given half-length portraits, or busts. The portraits are individual, and presumably were done before (sometimes long before) death, or according to the wishes of the heirs.

The Roman word for a tomb is regularly *monumentum*, a term which also implies that the tomb is a memorial and 'record' of an individual's life on earth. Another word used is *mausoleum*, which had its origin in the grandiose tomb constructed in the mid fourth century BC at Halicarnassus (Bodrum) on the seaboard of western Turkey, to house the body of Mausolus, the virtually independent kinglet of Caria in the Persian Empire. In the Graeco–Roman world the word came to mean a 'tomb', not necessarily of lavish proportions, and it is still used today.[7]

Not all the population would be buried immediately outside the town walls. Those who lived in the country might be commemorated in plots at crossroads or on their own land. A technical writer on land surveying comments on the possible confusion between boundary markers and gravestones if the latter had been erected close to the edges or corners of a survey grid.[8]

CITIES OF THE DEAD

It is important not to imagine tombs as necessarily standing individually. The roads leading away from any town were lined with tombs. Families bought a plot which remained for their use thereafter. Competition existed for the prime positions visible to travellers, who might read the inscriptions and reflect on the life and achievements of the deceased. Some had seating for the family to use when visiting the tomb, and for any passerby who wished to linger. A good example of a Roman cemetery is provided by the Street of the Tombs outside the Herculaneum Gate at Pompeii (Fig. 62). Here the modern visitor descends a tomb-lined avenue, on his way to visit the Villa of the Mysteries. We must avoid thinking always in terms of lines of upright tombstones. Rather, like many modern cemeteries in southern Europe, the visitor would see family tomb monuments, sometimes house-shaped or temple-shaped, or like altars, some massive in size. These were cities of the dead, as outside (for example) Naples or Genoa today, at Père Lachaise in Paris or Kensall Green in London. A street of house-type tombs also survives along the road leading from the harbour town of Portus, at the mouth of the River Tiber, near Fiumicino airport.

The spirits of the deceased were believed to continue to live in, or in the vicinity of, the tomb, and it was the duty of later generations to appease them. The Roman term for these spirits was the *Manes* or the *Di Manes* ('Spirits of the Dead'). The poet Propertius expressed a common view: 'The Manes *do* mean something. Death is not the end, and the pale ghost escapes the defeated pyre'.[9] In the same poem he imagines that his mistress Cynthia, taken from him by death, has suggested in a dream that he clear away the ivy which had already engulfed her tomb near Tivoli, and inscribe on a stone pillar a few lines of verse which the traveller on his way from Rome might read.

Cemeteries outside towns, which had been continually in use over many centuries, must have been very extensive by late antiquity. Soon they were to serve as ready sources of building materials (above, p. 30). An eighteenth-century writer refers to 3000 monuments outside the walls of Pula in Yugoslavia; now a solitary hexagonal plinth survives amid modern housing. Similarly the roads outside a legionary fortress or fort must have been lined with gravestones and tombs, for those of the garrison who had died or fallen in battle, as at some military depots today.

Some major concentrations of tombs can still be seen. In Turkey at Hierapolis (modern Pamukkale) upwards of a thousand tombs, gravemarkers, sarcophagi on plinths, and circular tumuli give a vivid impression of the extent and variety of a cemetery in late Roman times (see Fig. 69).

THE VATICAN NECROPOLIS
One of the (to us) less familiar streets leading out from Rome is the *Via Cornelia* which passed across

62 *'Street of the Tombs', outside the Herculaneum Gate, Pompeii, Italy. In the foreground are monuments to C.Munatius Faustus and C.Calventius Quietus, successful freedmen in Pompeian society.*

the flat ground of the *Campus Vaticanus* towards Cerveteri. Much of the zone was for a while in imperial ownership; Nero learned to drive a chariot on a private race-track there.[10] To the north of the road was a zone given over to tombs, which later extended over a wide area.[11] It was here that the body of St Peter was laid to rest during the reign of Nero. By the middle of the second century the site of the grave was marked by a small shrine, and in the early fourth century Constantine had a basilica constructed on top. Levelling the ground for the basilica, the predecessor of the present St Peter's, paradoxically ensured the survival of several nearby tombs which now lie below the nave of the present church.

The tombs, excavated from 1939 onwards and re-examined recently, lay to either side of a narrow alley. They were brick-built with gabled roofs and had wooden doors. Inscribed panels set above the doors gave details of those buried within (cf. below, p. 108). The compartments themselves were decorated with stucco and frescoes. Each mausoleum held the remains of a group of people, mostly freedmen or descendants of freedmen. Ash-chests for cremated remains lay alongside

sarcophagi; pagan and Christian burials are found in the same tomb. The street offers an excellent impression of the burial customs of moderately well-to-do Romans of the mid second century onwards. Constantine's workers removed the tops of some recently built tombs, which must still have been tended by families. The bodies and ashes were for the most part left undisturbed. But other tombs must have been completely removed, a procedure made necessary by the requirement of placing the high altar in the basilica directly over the Apostle's grave.

Less well known, undeservedly so, is a group of tombs and burials found all but intact, preserved by landslips and terracing, below the Vatican car park in 1956. Here is a bewildering variety of tombs, gravestones and grave-altars, closely packed. A small group of mausolea survives below the church of S. Sebastiano on the *Via Appia* outside Rome to the south-east.

THE TOMBS OF THE RICH

Some tombs were constructed on a very grand scale. A common architectural type, inspired in part by circular Etruscan tombs, as at Cerveteri,

63 Tomb of Caecilia Metella, Via Appia, Rome. Late first century BC.

64 Tomb of the Plautii, near Tivoli, Italy, early first century AD.

was a cylindrical masonry drum of grandiose dimensions, which found favour among wealthy Roman families in the Augustan age. A good example of the type, perhaps the best known, lies 5km (3 miles) outside Rome on the *Via Appia*. It is 29.5m (97ft) in diameter, set on a squared podium (Fig. 63). The tomb commemorated Caecilia Metella, daughter of Quintus Caecilius Metellus Creticus (consul in 69 BC), and wife of M.Licinius Crassus, a son of Caesar's partner in the First Triumvirate of 60 BC (cf. above, p. 20). The inscription reads:

Caeciliae | Q(uinti) Cretici f(iliae) | Metellae Crassi.[12] To Caecilia Metella, daughter of Quintus Creticus, (wife) of Crassus.'

The tomb has been a landmark for travellers since its construction in Augustus' reign.

On the *Via Valeria* at Ponte Lucano some 6.5km (4 miles) west of Tivoli is a similar monument, the splendid tomb of the Plautii (Fig. 64), used from Augustan to Flavian times.[13] The tomb itself bears the single inscription of the first family member to be buried there; other, massive slabs set on separate façades in front commemorated others, including Ti. Plautius Silvanus Aelianus, a successful governor in the later half of the first century AD, who had earlier been a 'companion' of Claudius during the invasion of Britain in AD 43.[14] A similar style of monument, on a quite massive scale, was chosen by Augustus (who may indeed have brought it into fashion), for his own mausoleum in the Campus Martius at Rome. Hadrian followed the custom for his own tomb, now the Castel S. Angelo. Smaller versions in the same style are found in cemeteries across the Roman world.

Other forms favoured by wealthy families were temple-tombs, with statues often placed between the columns; or lofty circular or square towers, perhaps with columns or pilasters, and topped by a pyramidical cone. The Tomb of the Julii at Glanum (St Rémy-en-Provence) and the Romano-

65 *Pyramid of Cestius, Rome, adjacent to the (later)* Porta Ostiensis, *late first century BC.*

Punic tombs at Dougga, Tunisia, are examples of this type. The bodies were placed in closed compartments in the base. Such monuments served both as a tomb and a commemoration of the family and its wealth.

There are a few examples of pyramid-tombs on the Egyptian model. Such a pyramid, some 30m (100ft) high, was built on the *Via Ostiensis* outside Rome, to hold the remains of Gaius Cestius, a magistrate at Rome in the last decades of the Republic or under Augustus (Fig. 65). The main text reads:

C(aius) Cestius L(uci) f(ilius) Pob(lilia tribu) Epulo pr(aetor) tr(ibunus) pl(ebis) | VIIvir Epulonum.[15] 'Gaius Cestius Epulo, son of Lucius, of the Poblilian voting-tribe, praetor, tribune of the People, member of the Board of Seven in charge of public feasts.'

A secondary inscription, placed lower down, states that the pyramid, constructed after his death according to Cestius' instructions in his will, took 330 days to build. A third text notes that it was restored on the instructions of Pope Alexander VII in 1663. The pyramid originally stood within a low-walled enclosure, with statues and columns in front and other tombs nearby. Access was from the side which now faces the modern Protestant Cemetery. In the later third century AD this pyramid, then one of a number of monuments on the *Via Ostiensis*, was incorporated into the Aurelianic walls of Rome: the walls have been butted on to the monument which stood in their path, and which it must have been impractical to remove.

BURIAL OF THE POOR

It would be misleading to concentrate only on the most magnificent monuments. Not everyone could afford to be commemorated at such expense. Memorials cost money. From the second century AD it became quite common to report, as part of the inscription, the cost of erecting it. Those who could not afford marble used limestone, those who could not afford limestone used brick or tufa, with marble or limestone facings. Sometimes only the inscribed panel itself will be in marble or limestone; the rest was in brick, which must have been plastered. One thing is clear: the size of the inscribed panel is not a sure indicator of the dimensions or pretentiousness of the monument – a quite modest block may derive from a substantial and elaborate tomb.

Communal burial within a single plot had always been normal practice if the people were related, or dependent freedmen or slaves. The less well-off could buy space in a communal tomb, sometimes termed a *columbarium* (literally, a dovecote).[16] Inside, the walls were lined with small niches each large enough to receive two urns, in stone, glass or terracotta. Often such communal tombs were subterranean. Trade organizations, some military units at Rome and slave or freedman members of the imperial and other large households had their own communal tombs in plots purchased for the purpose. Sometimes these burial clubs also organized the funeral itself, including hiring mourners, and kept faith with the deceased by arranging a feast on the anniversary of the person's death. Several such tombs at Rome have been found more or less intact. Individuals could

buy space in advance before the tomb was built, and even sell the space if they moved house and no longer needed a burial niche locally. Niches were identified by small inscribed plaques set below the urns. At Nîmes the chief official of an organization of freedmen paid for the construction of a communal tomb, which he terms a *mausoleum*, for its members, and enhanced the surrounding plot with trees, vines and rosebushes.[17] In return the members of the group offered him 'immunity', that is free membership of the group without having to pay its dues, and a special commemorative plaque to mark his generosity; he declined these honours, and 'was content with the inscription he had set up at his own expense'. Another such benefactor, who had organized the construction of a fine tomb at Rome (described simply as a *monumentum*) and provided a roofed dining room, was allowed to select niches for six urns, for himself, his family and friends.[18]

Poorer families might place the ashes in a simple pottery jar, which could be buried with no more than a painted inscription on the side of the container and a wooden marker above ground level. The poet Horace mentions a substantial area on the Esquiline Hill in Rome set aside for the burial of the poor, 'one thousand feet in length and 300 broad'; this offered a disconcerting view of whitening bones, and was the haunt of thieves, animals and witches.[19] The area was landscaped at the expense of Maecenas in the later first century BC and laid out as a public park.

SARCOPHAGI

From the time of Hadrian onwards there was an increasing tendency for the dead not to be cremated but buried. The precise reason for this change has never been satisfactorily explained. Burial of unburnt remains is known at every period of Roman history; but from the middle of the second century AD it became the favoured practice. The body was placed in the ground protected either by a coffin of stone, wood or lead, or a simple cover of terracotta tiles; sometimes it had no protection beyond the customary linen shroud. As before, our evidence favours the wealthier classes, though archaeological excavation of cemeteries in the provinces has helped somewhat to redress the balance.

66 Sarcophagus at the Christian basilica of Manastirine, Solin, Yugoslavia. It commemorated Petronia, who died as a baby, and her parents, fourth century AD.

The rich could afford substantial and artistically impressive coffins in marble or limestone, generally known as sarcophagi (Fig. 66), with a separate close-fitting lid, which might bear along the front face an inscription to the deceased. The finest sarcophagi were imports to Italy from Greece and Asia Minor. The decoration of the panels of the sarcophagi provided a whole new outlet for the sculptors of the age and opened up a new genre of artistic representation. Scenes from Graeco-Roman mythology or from the daily life of the deceased are shown, or later (for Christians) stories from the Old or the New Testaments. Others were decorated with garlands; sometimes the inscription was set within a wreath held by victory-figures or by cupids. At times sarcophagi were intended to stand proud in funeral enclosures visible to the passerby; at others they were placed within a tomb, or a catacomb, where the elaborate decorative details were protected from damage and from the elements, and seen only by the family (below, p. 120).

EPITAPHS

It is time to consider the inscriptions that are found on tomb monuments or gravestones. The most important information was of course the name or names of the deceased. Forename and family name may occur in the nominative case (so that the deceased is the 'subject' of the ensuing sentence), in the dative case (so that the dedication is *to* the individual, or in the genitive case (i.e. it is the grave *of* someone). After the name of the deceased will come that of his father (in the genitive case), then the voting-tribe and surname (cf. above, p. 19). Next, if the deceased has died away from home, there may be a reference to his birthplace; sometimes the latter is placed next to the voting-tribe and before the surname. The town of origin is often prefaced by the word *domo*; for instance *domo Parmā*, 'from Parma, [which was] his home-town'.

Then may come the age at death, indicated perhaps by the use of the word *annorum* followed by numerals; such as *annorum XXX*, 'of 30 years'. In the second century AD the phrase *vixit annos* or *vixit annis* became more common; e.g. *vixit annis XXX*, 'lived 30 years'. In the third century and after the age at death was more precisely indicated; for instance *vixit annis XXX, mensibus X, diebus XX*, 'he lived 30 years, 10 months and 20 days'. Sometimes the age appears to have been 'rounded up'; the heirs may not have had exact information available. A text may state *vixit plus minus annis XXX*, 'he lived 30 years, more or less'. It should be emphasized that many epitaphs do not give any information on age. Where a tomb monument or gravestone was prepared in advance of death, details of age were of course out of place, and so are not found. Finally can come details of the family, freedmen or heirs who may have set up the stone. Occupations are occasionally given. Offices held in local government, or in the emperor's service are usually listed, and priesthoods held. Military tombstones give the rank of the soldier, the legion or regiment he had served in, or was then serving in, and the length of that service to the nearest year. Such information was regarded as specially important where a soldier was buried at his place of service, in the presence of his comrades.

For the most part, two pieces of information which we might expect to encounter on a modern tombstone are lacking: the dates of birth and death (see Fig. 60 for an exception). Only in the third and fourth centuries AD was it common to specify the date and year of death, which could be expressed by the names of the consuls. Christian epitaphs are very often dated (below, p. 122). It was common, during the first century BC and first century AD, for a funerary inscription to end with the words *hic situs* (or *sita*) *est* (he *or* she lies here), normally abbreviated to H S E. From the mid first century AD

onwards a new formula became popular: the inscription now began with the words DIS MANIBUS ('To the Spirits of the Dead'), followed by the name of the deceased. When the formula first came into use, the words were fully written out, but they were soon abbreviated, to DIS MAN and then to D M. The name of the deceased can be given in the genitive case (so that the invocation is made to the spirit of the departed individual). The name can also appear in the dative case – there the dedication is both to the spirits of the departed in general, and to the particular individual. The name is found also in the nominative case, so that the phrase *Dis Manibus* serves solely as an introductory invocation.

The inscription may end with the formula *sit tibi terra levis* (abbreviated to S T T L), 'may the earth lie lightly upon you'. On occasion the inscription will incorporate a short homily, addressed to the family or to a passerby who has stopped to examine the stone. The epitaph can include a poem or be followed by some lines of verse. These lines can be very moving, expressing in a few words the closeness of a bond between father and son, between husband and wife. A particularly moving text is a funeral elegy delivered by a husband over the body of his wife, who (it seems) had aided his escape from capture, probably during the proscriptions of 42–41 BC, and who died before him. It has been argued, but not accepted by all, that the pair are Q. Lucretius Vespillo and his wife, whose story is told by the historian Appian.[20]

PREPARING FOR DEATH

Often, as already observed, the person commemorated had the stone cut or the monument erected during his lifetime. This is made clear by an inscription which has the name in the nominative case, and concludes with the words *vivus sibi fecit* ('had it made for himself while still living').[21] An inscription may commemorate a number of individuals, some still living when it was erected. For the reader's benefit a single letter V (abbreviated from *vivus*) can be inscribed beside the name or names of those still living; later the additional symbol θ (Greek theta) may be added, signifying that the person has since died.[22]

If a tomb was not prepared in advance the deceased could leave money for it in his will: the resulting inscription would record that the monument or tombstone was erected *ex testamento* (according to the provisions of the will). The following text was found in 1944, placed over the entrance to a tomb below St Peter's. 'You, my heirs, I ask and bid and trust to your good faith, to build me a tomb on the Vatican plain near the Circus, beside the monument of Ulpius Narcissus, at the cost of 6000 sesterces. . . . And there I wish placed my remains and those of Fadia Maxima my wife . . . . . of which monument I bequeath the legal control to my freedmen . . . . . they be allowed to enter the ground in order to offer sacrifices at this monument.'[23]

However, it was always advisable to begin work on your own tomb, to ensure that it was ready; your heirs might not have the same priorities. Augustus, frequently in poor health, began his *Mausoleum* (the name used for it by Augustus himself) in the Campus Martius in 28 BC.[24] In fact he was to live over 40 more years; others of his family preceded him within its encircling walls. The Younger Pliny reports a visit he made to the tomb of a friend, the ex-consul Verginius Rufus, ten years after his

67 *Mosaic panel, over a tomb chamber at Solin, Yugoslavia. The inscription commemorates T.Aurelius Aurelianus who died aged nine; third century AD. (Arheološki Muzej, Split.)*

death, and found it still incomplete, though it was of modest proportions, through the heir's neglect. No inscription had been set up, though Verginius himself had determined the wording of a two-line epitaph.[25] The deceased could leave instructions in the will for the wording of the inscription. Sattia, whose death at the age of 99 is noted by Seneca and others, stipulated that her remarkable age must be mentioned.[26] Frequently inscriptions on tombs mention public honours and special privileges decreed. The Younger Pliny mentions such a text in honour of Pallas, freedman secretary to the emperor Claudius, which he found particularly irritating.[27] In contrast, Julius Frontinus, one-time governor of Britain, wanted no monument at all erected to himself.[28]

DEATHS BY MISADVENTURE
Some epitaphs specify the circumstances of death, especially when they were unusual. Parents grieve for children who in the normal course of events would have grieved for them (Fig. 67).[29] One man fell from a ladder while fixing mosaic tesserae;[30] another was killed by a crush of people on the Capitoline Hill in Rome;[31] a bride died on her wedding day;[32] a slave seven days after being bitten by a snake;[33] a ten-year-old girl is killed for her jewellery.[34] People are burned to death;[35] mugged;[36] drowned by shipwreck;[37] and kidnapped.[38] A wife is murdered by her husband after 28 years of marriage.[39] A man, after escaping from a fire, goes back into the building to retrieve some possession and a wall falls on him.[40] A child drowns in a swimming pool.[41] Very occasionally there is hatred, but hardly ever any humour of the type encountered on seventeenth- or eighteenth-century gravestones.[42] At Ostia there is the monument to a soldier of the Praetorian Guard (whose name has not survived), for whom 'the people of Ostia gave the burial place and decreed a public funeral procession because he perished in putting out a fire.'[43] A promising young charioteer, only then graduating from 2-horse to 4-horse chariots, died, much to his chagrin, of a fever at the age of 22, rather than, as he would have wished, before the spectators in his beloved Circus at Tarragona.[44]

Many epitaphs accept that death is a final farewell, with no prospect of an afterlife.[45]

LYING IN PEACE
The concern for a lasting commemoration of one's life is also expressed in the formula with which a funerary text frequently concludes: *hoc monumentum heredem non sequitur* (H M H N S) –'this monument does not follow the heir'.[46] In other words, the tomb and its plot of ground were not a piece of heritable property that passed to the person's heirs, to be disposed of at their whim, or allocated to another use. The ground was sacred. The deceased could thus lie in peace and dignity. Certainly families were expected to care for the tomb. A sum of money could be left by the deceased to ensure that it was tended, and the inscription itself may warn off intruders and defilers.[47] A slab from Rome discourages anyone contemplating painting an election slogan on the tomb; the candidate was sure to lose![48] Others threaten even more dire penalties: 'anyone shitting inside the plot or damaging it, may he be blinded'.[49] Another text, to discourage such practices, refers to nettles growing around the monument.[50] And at Pozzuoli: 'whoever removes this inscribed plaque will make the spirits of those buried here very angry.'[51] There could be a map of the tomb-precinct and an inventory of its furnishings and ornamentation.[52] There are warnings against the reuse of a tomb, or the placing of other bodies in it,[53] or defacing or chiselling out the inscription itself.[54] A fine would be payable to a local cult or to the state treasury. Clearly abuses were all too common. Petronius has the humorous story of a soldier who went mad, and running about among the gravestones of his town, urinated five times in a circle and turned into a werewolf.[55] Cemeteries in the ancient world were convenient for prostitutes, for tramps and for brigands.[56] A tomb could be a hiding place for the living in dangerous times.[57] Sidonius Apollinaris bewailed the desecration of his grandfather's tomb by gravediggers (cf. above, p. 14), who failed to realize that the ground had already been used. He had them flogged.[58]

14

TRADE, ECONOMY
AND THE BUSINESS WORLD

Many of the preceding chapters have dealt with the private lives and careers of people; but other aspects of the Roman world are illuminated by inscribed texts, among them the financial and business world, and the movement of goods throughout the Roman economic market. Information about such economic activity was frequently inscribed not on stone, but written on other often less durable materials. Papyrus, wooden writing tablets and ostraca (i.e. broken potsherds or slivers of suitable stone) were employed. Sometimes the trade goods themselves, or the containers that held them, bear some message. As so often, it is a combination of different types of evidence which allows a picture to be built up.

Commerce is a subject repeatedly referred to in the literary sources. Some of the aristocratic classes at Rome adopted a rather sneering tone, as so often in more modern societies, to those who had made, or were making, their money in 'trade' instead of in agriculture and land ownership; but inscriptions frequently record the transactions involved and the personnel engaged in such activities. Epitaphs reveal the names of merchants and the location of their activities. The level of prosperity generated is reflected in the elaborate tombs and public monuments that graced the towns of Italy and the provinces. Commerce launched many a family on an upward climb on the social and political ladder. By law, senators were forbidden to participate directly in trade, but did so by means of partnerships and the efforts of their freedmen. To a section of the equestrian class at Rome commerce and moneymaking were its life's blood. Traders combined to form trade associations, *collegia*, which were prominent both locally and nationally. Inscriptions reveal a range of trade associations[1] and the occupations of many individual artisans and craftsmen.[2]

THE MARKET PLACE

The economy of most Roman towns was locally-based. Farmers raised animals, grew crops and vegetables which they brought to town for sale or exchange, and where they purchased other necessities or even luxury items. Local markets of this type survive throughout Europe even today. Prominently sited in the town forum would be public weights and measures. Many such weights and measures in stone, bronze or lead have survived, stamped with the weight and a date as evidence of authenticity.[3] Local magistrates, recognizing a real need, sometimes donated fresh sets of public weighing equipment inscribed with their names, as a guarantee of authenticity and accuracy.[4] A bronze corn-measure in the shape of a bucket (Fig. 68) was found at Carvoran on Hadrian's Wall in 1915.[5] The well-cut inscription reads:

Imp(eratore) [[Domitiano]] Caesare Aug(usto)

Germanico $\overline{XV}$ *co(n)sule | exactus ad S XVIIs | habet p(ondera) XXXIIX.* 'When Domitian Caesar Augustus, victor over the Germans, had been consul 15 times; tested to the capacity of $17\frac{1}{2}$ pints, it weighs 38 pounds.'

68 *Bronze corn-measure, with the names of the emperor Domitian partly erased, AD 90–91. (Museum of Antiquities, Newcastle.)*

The names of the emperor Domitian, later partially erased, served as a guarantee.[6]

In any town there were numerous workshops with craftsmen selling the goods made there. Mostly they were small, sometimes no more than the width and depth of a single room along the street frontages, with private housing behind or above. Visitors to Pompeii will be familiar with them, as will those who have seen the still functioning shops of medieval Dubrovnik. Very probably these workshops were run by a single family. At Pompeii the users seem often to have been freedmen of the owners of the houses behind. On the outer walls of houses at Herculaneum and Pompeii, and doubtless elsewhere, there were painted shop signs and frescoes illustrating the type of goods and services available within; the intending customer might also encounter graffiti left by less than satisfied past customers, offering an alternative view. In larger towns such as Ostia and Rome workshops are found in the ground floors of apartment blocks (as in Victorian tenements today). There were even shopping precincts; Trajan's Market in Rome, once hailed as the world's earliest hypermarket, had 150 small shops on three floors under a single roof.

Market-buildings for particular commodities, such as fish, meat, fruit and vegetables, wine and olive oil, lay close to the forum in each town. A very well-preserved market can be seen at Lepcis Magna in North Africa; inscriptions have been found which record those who paid for its construction, ornamentation and equipment.[7] The so-called Temple of Serapis at Pozzuoli on the Bay of Naples, whose ruins alternately emerge from and partially disappear into the encroaching waters, is in fact a market with a circular fountain at its centre.

TRADING WITH THE WIDER WORLD

As the Roman world expanded, Italian merchants travelled ever more widely, seizing the opportunities of preferred status. They and others traded the manufactured goods of the Mediterranean world into the as yet undeveloped territories of the west.[8] In 166 BC Rome declared the Aegean island of Delos to be a 'free port', and it enjoyed a brilliant, century-long existence as a meeting place of the merchants of east and west. Many Greek and Latin inscriptions record the presence there of Italian and Roman entrepreneurs who had formed themselves into associations.

The rapid growth of Rome into a vast capital city upset the neat balance between town and countryside; the demands of its growing population outstripped supply and distorted trading activities in the other towns of the region. The difficulty of obtaining an adequate and reliable food supply for the poorer citizens at Rome was a constant feature of political life. The city drew its corn supply first from Sicily and later from Tunisia and Egypt. Granaries and warehouses at Pozzuoli, Ostia and in Rome itself stored the accumulated reserves; the safe-passage of the grain fleets across the Mediterranean was watched anxiously. Transportation and supply of corn were state-regulated though not state-run; private enterprise was allowed full rein. In his *Satyricon* Petronius makes the freedman Trimalchio relate over dinner how he financed six corn ships, but they sank in a storm on the return journey. He had to start up his business again, helped by his wife who sold off her jewellery as a contribution.[9]

A fine tomb (Fig. 69) surviving at Hierapolis (Pamukkale) in Phrygia, Turkey, commemorates Flavius Zeuxis, a merchant 'who sailed 72 times round Cape Malea' (at the southern tip of the Peloponnese), from Asia Minor to Italy in the course of his life's occupation.[10] From Rome there is the memorial to 'honest' Onesimus who traded for many years along the *Via Appia*.[11] A long text, again from Rome, bewails a failed businessman's attempts to grow rich; he was betrayed by his 'friends'.[12] A shop-assistant asks for forgiveness if he ever gave short measures (and obviously he did); it was only to add to his father's belongings.[13]

Ostia was the chief entrepôt for goods arriving at the capital. A good picture of commercial life there is gained by a stroll in the so-called Piazzale delle Corporazioni, next to the theatre, round which trading companies and shippers, many of them with headquarters in North Africa, maintained offices. The floors are decorated with mosaic designs advertising their activities and destinations. Here is one text: *navicul(ari) et negotiantes | Karalitani*.[14] 'Shippers and traders from Karales' i.e. from Cagliari in Sardinia (Fig. 70).

The study of shipwrecks has uncovered invaluable details of cargoes which never reached their destinations.[15] A wreck of the mid first century BC located south-west of Toulon included amphorae stamped with the name of an owner of vineyards near Terracina in southern Italy. Another found off Marseilles in 1952 was laden with nearly 1700 amphorae, mostly stamped with the letters SES, abbreviated from the name Sestius, which recent research has linked to estates near Cosa in Tuscany. Anchors too can bear a maker's name.[16]

BANKING

The Roman world had no national or private banks with premises in every High Street. However, the system of financing business ventures and of providing private finance was well developed. Individuals practised as money-lenders; sometimes they were freedmen of rich families who could have their patrons' fortunes as reserve capital. Credit transfers could be arranged over long distances through a network of middlemen.

69 *Tomb of the merchant Flavius Zeuxis, Hierapolis (Pamukkale), Turkey.*

70 *Mosaic floor, Piazzale delle Corporazioni, Ostia, Italy, AD 190–200.*

At a basic level we hear much of debt- and rent-collectors, the *coactores* (an English translation might be 'enforcers').[17] Vespasian's grandfather, an ex-centurion, became a debt-collector; his father was a tax-collector and then later a money-lender.[18]

The money-lenders themselves were the *argentarii* (from *argentum*, silver). In Rome they could be found at various locations, especially at the markets, chiefly the *Macellum Magnum* (Great Market) on the Caelian Hill. In 204 the *argentarii* and other merchants based at the *Forum Boarium* (Cattle Market) beside the Tiber dedicated an arch (Fig. 71), which now bears their name, to the reigning emperor Septimius Severus, his wife and family.[19] The arch is now partly incorporated into the church of S. Giorgio in Velabro.

The inscription was cleverly altered at least twice within a few years, evidently to delete the name of Plautianus, praetorian prefect, then of his daughter Plautilla, married to the emperor's elder son Caracalla, finally that of the younger son, Geta. The ornamental details of the Arch were adjusted too, to remove the sculptured figures of Geta, Plautianus and Plautilla, and the head of Geta from a group of images on military standards.

The *argentarii* usually operated on a fairly small scale, supporting small businessmen and traders, with the merchandise itself forming the security. A fine tombstone from Rome commemorates L. Calpurnius Daphnus (probably a freedman) who was an *argentarius* at the *Macellum Magnum*. Below the inscription is a sculptured scene showing Daphnus between two heavily burdened fish-porters.[20]

In 1875 excavation of a house at Pompeii belonging to Lucius Caecilius Jucundus revealed in a wooden chest some 150 carbonized wax writing-tablets. Many were receipts for rent payments or for moneys paid out to his clients after auctions Jucundus had organized, in the period 52–62 AD.[21] Caecilius Jucundus was presumably an *argentarius*. The tablets provide names of many local people with whom he had dealings or who acted as witnesses to the transactions. From Herculaneum has come a tablet relating to the purchase of a slave; the deal was 'transacted in the Pompeian territory, at the *Arriani* tileworks belonging to Poppaea Augusta, in the consulship of C. Memmius Regulus and L. Verginius Rufus' (i.e. AD 63).[22] Nero's empress Poppaea had family estates near Pompeii; indeed she may have been the owner of the palatial villa found at nearby Oplontis.[23] More recently, from excavations at Murecine to the east of Pompeii, has come a substantial

71 *Arch of the Argentarii, Forum Boarium, Rome, AD 204.*

number of tablets, preserved in waterlogged conditions, relating to bail-sureties at Pozzuoli in the reigns of Claudius and Nero.[24] Such material offers valuable insights into financial activities of which we otherwise hear very little, except on papyri recovered from the dry sands of Egypt.

The goods themselves might bear a stamp or mark indicating origin or the manufacturer's name. The large earthenware amphorae were stamped on the rim or handle with the name of the kilns where they were made or the owner of the estate where the contents – usually wine or olive oil – were produced.[25] Production was very localized; vineyards were often family-run, with merchants arranging the transportation and shipping to intended markets. Sometimes the amphorae also bear painted or inked on them a note of the contents, the date of filling, or the destination of a particular consignment. At other times the precise meaning of the notation was only known to the people involved. Careful study of this material and controlled excavation of production sites provide a chronological framework for the manufacture of amphorae-types and the life-span of different estates. Just behind the Aventine Hill in Rome is an enormous dump of broken amphorae, now 30m

(100ft) high, the so-called Monte Testaccio.

Other types of pottery might bear a maker's name: samian ware, the Roman 'best china', was produced in factories in Gaul and Germany; *mortaria* (mixing bowls) were used in cooking and preparing vegetables.[26] A study of their distribution can demonstrate how markets were opened up, dominated and then lost; the handiwork of particular potters or factories can sometimes be recognized from the smallest fragments, even where no stamp has survived. Detailed study may also provide close dating for archaeological sites where the products are found. The stamps themselves, of clay, wood, metal or bone with the letters in 'retrograde' do not survive very often; but they must originally have been common. At the samian production site of La Graufesenque (Millau, France) sherds bear details, scratched with a sharp point, of the contents of a kiln on a particular day, the numbers of pots being produced and the names of the potters who had an interest in the successful firing of the batch. Such evidence provides valuable information on day-to-day procedures at the site.

People who bought the products of such kilns often scratched their names or initials on them, as proof of ownership. A study of such graffiti on pottery found at the short-lived Augustan legionary base of Haltern, east of the Rhine, provides a useful guide to the names and origins of soldiers who served there.[27] A consignment of some 90 decorated samian bowls from southern Gaul was found still in its packing case during excavation of a house at Pompeii in 1881; the consignment must have arrived in the town very shortly before the fatal eruption of AD 79.[28]

There are also many inscribed lead sealings, and seal-boxes, which authenticated the goods and guaranteed their genuineness until the destination was reached.[29] Oblong bronze stamps were used by oculists to mark blocks of eye-salve and other medicines in solid form.[30] Metal vessels frequently bore a stamp in relief. For example, the products of P.Cipius Polybius, maker of bronze saucepans at Capua in the first century AD, found their way to the western provinces, up to the northern frontiers.[31] Even bread could bear a stamp with the baker's name: loaves from Pompeii have the stamp *Celeris Q(uinti) Grani Veri ser(vus)* 'Of Celer, slave of Q.Granius Verus'; the Granii were an important business family at Pozzuoli.[32] Lamps were sometimes signed with the maker's name, a guarantee of quality or a claim to it.[33] Leather shoes could also have the maker's name. Slaves, themselves a traded commodity, might be branded, or have to wear bronze name-discs, rather like dog-tags today, or collars with the name and address of their owners, sometimes offering a reward if the slave was found to have absconded.[34] The products of mining – copper, tin, gold and silver, and lead – could be marked with an estate name and a date, sometimes expressed using the current titulature of the reigning emperor.[35] Quarrying of stone is documented by tally-marks on the quarried blocks, and graffiti and religious dedications were inscribed on living rock and on abandoned quarry faces (above, p. 88).[36]

The brick and tile industry has been studied in great detail. Examination of debris from buildings and of standing structures in Italy reveals many bricks stamped with the names of senatorial and equestrian families, and producers whose works had passed into imperial ownership.[37] Sometimes the products can be linked to known centres of manufacture. Great companies such as the Domitii at Rome or that of Pansa in Istria catered for a rapidly expanding demand for bricks in the Early Empire. Stamps could be rectangular, crescent-shaped or circular, and may bear the name of the owner of the brickworks, together with the names of the consuls or the titles of the emperor. Brick-stamps are useful for dating: for example, examination of bricks on the Pantheon revealed that the structure we see today is almost entirely Hadrianic in date rather than of the time of Augustus (above, pp. 24, 29). In the provinces, the army – which spent part of its time on construction projects – sometimes identified its work by marking roof tiles or bricks with the name of the legion or the auxiliary regiment involved. Other, less official, details could be added by hand while the clay was still wet.

DIOCLETIAN'S PRICES EDICT

A lengthy document of great importance in providing a picture of the economic life of the Empire is the so-called *Prices Edict* issued by Diocletian and his colleagues in AD 301 (see below, p. 125f).[38] The intention was to set maximum levels for certain specified wages and salaries, and maximum prices for goods and services throughout the Roman world. The surviving sections of the Edict list some 2000 items. Copies in stone were set up in many towns in the eastern provinces of the Empire, with slight variations in the text. No complete text survives, but numerous fragments, some substantial, others very small, are known, both in Greek and in Latin. The information on the range of manufactured goods and the variety of foodstuffs and services which were available is extremely interesting, as is the guidance on relative valuations of their worth. It seems that, despite the care taken to specify prices at the time of its issue, the Edict was no more successful than modern attempts to hold down prices in an age of inflation.

15

POPULUSQUE ROMANUS

The inclination of literate man to write on any available surface, with or without authorization, is a perennial habit and, sometimes, a nuisance. The passerby at Pompeii, Herculaneum and elsewhere expressed on the walls his opinions on many subjects: the drink on offer at a bar, the quality of a brothel, hopes and aspirations, love gained and lost,[1] letters of the alphabet, quick arithmetic calculations, lines of Vergil and other literary quotations, praise or dislike of the emperor, today's date, messages to friends. 'I'm amazed, wall,' wrote one humourist at Pompeii, 'that you have not collapsed under the weight of so many boring scribblers.'[2] The messages written on the walls of public baths confirm the indications from literature that a wider variety of activities took place there than simply washing.[3] The range of obscenities encountered is breathtaking.[4] A satisfied user of a latrine at Pompeii lauds the achievement of a good bowel movement.[5] In Plautus' play *Rudens* (The Rope), the slave Gripus, who has found a trunk brimming with gold and silver, proposed to put notices up 'all over town, in huge letters, a cubit high', seeking the owner.[6] In Domitian's reign, a humourist, reacting to popular dissatisfaction at the number of arches (*arcus*) the emperor had constructed to publicize his military successes, scribbled the Greek word *arkei* (enough) on one of them.[7]

Visitors to ancient monuments left their mark, for instance on the pyramids at Gizeh.[8] It was almost obligatory for the visitor to Thebes in Upper Egypt to cross the River Nile in the early morning to the two massive statues of Amenhotep III beside the Nile.[9] As the result of a fissure in one of the statues (first reported after an earthquake in about 27 BC), when the early morning sun caused the stone to expand slightly, especially (it seems) in February or March of each year, the statue gave out a peculiar whistling sound. It was known as the Colossus of Memnon. Distinguished visitors who had 'heard' the statue singing recorded the fact on its feet and legs; over 100 such messages are known in both Greek and Latin (Fig. 72). Severus, Hadrian and Germanicus were among the visitors, as was the prefect of Egypt, T.Haterius Nepos, who 'in the fifth year of our lord Hadrian heard Memnon on the 12th day before the 1st of March at 7.30 in the morning.'[10] A centurion of legion III *Cyrenaica*, based at Alexandria, heard Memnon 13 times between November 80 and June 81, and gives the dates precisely; we could suppose that he had been stationed nearby.[11] Officials brought their wives and children.[12] Some time during or after Severus' reign, the crack was repaired; the statue's singing days were over.[13]

It is a tendency for any handbook on Roman inscriptions to concentrate on stones which record important historical events, or famous people, and in general on inscriptions with out-of-the-way information or from unexpected localities. But, as I hope the reader has realized, not all inscriptions

72 Texts inscribed on a leg of the Colossus of Memnon, near Thebes, Egypt. (Reproduced from A. and E.Bernand, Inscriptions grecques et latines du Colosse de Memnon, *Le Caire, 1960.)*

were set up by the rich and influential. Many thousands of inscriptions from Rome itself report the lives and occupations of its huge population and the diversity of their origins; they massively enrich the picture of city life obtained from such authors as Juvenal and Martial. Tickets from gladiatorial spectacles are known from Rome and indeed from elsewhere, as well as details of the lives and careers of the gladiators themselves, and other performers. Where large bodies of inscriptions survive, illuminating the population of a town or a region, demographic trends can be studied.

Yet there were groups in any ancient society who could not afford to erect an altar or have a stone gravemarker. Such groups can easily be ignored,

omitted or just forgotten. Only a minute percentage of a town's population had a statue erected in the main square or a monumental tomb outside one of its gates.

We should beware of over-estimating the percentage of the population who were literate. Even in Italy there must always have been people who could neither read Latin nor write it. These groups must have been sizeable in many of the provinces. Not everyone acquired the 'epigraphic habit'. The erection of an altar or a tombstone with a Latin text was itself a mark of the acceptance of Roman ways or an aspiration to them. In some frontier provinces, inscribed texts congregate at military bases, where the impulses to erect them were more pressing, with a noticeable dearth in the surrounding region.

Something of an alternative society briefly surfaces, and with it the use of slang words, obscure terms and slurred pronunciation, giving insights into a world far removed from monumental capitals and honorific epithets. At Pompeii scratched messages on tiles, potsherds and wall-plaster abound. A boorish guest at Trimalchio's banquet boasted that while he knew nothing about mathematics or literary criticism, he did know his 'lapidary letters', could count money and do fractions; that was enough for any man to make his way in the world.[14]

An interesting but somewhat neglected category of inscriptions is that on stone gaming-boards, the *tabulae lusoriae*, marked with two sets of three six-letter words, neatly set side by side. The inscriptions often reflect political aspirations or the realities of the age. Notice this example, on a sizeable stone tablet found in the Catacombs of Saints Marcus and Marcellianus at Rome (see Fig. 73). The text reads:

Parthi occisi | Br[i]tt[o] victus | ludit[e R]omani.[15] 'Parthians slaughtered, Briton conquered, Romans play!' (cf. below, Fig. 79).

An intriguing aspect of ancient custom and belief was the practice of inscribing small lead plaques with derogatory messages directed against an enemy or rival in litigation, in the arena or in love. Such plaques are generally known as curse tablets (*tabellae defixionum*).[16] Many hundreds are known throughout the Roman world. They could be placed either in the temple of a particular deity or even inside the recipient's tomb. There was always a connotation of 'fixing' or nailing of one's enemy, which has parallels in religious belief both before

and since. Sometimes the tablets, folded in the form of a papyrus roll or as a writing tablet, were attached by a nail to a monument or wall or were thrown into a well. In Britain the corpus has been recently enlarged by discoveries at Uley in Gloucestershire and at Bath, some of which implore the resident deities to bring punishment, unhappiness or illness to suspected thieves of clothing, jewellery and money, or seek their assistance in the recovery of lost goods.[17]

The Romans were surrounded by inscriptions in their world, just as we are in ours. Street signs and public information abounded. 'Be on your way, ye who linger; this is not a place of men of leisure'.[18] 'No defacing of notices'.[19] A reward is offered for the return of a bronze vessel stolen from a shop.[20] In Petronius' account of Trimalchio's banquet, when the hero arrives at the host's house he sees first a tablet affixed to a doorpost: 'No slave to go out without the master's permission'. Immediately after, just inside the door, a great chained-up dog was painted on the wall, with the words, in large capitals, CAVE CANEM (Beware of the dog). The hero, true to form, took fright and thought the dog was real.[21] The same inscription is familiar to modern visitors to Pompeii on mosaic floor-surfaces at the entrances to several houses.

Slaves scratched their names too, and sometimes were wealthy enough to have tombstones erected by their fellows. More often the owner of a particular slave erected a memorial, but we cannot suppose that every slave was so commemorated. Freedmen of the emperor and of individual families are attested in large numbers; a few died rich men. It is less easy to record the activities of slave-gangs and labourers who worked daily in the fields, far from an urban centre.

16
CHRISTIANITY

A small Jewish sect, formed round a leader crucified in Judaea under Tiberius, developed within a century into a cult with adherents in many provinces, and became from AD 325 onwards the official religion of the Roman state. The details of its early history do not concern us here, but many thousands of inscriptions have survived which, from their simple wording, imagery or findspots, can confidently be ascribed to the Christian communities.

The early Christians did not set up altars or erect temples in the traditional sense;[1] most surviving inscriptions before the sixth century are funerary. Christian inscriptions are an important and distinctive category worth special study. Yet handbooks on mainstream Roman epigraphy rarely accord them much attention, preferring to relegate them to specialist scholars (see Bibliography). A corpus of Christian inscriptions from Rome begun by G.B. de Rossi (1822–94), the Mommsen of early Christian epigraphy, was continued by Silvagni and Ferrua. A valuable selection, an equivalent to Dessau's *ILS*, was prepared by E.Diehl.

There have been several introductory handbooks, and corpora of Christian inscriptions from various parts of the Graeco-Roman world have been published or are in preparation. The inscriptions range widely in date from, it is judged, the later second century onwards, and they continue to appear throughout the Mediterranean world long after the fall of the Roman Empire in the West.

Perhaps the most famous 'Christian' inscription is also the earliest: the notice nailed on Pilate's orders to the Cross at the Crucifixion of Jesus. The text was in Greek, Latin and Hebrew. The Latin version read *Iesus Nazarenus Rex Iudaeorum*. 'Jesus of Nazareth, King of the Jews.'[2]

CATACOMBS AND CEMETERIES

A great many of the texts available for study derive from catacombs in the immediate vicinity of Rome itself. The catacombs were sets of subterranean passageways, in use mainly from the third to the fifth centuries, cut out of soft volcanic rock. Into the walls of the passageways thus created were carved oblong compartments (*loculi*) in several layers from floor to ceiling; into them were placed the linen-wrapped and unburnt bodies of the faithful.

Today's visitors to the catacombs are warned not to stray, in case they become lost in the intersecting sequence of passages. Some catacombs contained two, three or more levels, connected by staircases. Subterranean burial was not of course a Christian innovation. It had been widely employed in the Near East and Egypt, in Asia Minor and in Greece, and in Italy by the Etruscans (above, p. 100), whenever the underlying geology made this feasible. Around Rome the soft volcanic rock was easily dug into.

For the Christians cremation of the body was not an option; their religious beliefs required the body

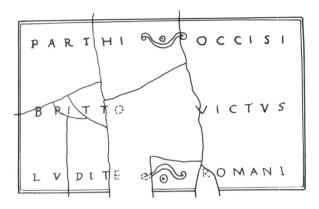

73 Stone gaming-board, from the Catacombs of Saints Marcus and Marcellianus, Rome, 90 × 64cm (36 × 26in.), fourth century AD. (After Hülsen.)

to be preserved intact, resting until Judgement Day and the Resurrection. Each recess in a catacomb was sealed by a thin limestone or marble plaque on which were usually inscribed brief details of the person whose body lay within. Some niches were deep enough to contain two or more bodies, presumably of the same family. Smaller recesses held the bodies of children. Many were robbed long ago by barbarian raiders, from the fifth century onwards, in search of valuables. The inscriptions have often been recovered from the debris-filled passageways.

The catacombs (some 40 systems are known from Rome itself) lay along the major roads leading away from the city in accordance with legislation on burial; we could suppose that they often underlay a plot of land owned by or bought by Christian groups, among the tombs and enclosures of their pagan contemporaries. The martyr S. Cecilia was buried in the catacombs of S. Callistus, which may well have occupied land belonging to the Caecilii, not far from the well-known monument to Caecilia Metella (above, p. 102). The catacombs offered a fairly secure form of burial in areas where land was expensive; they were in effect a Christian equivalent of the communal tombs (*columbaria*; see above, p. 105).

Most bodies were placed in simple recesses sealed by stone slabs, though sometimes the alcove was closed up with bricks, and plastered over, with a painted text. In the catacombs of North Africa the fronts of many recesses were decorated with mosaic *tesserae*, incorporating the epitaph (cf Fig. 67). As in a pagan cemetery there were gradations according to wealth; better-off members of the community were buried in arched alcoves (*arcosolia*) in the passage-walls. Here an inscribed slab was sometimes set horizontally into the top of the recess rather than vertically at its front; or the body was placed under the arch in a sarcophagus. Some families could afford a separate room called a *cubiculum*, which opened off the main passageways and was in effect a private burial chapel. These more elaborate burial places were decorated with frescoes on the walls and ceilings depicting scenes from the Old or New Testaments. Christians, like their pagan contemporaries, often took care to purchase in advance recesses in the catacombs for themselves or for their family as a whole. In the third century they could seemingly buy them direct from a *fossor* (literally, 'digger'), evidently when the catacomb was being dug or extended.[3] The popular view that early Christian communities assembled for prayer and worship in the catacombs cannot be maintained – the narrow passageways were dark and sometimes damp and several miles outside the city; but small family groups could and did gather at a grave on the anniversary of death.

By the early fifth century the catacombs had ceased to be used. The remains of martyrs were often transferred to churches within the city for veneration and safekeeping, and burial of the faithful at these churches became the norm. With a few exceptions knowledge of the whereabouts of catacombs faded from memory. But from the fifteenth century pilgrims began to visit them and to inscribe their own graffiti on the walls of the stairs and passageways. Soon the Popes began to amass a collection of interesting texts; scholarly compilations were made during the sixteenth century and after.

Though we often think of all Christian cemeteries as taking the form of catacombs, they are concentrated at Rome, some other Italian towns, in Sicily, Malta and parts of North Africa. The majority of Christian cemeteries were at ground level, often in the vicinity of basilicas or churches.

At Salona (modern Solin on the outskirts of Split, Yugoslavia) substantial cemeteries were laid out within and beside several extra-mural basilicas, the epitaphs ranging in date from the early fourth century to the end of the sixth century; in the basilica at Manastirine where a large number of sarcophagi can be seen today a century after their discovery (Figs. 66, 74), it is clear that many were placed below the floor of the church, as close as possible to a martyr's tomb in the apse; the western half of the church was hardly used at all for burials. Poorer Christians, however, were buried outside the church.

The desire for proper and lasting commemoration after death inspired Christians as well as pagans, when they could afford it. A celebrated inscription in Greek from Lycaonia in Turkey records M.Julius Eugenius who resigned an army commission in the early fourth century and became bishop of Laodicea for 25 years, where he built a church. 'Having completed all this, I contemplated the span of human life, wrought myself a marble sepulchre and had the aforesaid information inscribed on it for the adornment of the Church and my family.'[4]

CHRISTIAN FORMULAE

Most epitaphs of early Christians are extremely simple, with perhaps no more than the name of the deceased and the age at death (Fig. 75). The traditional sequence of names, involving a forename, family name and surname (above, p. 19) is hardly ever found, and individuals were content with one name or two. Often the Faithful took or were given at birth or baptism the name of a pope or martyr, or a name reflecting Christian doctrine or beliefs, for instance *Redemptus* (Redeemed) or *Adeodatus* (God's gift), or one which reflected their humility, such as *Projectus* (Outcast). In line with changing epigraphic habits in the third-century

74 Sarcophagus from the Christian basilica at Manastirine, Solin, Yugoslavia. It held the body of Viventia who died aged 65, fourth century AD.

75 *A selection of Christian texts (not to scale). 1 Rome (Lateran Galleries); 2 Trier; 3 Catacomb of Cyriaca; 4–6 Catacomb of S. Callistus.*

world, care was taken to state the precise length of life, to the nearest year, month and day. From North Africa comes an epitaph of a baby who was born at midday and whose life lasted just nine sighs.[5] Frequently the year of death is given by using the names of the consuls, and sometimes the individual day of death, which facilitated the commemoration of anniversaries.

Some of the earliest Christian texts are in Greek, even in Italy and the Latin-speaking west, reflecting the origin of both the cult and its first adherents, who had migrated from the eastern Roman world. Christians were as concerned as most pagans that their bodies should lie undisturbed and that the ground should not be reused. Take for example this text (from Rome): 'May he, who wishes to violate the tomb, incur the fate of Judas';[6] or (from Como) 'All you Christians, keep this tomb safe to the end of the world, so that I may return to life without impediment, when He who comes will judge the living and the dead'.[7] Many texts exhibit a piety often lacking in pagan inscriptions and a hope for a better life to come. Parents mourning dead twins at Lyon considered that they had not been bereaved; rather they had given the twins as gifts to God.[8] Occasionally some brief details of doctrine and dogma are included, and something can be learned about early Church hierarchy.

At a more elevated level the catacombs also contained the bodies of popes (who were – and are – the bishops of Rome) and martyrs – the latter being those who had died as 'witnesses' to their faith in a period of persecution.[9] Later there was competition among worshippers to be buried close to the grave of a martyr (above, p. 121), which was felt to enhance the chances of their admission into heaven. The length of a life was sometimes reckoned not from birth but from the moment of baptism; such new converts were known as neophytes.[10] The use of particular phraseology may help to identify a text as Christian: for instance *vivas in deo* ('may you live in god'); or *requiescat in pace* ('may he/she rest in peace'). The deceased was envisaged as 'sleeping' and the body as 'laid to rest' (*depositus*).

The literal meaning of the Greek word 'cemetery', which now comes into more common use, is 'resting place'.[11] Decorative details, drawn from the repertoire of Christian symbolism, are often found in addition to the brief texts, including a dove, a fish or an anchor, the figure of the Good Shepherd, or the famous chi-rho symbol (☧) which began as an abbreviation of the word *Christus*, but later functioned as an independent symbol. Those texts inscribed before the legitimization of the Church under Constantine tend to be brief; later the texts can become effusive. The lettering in itself is hard to date exactly; as early texts often commemorate apparently poor families, the standard of workmanship is unfortunately often indifferent.

Large numbers of slabs survive in the catacombs not so much because of the piety of later generations, but because they were not so accessible or of obvious constructional value in later imperial times and after, when so many monuments were broken up to provide building material for defensive walls, though slabs could be re-employed in the pavements of churches. In the later fourth century

Pope Damasus identified and restored the graves of many martyrs and early popes in the catacombs outside Rome, replacing the original inscriptions with ornamental marble slabs and providing lengthy new texts (in high quality lettering), usually in verse, with details of their lives and sufferings.[12] It would be wrong to over-emphasize the differences between Christian and pagan texts of the third and fourth centuries, or to imagine that all late texts are Christian. But study of this material is a valuable guide towards the changes in Latin syntax and grammar as the Middle Ages drew near.

From the *Via Labicana* outside Rome comes a sarcophagus-text dated to AD 217. It honours Marcus Aurelius Prosenes, a freedman who held a sequence of posts in the imperial household, from procurator of the wine-cellar under Commodus, to master of the emperor's bed-chamber under Caracalla.[13] His own freedmen had the sarcophagus prepared at their expense. On an end-panel a separate inscription identifying him as a Christian reports that 'Prosenes was taken unto God on the 5th day before the Nones of [name of month lost] in the consulship of Praesens and Extricatus, the latter holding the post for a second time, when he (Prosenes) was returning to Rome from the overseas expeditions'.

Epitaphs form the vast majority of surviving inscriptions of the early Church. Others, from baptisteries or other church buildings, record ceremonies that took place there or commemorate the construction of their component parts.[14] More common are inscriptions in mosaic *tesserae* from the floors or walls of basilicas, which report pious sentiments, beliefs or doctrine, or the names of those who had financed the laying of the floor itself, for instance at Aquileia or nearby Grado in the fourth century, or (from a later time) at the Basilica of Euphrasius in Poreč.[15] The ornamentation with texts of a basilica at Lyon is recorded by Sidonius Apollinaris in the mid fifth century; they praised the architect and described the chief features of his edifice.[16]

A famous 'Christian' text is the five-line word-square or acrostic found at Cirencester in 1818 scratched on a piece of painted wall-plaster (Fig. 76). The text reads:

```
R   O   T   A   S
O   P   E   R   A
T   E   N   E   T
A   R   E   P   O
S   A   T   O   R
```

A rough translation is 'Arepo the sower of seed holds the wheels by his efforts.'[17] The belief that the word-square has a Christian significance was advanced first by Felix Grosser in 1926, who pointed out that the letters could be used to spell out twice the words *pater noster*, in the form of a cross; the superfluous letters, two As and two Os, were intended as alpha and omega, 'the beginning and the end' of the Greek alphabet. However, this interpretation has been vigorously disputed, and a connection with Mithraism or Judaism is now advocated.[18]

76 Arepo-Sator word-square, on a fragment of painted wall-plaster, Cirencester, England. (Corinium Museum, Cirencester.)

17

THE
LATER ROMAN EMPIRE

For the Roman world the later third century was a period of insecurity and chaos, with emperors often reigning for brief periods before meeting a violent end. But Diocletian (emperor 284–305) put the Empire on a road to recovery, and his reign and that of Constantine I (306–37) are taken as marking the transition from the Early (or High) Empire to the Late (or Low) Empire. Undoubtedly to observers at the time the transition would have seemed more gradual, but there can be no doubt that the years between 285 and the 330s saw important administrative as well as religious changes. The Empire, as Diocletian realized, was often too beset by internal disorders and external threats for a single emperor, however energetic and resourceful, to govern alone. It had not grown any larger in the preceding century and a half, but was increasingly buffeted by foes. The solution, as Diocletian saw it, was an element of power-sharing, which had indeed been tried before between an emperor and a son or brother. In 286 Diocletian selected as co-Augustus a fellow-soldier Valerius Maximianus (Maximian) and a few years later each Augustus appointed a Caesar to assist him. This was government by committee, with a clear hierarchy and spheres of geographical responsibility.

New forms of address for emperors became common: the phrase *d(ominus) n(oster)*, 'Our Lord', already frequent in correspondence and in direct address, began to replace *imperator Caesar* as the opening formula in official texts. *Dominus noster* was used as a title of the emperor even by Christians after Constantine. The titulature of emperors and their deputies became lengthier, not only because of extra elements (see below) but because, in the case of building work and administrative edicts, the task was regarded as undertaken by the four rulers jointly in their spirit of partnership.

A splendid example of this collegiality comes in the preamble to Diocletian's *Prices Edict* (above, p. 115 of AD 302.[1] The preamble (with the various abbreviations expanded) reads:

[Imp(erator) Caesar C(aius) Aurel(ius) Val(erius) Diocletianus p(ius) f(elix) inv(ictus) Aug(ustus) po]nt(ifex) max(imus) Germ(anicus) Max(imus) VI Sarm(aticus) Max(imus) IIII Persic(us) Max(imus) II Britt(annicus) Max(imus) Carpic(us) Max(imus) Armen(iacus) Max(imus) Medic(us) Max(imus) Adiabenic(us) Max(imus) trib(unicia) p(otestate) XVIII co(n)s(ul) VII imp(erator) XVIII p(ater) p(atriae) proco(n)s(ul) et imp(erator) Caesa[r] M(arcus) Aurel(ius) Val(erius) Maximianus p(ius) f(elix) inv(ictus) Aug(ustus) pont(ifex) max(imus) Germ(anicus) Max(imus) V Sarm(aticus) [Max(imus) IIII Persic(us) Max(imus) II Britt(annicus) Max(imus) Carpic(us) Max(imus) Medic(us) Max(imus) Adiabenic(us) Max(imus) tri]b(unicia) p(otes-

tate) XVII co(n)s(ul) VI imp(erator) XVII p(ater) p(atriae) proco(n)s(ul) et Fla(vius) Val(erius) Constantius Germ(anicus) Max(imus) II Sarm(aticus) Max(imus) II Persic(us) Max(imus) II Britt(annicus) Max(imus) [Carpic(us] Max(imus) Armeni(a)c(us) Max(imus) Medic(us) Max(imus) Adiabenic(us) Max(imus) trib(unicia) p(otestate) VIIII co(n)s(ul) III nobil(issimus) Caes(ar) et G(alerius) Val(erius) Maximianus Germ(anicus) Max(imus) II Sarm(aticus) [Max(imus) II Persic(us) Max(imus) Britt(annicus) Max(imus) Carpic(us) Max(imus) Armeni(a)c(us) Max(imus) Medic(us) Max(imus) Adia]b(enicus) Max(imus) trib(unicia) p(otestate) VIIII co(n)s(ul) III nobil(issimus) Caes(ar) dicunt, etc.*

The four persons whose names and titles precede the main text are Diocletian and Maximian, and their Caesars, Constantius (the father of Constantine) and Galerius. The two Augusti were *pius* (Loyal), *felix* (Fortunate) and *invictus* (Unconquered); each is *pontifex maximus*. All four had the *tribunicia potestas* (for different periods, according to the date of their elevation to imperial status), had been consul and had taken imperatorial salutations. Each was a 'great conqueror' over the Germans, the Sarmatians, the Persians, the Britons, the Carpians (of Thrace), the Armenians and the peoples of Mesopotamia. Simple imperial salutations were no longer an adequate record: victories needed emphasizing in an age when they were no longer the norm. Honours were taken in common regardless of personal involvement. All

77 Panels reporting the official response by the emperors Valentinian, Valens and Gratian, to a petition from the proconsul of Asia, displayed on Curetes Street, Ephesus, Turkey, AD 371–72.

took credit for victories won over the Empire's enemies. The emperor was no longer merely *Augustus*, but could be *semper Augustus*, 'the everlasting Augustus'; he was *restitutor urbis Romanae*, 'restorer of the city of Rome', or *victor et triumphator*, 'winner of victories and celebrator of triumphs'. Fresh abbreviations came into use to shorten the new titulature: if two (or more) emperors were being honoured, the plural word *Augusti* might be reduced to AVGG, *Caesares* to CAESS, *domini nostri* to DD NN. Coins of the usurper Carausius, who set up an independent government in Britain in the later third century, laud the *pietas Augustorum*, 'the loyalty of emperors' (to the state and to their ancestors), using the abbreviation AVGGG, that is of three *Augusti*, who are the two legitimate emperors (Diocletian and Maximian) together with Carausius who is cheekily equated with them.

The same collegiality is reflected in imperial responses to petitions and requests by officials and communities. On Curetes Street in Ephesus, Turkey, stands a substantial text, one of several such documents (Fig. 77), reporting the response of the emperors Valentinian, Valens and Gratian to a petition from the proconsul of Asia (the historian Eutropius), in AD 371–72.[2]

In front of the so-called Temple of Hadrian at Ephesus (Fig. 78) stand four statue bases.[3] Three honour Diocletian, Galerius and Constantius. There must have been a fourth honouring Maximian; but this was removed, and its place taken later in the century by a base in honour of Count Theodosius, father of the emperor Theodosius.

78 Temple of Hadrian, Curetes Street, Ephesus, with statue bases in honour of (left to right) Galerius, Count Theodosius, Diocletian and Constantius Chlorus.

DIOCLETIAN'S REFORMS

Diocletian vigorously overhauled the government of the provinces in order to realign responsibilities more exactly with realities. The tide was beginning to run against the Romans, and peaceful tenure of a post was a rarity rather than the norm. Diocletian increased the number of provinces by splitting up existing entities; thus new geographical names appear in the epigraphic record. The overall responsibilities of a governor were thus lessened. Secondly, Diocletian introduced a new hierarchy into provincial command: the Empire was divided into 12 dioceses, each under a *vicarius*.[4] (The names are familiar in a separate, ecclesiastical context.) Each *vicarius* reported to one of four Praetorian Prefects who oversaw even wider geographical areas. Each diocese contained a number of provinces, mostly under a *praeses*. For example, Britain formed one diocese, and was divided into four provinces.

These administrative changes were linked to reform of army organization. Many of the details are obscure, and the timing and sequence of the reforms continue to be debated. The previous half century had seen the frontier garrisons weakened in the interest of strong forces marching with the emperor. Diocletian redressed the balance by forming many new legions to bolster provincial garrisons and providing machinery for the swift concentration of the principal elements in detachments (*vexillationes*). This constituted a honing of the traditional system. A few of the new legions were designated as a permanent accompaniment for the emperors themselves. Detachments must have been separated from their parent units for extended periods.

Constantine carried this system to a logical conclusion by distinguishing two categories of troops: static frontier forces defending the outer limits of the Empire who were entitled *ripenses* (of a river bank) or *limitanei* (of a land frontier); and mobile armies available to the Augustus or his Caesar. Soon the latter groups gained the name *comitatenses* (companions). Sometimes legions of the early Empire continued in a double existence, in a frontier base and as a mobile unit; but many new formations make their appearance now, especially cavalry regiments. Within each diocese the military and civil commands were separated, responsibility for all the army units permanently stationed there falling to a *dux* (lit., commander), with independent commands assigned by the emperors on an *ad hoc* basis being undertaken by *comites* (lit., companions). These titles, *dux* and *comes*, are familiar to us as medieval 'dukes' and 'counts'. The Praetorian Guard was disbanded by Constantine, and replaced by selected troops from his victorious army, who gained the designation *Palatini* (i.e. household troops), stationed on the Palatine Hill in Rome.

A substantial cemetery of the fourth and fifth centuries was unearthed from 1873 onwards at Concordia, in north-east Italy, near modern Portogruaro. The graves lay along the *Via Annia*, east of the town; flooding of the area from the fourth century onwards paradoxically preserved them from disturbance (cf. at Šempeter above, p. 34).[5] Both pagan and Christian graves were present here; many bodies had been placed in sarcophagi. In the Late Empire the town was a production centre for military equipment (hence the name then in use: *Concordia Sagittaria*, 'Concordia of the Arrows'); many memorials to military personnel have survived.

CHANGING TIMES

The increasing obsession with status and hierarchies is reflected in the epigraphic record from the end of the second century AD at all levels: officials drawn from the senatorial order had come to be designated *vir clarissimus* (most distinguished gentleman, abbreviated to *v.c.*), and those of the equestrian order might use the phrases *vir eminentissimus* (most eminent gentleman, abbreviated to *v.e.*), *vir perfectissimus* (most perfect gentleman, abbreviated to *v.p.*) or *vir egregius* (distinguished gentleman, abbreviated to *v.e.*), according to the seniority of the posts held. These fashions were carried forward into the Late Empire when many new titles and designations came into use.

A magnificent sarcophagus, now in the Lateran Galleries of the Vatican Museums, commemorates a senator, Junius Bassus, *v(ir) c(larissimus)*, who *in ipsa praefectura urbis neophytus iit ad deum Eusebio et Ipatio conss* ('while he was serving as Prefect of the City, he went to God as a new convert, in the consulship of Eusebius and Hypatius'). Junius Bassus 'went to God', that is died, in AD 359.[6] He had only recently been baptised as a Christian. Another inscription, found more recently, identifies Bassus as the son of a praetorian prefect of the same name; other posts we now know that he held were the otherwise unattested *comes primi ordinis* (Count of the First Rank), and *Vicarius* of the city of Rome.[7]

There is a clear falling away in the number of civic benefactions reported on stone panels; the wealthy turned their backs on urban life, it has been argued, to concentrate on their rural estates. Society in both town and country became increasingly rigid, with (for example) the sons of councillors required to serve in turn on the *ordo decurionum* (and to contribute to the costs of amenities and shows), and the sons of soldiers condemned to hereditary military service.

The Roman inscriptions of the Late Empire seem less numerous than those of earlier centuries; often they are also more poorly executed. To us there seems an evident decline in standards; but lettering which may appear less aesthetically satisfying was perhaps felt to be more modern. The changes in lettering (above, p. 28), style and spelling which are evidenced on inscriptions did not occur suddenly; this was a gradual process, beginning in the late second century and continuing into the fourth and beyond.

The granting of universal citizenship under

79 Bronze dice-dispenser from a villa at Froitzheim, between Aachen and Bonn, fourth century AD. *(Rheinisches Landesmuseum, Bonn).*

Caracalla (Marcus Aurelius Antoninus Pius Felix) in the early third century led to a tremendous rise in the number of families with the name *Aurelius*, who had acquired it from the emperor. In the fourth century we encounter *Valerii* and *Flavii* in great numbers; these are the family names of the royal houses of Diocletian, Maximian and Con-stantine. (Flavius was also the family name of Vespasian and his sons.) Since the range of family names (*nomina*) became more confined, people used their surnames (*cognomina*) as an easier method of identification; we find forenames (*prae-nomina*) appearing in the role of surnames; for instance, Aurelius Marcus or Aurelius Gaius.

A dice-dispenser, 22cm (9in.) high (Fig. 79), recently found at a villa between Aachen and Bonn, takes the form of a bronze tower;[8] the Latin term, known from the poet Martial, is a *turricula*.[9] Round the 'battlements' of the tower are the Latin words VTERE FELIX VIVAS. 'Use (me) well. Live life (to the full)'. One side of the dispenser bears the optimistic message PICTOS VICTOS, HOSTIS DELETA, LVDITE SECVRI. 'Picts beaten, enemy destroyed, relax and play'. The peculiar selection of case endings in the Latin is necessitated by the need to use words of the same length throughout. The wording recalls the messages cut on stone gaming-boards (above, p. 118). A mid-fourth-century date is likely.

Standing in the Forum at Rome near the Arch of Septimius Severus is a substantial marble block carved on one face with 15 lines of text in good capitals, of which two lines are erased. Closer inspection reveals that the block is the base for an equestrian statue, up-ended, but no trace of an original dedicatory inscription has been observed on any of the visible faces (Fig. 80). The visible text reads:

> *Fidei virtutiq(ue) devotissimorum | militum dom-*
> *norum nostrorum |Arcadi Honori et Theodosi |*
> *perennium Augustorum | post confectum Gothi-*
> *cum | bellum felicitate aeterni | principis domni*
> *nostri Honori | consiliis et fortitudine | inlustris*
> *viri comitis et* [two lines erased] *S(enatus)*
> *P(opulus)q(ue) Romanus | curante Pisidio*
> *Romulo v(iro) c(larissimo) | praef(ecto) urbi*
> *vice sacra | iterum iudicante.*[10] 'To the loyalty
and virtue of the most devoted soldiers of our lords Arcadius, Honorius and Theodosius, perpetual *Augusti*, after the Gothic War had been brought to an end through the good fortune of

80 Re-used statue base, up-ended, inscribed in honour of the emperors Honorius, Arcadius and Theodosius II. The Forum, Rome, AD 402–6.

our eternal ruler and lord Honorius, and by the good counsel and the bravery of the illustrious gentleman, Count and .... The Senate and the People of Rome, under the care of Pisidius Romulus, most distinguished gentleman, prefect of the city, who has charge for the second time of judging appeals.'

The date range is AD 402–406, and the name of the erased Count is Stilicho, the Vandal general whose abilities had done much to shore up the weakening Empire in times of great stress. He fell from power in AD 408. Two years later Rome was sacked by the Visigoths.

18

CONCLUSION: THE VALUE
OF ROMAN INSCRIPTIONS

These chapters began with R.G.Collingwood's generous verdict on inscriptions and their value for the historian of the Roman world. Was his praise justified? If nothing else has been achieved here, the reader should have become aware of the information that inscriptions, as a distinct but wide-ranging class of evidence, can add to our knowledge.

Yet some caution will not be out of place. Many inscriptions were composed as a deliberate act for others to see – the details of a career or a life of public service, or an altar expressing the dedicator's gratitude to the gods. There is a fine line between an unbiased record of fact and self-glorification and congratulation. 'The writer of an epitaph' Dr Johnson observed 'should not be considered as saying nothing but what is strictly true. Allowance must be made for some degree of exaggerated praise. In lapidary inscriptions a man is not upon his oath.'[1] Should we be similarly suspicious of Roman epitaphs and indeed of other types of inscriptions? Many categories provided a ready opportunity for an individual to make a statement in a way which suited the dedicator. Yet, for the most part, such hypercriticism seems unnecessary. Most epitaphs, for example, are bare records of a lifetime's public service or of family relationships, impressive perhaps, but unembellished by personal comment or self-promotion.

There are, however, occasions when it is wise to read not only the lines of text, but between them

too. The emperor Augustus composed a lengthy text, his *Res Gestae* (Achievements), which was inscribed after his death on bronze pillars outside his mausoleum in Rome; copies were inscribed on temples dedicated to him elsewhere. An almost complete version and a virtual translation in Greek were inscribed on a wall of the temple to 'Rome and Augustus' at Ankara, the capital of the Roman province of Galatia (Fig. 81); the Latin text, a total of 285 lines, is spread over six columns.[2] Students often fail to realize that this important text is on stone rather than surviving in manuscript form through the ages. We have here an emperor effectively writing his own obituary notice, presenting himself in the way he hoped posterity would remember him and his achievements. Here is the truth, but not all of it, with awkward events glossed over. Cornelius Gallus, first holder of the post of prefect of Egypt under Augustus, erected at Syene in 29 BC a boastful text, in Latin, Greek and hieroglyphics, which emphasized his recent military successes.[3] Three years later he fell from favour and committed suicide. But such exercises in blatant self-promotion are rare.

Those inscriptions which have come down to us from antiquity do not constitute a complete record. It should be remembered that we have only chance survivals, albeit in some quantity. Perhaps only at Pompeii and Herculaneum, and a few other sites, can we begin, with some confidence, to study the epigraphic material in relation to the towns and

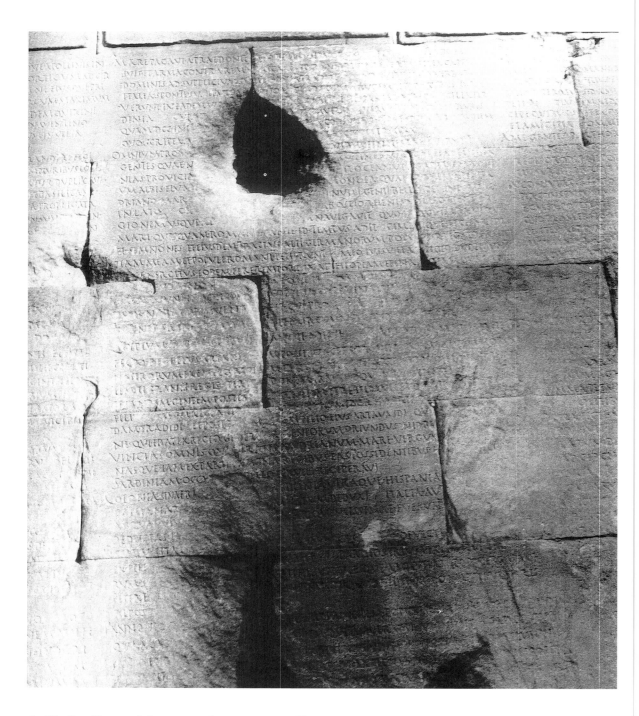

81 The Res Gestae *of the emperor Augustus, on a wall
of the temple of Rome and Augustus, Ankara, Turkey,
soon after* AD *14. This photograph shows paragraphs
(chapter 25 onwards) detailing Augustus' military
achievements and foreign policy successes.*

RESTITVTIONEM MVSAEI LEGIONARII
QVOD ERAT RVINIS PAENE OPPRESSVM
COMMEMORAVIT SVA ALTITVDO REGALIS
RICARDVS DVX GLOCESTRIAE
DIE II · IVNII · MCMLXXXVII

82 The Duke of Gloucester unveiling an inscribed plaque at the Legionary Museum, Caerleon, Gwent. 1987. (National Museum of Wales.)

their monuments, and other evidence for economy and society. Moreover, inscriptions constitute only one branch of ancient evidence, and any reconstruction of antiquity is best achieved through the use of different types of both source material and approaches. The Romans did not distinguish between what they wrote down on papyrus, or parchment, or inscribed on stone. We should beware of modern compartmentalization in scientific study of the ancient world.

The scholar must also be watchful for forgeries, in both Roman times and (in particular) in more recent centuries. Some early antiquarians did not flinch from adding to the number of stones reported in their publications. Prominent families might wish to emphasize, or rather invent, links with the aristocracy of ancient Rome. Most of these inventions were long ago exposed, though a few texts were unjustly condemned as forgeries.

On a more positive note it can be observed that inscriptions mostly stand as inscribed up to 2000 years ago, and where they survive have not been subject to the vagaries of copying and the accidents of survival of manuscripts. Inscriptions on stone or bronze could be utilized as source material by the Roman historians themselves, along with written documents preserved in public record offices. A historian's verdict is, however, coloured by later events, his own preconceptions and attitudes. A very illuminating testimony to the methods of the historian Tacitus is provided by a large bronze panel (it is 2m (6½ft) wide) from the Altar of the Three Gauls near Lyon, which reports a speech made by the emperor Claudius advocating the admission to the Senate of Gallic nobility.[4] Tacitus reports the event in his narrative of the year AD 48, with a text of Claudius' speech.[5] Assuming that the inscription represents a fairly accurate record written down soon after the event, it is interesting to see how freely Tacitus has altered the content, even allowing for the summarizing and necessary stylistic changes required to convert a rhetorical text into a literary version.[6]

For the archaeologist inscriptions provide special details, sometimes closely datable, that no other form of evidence offers. But two pieces of advice are in order: the need both to see the stone and record accurately what it says; and secondly to know precisely the context in which it was recovered.

Latin is still used for inscriptions today, most obviously in ecclesiastical dedications at the Vatican City, though modern languages are gradually taking its place. The recent reopening of the legionary museum at Caerleon, Gwent, was marked by the unveiling of an inscribed plaque in Latin, its message in a mixture of classical and modern phraseology (Fig. 82). The text reads:

Restitutionem musaei legionarii | quod erat ruinis paene oppressum | commemoravit sua altitudo regalis | Ricardus dux Glocestriae | die II Junii MCMLXXXVII. 'His Royal Highness, Richard Duke of Gloucester, marked the restoration of the Legionary Museum, which had fallen into almost complete decay, on 2 June, 1987.'

In many cathedrals, churches and schools, slabs with Latin texts commemorate the careers and achievements not only of clerics but very often also of the military commanders and administrators of the British Empire. Classical erudition has been used to devise inscriptions down to modern times. Let me conclude by referring to a potentially misleading text, noticed recently at Nablus in Palestine:[7]

Paci Britannicae | leg(io) LXXII Colpica | Monticola Albanica | et cohors II fabrum | ob burg(um) explicatum | contra Arabos rebel(les) | v(otum) s(olverunt) l(ibentes) m(erito). 'To Pax Britannica, the 72nd Legion *Colpica Monticola Albanica* and the 2nd Cohort of Engineers, to mark the laying out of a blockhouse against rebellious Arabs willingly and deservedly fulfilled their vow.'

At first sight this could be a genuine record from the early centuries AD, erected by a legion numbered LXXII, and an auxiliary cohort; but there was never a Legion LXXII in the Roman army. On the other hand, the British Army had a 72nd Regiment, the Seaforth Highlanders, the Duke of Albany's Own, which served in Palestine in 1935–36 and inscribed the pillar (which may in origin be of Roman date), along with a Field Company of Royal Engineers (the *Cohors Fabrum* of the inscription).[8] Their policing duties were similar to those of their Roman forebears.

APPENDICES

Gallienus (*Imp. Caesar P. Licinius Egnatius Valerianus Gallienus Augustus*) 253–68

Claudius II (*Imp. Caesar M. Aurelius Claudius Augustus*) 268–70

Quintillus (*Imp. Caesar M. Aurelius Claudius Quintillus Augustus*) 270

Aurelian (*Imp. Caesar L. Domitius Aurelianus Augustus*) 270–75

Tacitus (*Imp. Caesar M. Claudius Tacitus Augustus*) 275–76

Florianus (*Imp. Caesar M. Annius Florianus Augustus*) 276

Probus (*Imp. Caesar M. Aurelius Probus Augustus*) 276–82

Carus (*Imp. Caesar M. Aurelius Carus Augustus*) 282–83

Carinus (*Imp. Caesar M. Aurelius Carinus Augustus*) 283–85

Numerian (*Imp. Caesar M. Aurelius Numerius Numerianus Augustus*) 283–84

Diocletian (*Imp. Caesar C. Aurelius Valerius Diocletianus Augustus*) 284–305

Maximian (*Imp. Caesar M. Aurelius Valerius Maximianus Augustus*) 286–305

Constantius (*d.n. Caesar Flavius Valerius Constantius Augustus*) 305–06

Galerius (*d.n. Caesar C. Galerius Valerius Maximianus Augustus*) 305–11

Severus (*d.n. Flavius Valerius Severus Augustus*) 306–07

Maxentius (*d.n. M. Aurelius Valerius Maxentius Augustus*) 306–12

Constantine (*d.n. L. Flavius Valerius Constantinus Augustus*) 307–37

Licinius (*d.n. Valerius Licinianus Licinius Augustus*) 308–24

Constantine II (*d.n. Flavius Claudius Constantinus Augustus*) 337–40

Constans (*d.n. Flavius Julius Claudius Constans Augustus*) 337–50

Constantius II (*d.n. Flavius Julius Constantius Augustus*) 337–61

Magnentius (*d.n. Flavius Magnus Magnentius Augustus*) 350–53

Julian (*d.n. Flavius Claudius Iulianus Augustus*) 360–63

Jovian (*d.n. Flavius Iovianus Augustus*) 363–64

Valentinian (*d.n. Flavius Valentinianus Augustus*) 364–75

Valens (*d.n. Flavius Valens Augustus*) 364–78

Gratian (*d.n. Flavius Gratianus Augustus*) 367–83

Valentinian II (*d.n. Flavius Valentinianus Iunior Augustus*) 375–92

Theodosius (*d.n. Flavius Theodosius Augustus*) 379–95

Honorius (*d.n. Flavius Honorius Augustus*) 395–423

Arcadius (*d.n. Flavius Arcadius Augustus*) 395–408

Theodosius II (*d.n. Flavius Theodosius Augustus*) 408–50

Valentinian III (*d.n. Flavius Placidus Valentinianus*) 425–55

Marcian (*d.n. Flavius Marcianus Augustus*) 450–57

Petronius Maximus (*d.n. Flavius Petronius Maximus Augustus*) 455

Avitus (*d.n. M. Maecilius Flavius Eparchius Avitus Augustus*) 455–56

Majorian (*d.n. Flavius Julius Valerius Maiorianus Augustus*) 457–61

Libius Severus (*d.n. Libius Severus Augustus*) 461–65

Anthemius (*d.n. Procopius Anthemius Augustus*) 467–72

Olybrius (*d.n. Flavius Anicius Olybrius Augustus*) 472

Glycerius 473

Julius Nepos 475–76

Romulus 475–76

Leo I (*d.n. Flavius Novus Leo Augustus*) 457–74

Leo II (*d.n. Flavius Leo Iunior Augustus*) 474

Zeno (*d.n. Flavius Zeno Augustus*) 474–91

—APPENDIX 2—

SOME COMMON ABBREVIATIONS

A	*Aulus*	Aulus
	annus	year
A A A F F	*Aere argento auro flando feriundo*	for minting and striking gold, silver and bronze coins
A D A	*Agris dandis adsignandis*	for giving and assigning land
AED	*Aedilis*	aedile
ANN	*annos/annis*	years
	annona	corn supply
ANT	*Antonius*	Antonius
APP	*Appius*	Appius
AVG	*Augustus*	Augustus
	augustalis	Priest of Augustus
	augur	augur
AVGG	*Augusti*	emperors
AVG N	*Augustus noster*	our emperor
B M	*benemerenti*	well-deserving
C	*Gaius*	Gaius
	Caesar	emperor (see p. 42)
	centuria	century
	cohors	cohort
C A	*curam agens*	taking care
CAP	*capitalis*	magistrate overseeing executions
C V	*clarissimus vir*	distinguished gentleman
CN	*Gnaeus*	Gnaeus
COH	*cohors*	cohort
COL	*colonia*	colony
COS	*consul*	consul
C R	*cives Romani*	Roman citizens
CVR	*curavit*	took care of
D	*Decimus*	Decimus
	dat(dedit)	give (gave)
	denarius	coin
	dominus	master
	domo	from the town of
D D	*decreto decurionum*	by decree of the town councillors
DEC	*decurio*	town-councillor
	decreto	by decree
DED	*dedit*	gave
DES	*designatus*	designate(d)
DE S P	*de sua pecunia*	from his own money
D I M	*deo invicto Mithrae*	to the invincible god Mithras
D M	*Dis Manibus*	to the spirits of the dead
D N	*dominus noster*	our emperor
D S	*de suo*	from his own money
EQ	*eques*	knight
	equitata	with a cavalry attachment
EQ P	*equo publico*	member of equestrian order
EX S C	*ex senatus consulto*	by decree of the Senate
EX TEST	*ex testamento*	according to the will
F	*fecit/faciundum*	did/to be done
	filius/filia	son/daughter
FAC COER	*faciundum coeravit*	saw to it being done
FEC	*fecit/fecerunt*	did
FID	*fidelis*	faithful
FL	*Flavius*	Flavius
GEN	*genius*	presiding spirit
H	*heres*	heir
	hic	here
H S E	*hic situs (sita) est*	he/she lies here
H F	*heres fecit*	the heir did it
H M	*hoc monumentum*	this tomb
H M H N S	*hoc monumentum heredem non sequitur*	this tomb does not pass to the heir
I D	*iure dicundo*	for administering the law
IMP	*imperator*	emperor
IN AG	*in agro*	to the rear
IN FR	*in fronte*	across the front
I O M	*Iupiter Optimus Maximus*	Jupiter Best and Greatest
L	*libertus*	freedman
	laetus/libens	gladly/willingly
	Lucius	Lucius
LEG	*legio*	legion
	legatus	legate
LEG AVG PR PR	*legatus Augusti pro praetore*	emperor's legate with powers of a praetor
L D D D	*loco dato decreto decurionum*	place given by decree of the town-councillors
L M	*locus monumenti*	the site of the tomb
LOC	*locus*	place
M	*Marcus*	Marcus
	Mithras	Mithras
M'	*Manius*	Manius
MIL	*miles*	soldier
	militavit	served in the army
MON	*monumentum*	tomb

N	*noster*	our	S P Q R	*Senatus Populusque Romanus*	The Senate and People of Rome
NAT	*natus*	born/aged			
NN	*nostri*	our (plural)	S T T L	*sit tibi terra levis*	may the earth lie lightly on you
NOB CAES	*nobilissimus Caesar*	most noble Caesar	STIP	*stipendia*	years (of military service)
O H S S	*ossa hic sita sunt*	the bones lie here			
OPT	*optimus*	best	T	*Titus*	Titus
	optio	centurion's deputy	TEST	*testamentum*	will
			TI	*Tiberius*	Tiberius
P	*Publius*	Publius	T P I	*testamento poni iussit*	ordered its erection in his will
	passus/pedes	paces/feet			
PAR	*parentes*	parents			
PAT PAT (*or* P P)	*pater patriae*	father of his country	TRIB POT (*or* TR P)	*tribunicia potestate*	with tribunician power
P F	*pia fidelis*	loyal and faithful	TR MIL	*tribunus militum*	military tribune
P M (*or* PONT MAX)	*pontifex maximus*	chief priest	TR PL	*tribunus plebis*	tribune of the People
POS	*posuit*	set (this) up	TRIB	*tribunus*	tribune
P P	*primus pilus*	chief centurion			
PRAEF	*praefectus*	prefect	V	*Vibius*	Vibius
PRAET	*praetor*	praetor		*vir*	man
PROCOS	*proconsul*	proconsul		*vivus*	alive
PROC	*procurator*	procurator		*vixit*	lived
PROV	*provincia*	province		*vovit*	vowed
PR PR	*pro praetore*	with powers of a praetor	V C	*vir clarissimus*	most distinguished gentleman
Q	*Quintus*	Quintus	V E	*vir egregius*	distinguished gentleman
	quaestor	quaestor			
	quinquennalis	with censorial powers		*vir eminentissimus*	most eminent gentleman
QQ	*quinquennales*	*as above* (plural)	VET	*veteranus*	veteran soldier
			VEX	*vexillatio*	detachment
R	*Romanus*	Roman	V F	*vivus fecit*	did it while alive
REST	*restituit*	restored	VIG	*Vigiles*	night-watch
R P	*res publica*	the state	VIX	*vixit*	lived
S	*Servius*	Servius	VOT	*votum/vota*	vow(s)
SP	*Spurius*	Spurius	V P	*vivus posuit*	erected it while alive
SAL	*Salvius*	Salvius			
S C	*senatus consulto*	by decree of the Senate	VRB	*urbana*	urban
			V S L L M	*votum solvit laetus libens merito*	paid his vow gladly, willingly and deservedly
S P	*sua pecunia*	with his own money			

—APPENDIX 3—

THE ROMAN VOTING-TRIBES

AEM	*Aemilia*	PAP	*Papiria*
ANI	*Aniensis*	POB	*Poblilia*
ARN	*Arnensis*	POL	*Pollia*
CAM	*Camilia*	POM	*Pomptina*
CLA	*Claudia*	PVP	*Pupinia*
CLV	*Clustumina*	QVI	*Quirina*
COL	*Collina*	ROM	*Romilia*
COR	*Cornelia*	SAB	*Sabatina*
ESQ	*Esquilina*	SCA	*Scaptia*
FAB	*Fabia*	SER	*Sergia*
FAL	*Falerna*	STE	*Stellatina*
GAL	*Galeria*	SVC	*Suburana*
HOR	*Horatia*	TER	*Teretina*
LEM	*Lemonia*	TRO	*Tromentina*
MAE	*Maecia*	VEL	*Velina*
MEN	*Menenia*	VOL	*Voltinia*
OVF	*Oufentina*	VOT	*Voturia*
PAL	*Palatina*		

For variations in spelling and abbreviations employed, the reader is referred to L.R. Taylor, *The Voting Districts of the Roman Republic* (Rome, 1960).

—APPENDIX 4—

THE CORPUS OF LATIN INSCRIPTIONS (CIL): contents of the volumes

I	Inscriptions of the Roman Republic (to 44 BC).
II	Spain.
III	Northern and eastern provinces of the Empire (Noricum and Rhaetia; Pannonia and Moesia; Dacia; Thrace; Greece; Crete; Asia Minor; Syria; Judaea; Arabia; Cyrenaica and Egypt).
IV	Pompeii, Herculaneum and Stabiae: inscriptions painted on house-walls.
V	Northern Italy (Cisalpine Gaul).
VI	The city of Rome: inscriptions on stone.
VII	Britain.
VIII	North Africa, from Tripolitania to Morocco.
IX	Central and south-east Italy.
X	Campania and SW Italy, Sardinia, Sicily.
XI	North-central Italy.
XII	Southern Gaul (*Narbonensis*).
XIII	Central and northern Gaul, Roman Germany.
XIV	Latium, and the environs of Rome, including Ostia.
XV	The city of Rome: inscriptions on clay, glass, metal, etc.
XVI	Military Diplomas
XVII	Milestones.
XVIII	Pagan inscriptions in verse (no fascicules yet published).

APPENDIX 5

SOME EPIGRAPHIC CONVENTIONS

(abc) Letters within round brackets are those omitted by the stonecutter, but printed by the modern epigraphist to fill out an abbreviation; e.g. *leg(ionis)*.

[abc] Letters within square brackets are those lost on the stone, because of damage or weathering, but which can be restored with certainty; e.g. *Sept[imio Severo]*.

[....] Letters lost on the stone, by damage or weathering, which cannot be restored; each dot to represent one missing letter.

[----] Letters lost on the stone, by damage or weathering, which cannot be restored; the number of missing letters is uncertain.

⟨abc⟩ Letters accidentally omitted on the stone; e.g. *Ben⟨ev⟩entum*.

{abc} Superfluous letters inscribed on the stone, in error, when they are not needed, e.g. *Imp{p}eratori*.

[[abc]] Letters deliberately erased, as for example following *damnatio memoriae*: e.g. [[*P. Septimio Getae*]].

a̤ḅc̣ Letters underdotted are doubtful because of damage or weathering; they cannot be restored with certainty.

[\\\\\] Letters deleted on the stone, but not able to be restored with confidence. Each \ represents a single letter.

ABC Letters which appear on the stone, which are not understood by the epigrapher.

1 (etc.) Division between lines in the original text, with the number placed at the beginning of each e.g. 1, *Imp(eratori) Caes(ari)*, 2, *Hadr(iano) Antonino Aug(usto)*, 3, *Pio* etc. More frequently line-numbers are given only at five-line intervals. When inscriptions are printed in minuscule type, it is normal to indicate all line divisions with a slanted line (/).

v. represents a letter-space left blank on the stone; *vvv* represents three spaces, etc. The word *vac.* or *vacat* may be written in full to represent a longer space left blank, or a whole line.

FOOTNOTES

—ABBREVIATIONS USED IN THE FOOTNOTES AND BIBLIOGRAPHY—

AIEGL	L'Association Internationale d'Épigraphie Grecque et Latine
AE	l'Année épigraphique
AJA	American Journal of Archaeology
AJP	American Journal of Philology
ANRW	Aufstieg und Niedergang der römischen Welt (Berlin/New York 1972–)
CIL	Corpus Inscriptionum Latinarum
CIG	Corpus Inscriptionum Graecarum
CRAI	Comptes rendus de l'académie des inscriptions et des belles-lettres
EJ	V. Ehrenberg and A.H.M. Jones, Documents illustrating the Reigns of Augustus and Tiberius (Oxford 1949; 2nd ed. 1976)
G	A.E. Gordon, Illustrated Introduction to Latin Epigraphy (Los Angeles/London, 1983)
HTR	Harvard Theological Review
ILCV	Inscriptiones Latinae Christianae Veteres
IG	Inscriptiones Graecae
ILG	Inscriptions Latines de Gaule
ILS	Inscriptiones Latinae Selectae
ILLRP	Inscriptiones Latinae Liberae Rei Publicae
ILJ	Inscriptiones Latinae quae in Jugoslavia . . . repertae et editae sunt
JRS	Journal of Roman Studies
MAAR	Memoirs of the American Academy at Rome
MEFR	Memoires d'École française de Rome
MW	M. McCrum and A.G. Woodhead, Select Documents of the Principates of the Flavian Emperors (Cambridge, 1961)
Nash, TDAR	E. Nash, Topographical Dictionary of Ancient Rome (London, 1961)
PBSR	Papers of the British School at Rome
PLRE	Prosopography of the Later Roman Empire
RE	Real-encyclopädie der classischen Altertumswissenschaft
RIB	Roman Inscriptions of Britain, vol. 1 (Oxford, 1965), ed. by R.G. Collingwood and R.P. Wright
SHA	Scriptores Historiae Augustae
Smallwood, GCN	E.M. Smallwood, Documents illustrating the Principates of Gaius, Claudius and Nero (Cambridge, 1967)
Smallwood, NTH	E.M. Smallwood, Documents illustrating the Principates of Nerva, Trajan and Hadrian (Cambridge, 1966)
ZPE	Zeitschrift für Papyrologie und Epigraphik

Note: Inscriptions published in the *Corpus Inscriptionum Latinarum (CIL)* are referred to by volume and number only, e.g. X 3669.

—FOOTNOTES—

Chapter 1 (pp. 9–11)

1. *The Archaeology of Roman Britain* (Oxford, 1930), 162.
2. *Res Gestae* 20.1; *ILS* 7216.
3. Livy 28.46.16; Suetonius, *Dom.* 5; *ILS* 5466.
4. Note the dedication to the ancestral gods of Egypt and to the Nile, inscribed in hieroglyphics, Latin and Greek, erected at Syene by Cornelius Gallus, first prefect of Egypt, in 29 BC; *ILS* 8995 = *G* 22; above, p. 131.
5. *ILS* 244, 7216; Pliny, *Nat. Hist.* 16.237, 34.99.
6. Suetonius, *Vesp.* 8.5.
7. Horace, *Odes* 3.30.1
8. On the need, appreciated in antiquity, for the maintenance of the bronze panels used to record such important matters, see Pliny, *Nat.Hist.* 34.99.
9. Suetonius, *Caes.* 37.2.
10. Old Testament, *Daniel* 5.25.
11. The genuineness of the so-called *Fibula Praenestina*, once thought to belong in the seventh century, is now seriously questioned; *ILS* 8561 = *G* 1.
12. S.Butler, *The Life and Letters of Dr. Samuel Butler, Headmaster of Shrewsbury School* (London, 1896), 255. Strictly speaking the allusion is only to the contemporary fashion of composing Latin epitaphs.

Chapter 2 (pp. 12–16)

1. G.Susini, *The Roman Stonecutter* (Oxford, 1977), 9ff. See the excellent brief statement by R.Ireland, 'Epigraphy', in M.Henig (ed.), *A Handbook of Roman Art* (Oxford, 1983), 220–33.

2. G.M.Brown *et al. The Oxyrhynchus Papyri*, vol. 41 (London, 1972), no. 2950, with pl. 3 (full-size). An alternative interpretation would be that, in a country where wood was scarce, the sheet was in some way intended for public display in its own right. For the epigraphic 'conventions' used here in the text and in the following pages, see Appendix 5.

3. Varro, *de Ling.Lat.* 8.62; *ILS* 7675, 7675a, 7676.

4. *Satyricon* 65.6.

5. VI 9557; X 6193; *AE* 1940, 147, 153; *ILS* 7681.

6. IV 3884, 3775; latter lays a curse on whoever should deface what he had written; cf V 7160.

7. III 633, I and II = *ILS* 5466. Cf. *ILS* 139, lines 30–32: 'on a large pillar next to the altar, this decree, together with the above decrees, should be inscribed or carved' (*incidatur insculpaturve*).

8. X 7296 = *ILS* 7680; *IG* XIV 297. It can hardly be a coincidence that the only line scored with a horizontal guideline contains the word ORDINANTVR. Errors in the grammar of both Greek and Latin are not such as to inspire confidence in the discerning customer! The stonemason was perhaps a native Sicilian seeking business from as wide a range of clients as he could attract.

9. VI 9556 = *ILS* 7679. The full text reads: D M TITVLOS SCRIBENDOS VEL SI QVID OPERIS MARMORARI OPVS FVERIT HIC HABES. The letters D M for *Dis Manibus* (see p. 101ff) indicate that gravestones were among the handiwork on offer.

10. *RIB* 330. Information from Mr Richard Brewer and Mr David Zienkiewicz.

11. Notice (inter alia) *legio II Troiana*, the Second Trojan Legion, XIV 3626, for *Traiana*, Trajanic; *tribunus cohorte prima voluptaria Campanorum*, tribune in the First Voluptuary Cohort of Campanians, VI 3520, for *voluntaria*, Voluntary.

12. *Epis.* 3.12.5.

13. Here the stonecutter is called a *lapidicida* and later a *quadratarius*, a 'squaring-off man'; cf. VI 30865.

14. Aulus Gellius, *Noctes Atticae*, 10.1; notice COS TERTIVM on the Pantheon, below, Fig. 6.

15. Aulus Gellius, ibid. 10.1.9.

16. V 1183, 7388, IX 3906, XI 961, XII 3355; G. Susini, *op.cit.* (n.1), pl. 2.

17. Pliny, *Nat.Hist.* 33.122.

18. X 7852, line 2: *codex ansatus*.

19. E.g. *RIB* 316, 330.

20. F.H.Thompson, *Antiquaries Journal* 48(1968), 47–58.

21. Suetonius, *Aug.* 97.

22. II 5055.

23. In the recently opened *Musée Saint Jacques* at Béziers is a panel (XII 4247) from a tomb monument where tin has been poured into the inscribed letters and into the word-stops; some considerable traces have survived. On *RIB* 2059 the dedicator promises to gild the inscribed letters on an altar if his prayers are answered.

24. *ILS* 5726.

Chapter 3 (pp. 17–24)

1. There was an early stage when the Roman alphabet had only 20 letters; C and G were represented by the single letter C. As a result, the forenames (*praenomina*) Gaius and Gnaeus, when abbreviated, were represented by C. and Cn. This practice continued even after C and G were recognized as separate letters in the alphabet.

2. The inscription on the base of Trajan's Column at Rome (dated to AD 113) is often cited; *ILS* 294 = *G* 57.

3. For the sequence used when citizens were registered at a census, see *CIL* I² 593, line 146: *eorumque nomina, praenomina, patres aut patronos, tribus cognomina et quot annos quisque eorum habet* ('their names, forenames, their fathers or patrons, their tribes, surnames and how old they are').

4. Gaius, *Inst.* 1.64.

5. From the mid second century AD the custom developed of using or being given a nickname (*signum*), which can appear in the text of an inscription, or sometimes be given prominence at its head. For an example, *ILS* 1281; cf. Mommsen, *Hermes* 37(1902), 443–55; R.Cagnat, *Cours d'épigraphie latine* (Paris, 1914), 55–59; *CRAI* 1933, 563.

6. C. Starr, *The Roman Imperial Navy* (New York, 1941), 79.

7. Varro, *de Ling. Lat.* 8.21.

8. *RIB* 91; below, p. 41.

9. See J.S. and A.E.Gordon, *Contributions to the Palaeography of Latin Inscriptions* (Los Angeles, 1957), passim.

10. VIII 6982; cf. H.Hommel, *ZPE* 5(1970), 293–303.

11. Quintilian, *Inst. Orat.* 1.7.

12. R.P.Oliver, *AJP* 81(1966), 129–70. The long I may have originated as a normal I with *apex* superscribed.

13. *AE* 1956, 160; some coins and stamped tiles of legion XXII *Primigenia* have the numerals written as IIXX, where it is clear that the dies are not retrograde.

14. E.g. *ILS* 5494.

15. Cassius Dio 60.4.5; 74.2; Suetonius, *Dom.* 23; Pliny, *Pan.* 52.4; SHA, *Comm.* 20. Sculptured reliefs and statue-heads might also be adjusted to depict the succeeding emperor. C.L.Babcock, *Classical Philology* 57(1962), 30–32.

16. *AE* 1973, 137; H.Kähler, 'Der Trajansbogen in Puteoli', in *Studies presented to D.M. Robinson* (Saint Louis, 1951–53), 430–39.

17. Removal of references to a cult, *RIB* 1137; of the name of a legion, VIII 2534; 2535 etc. (III *Augusta*); XIII 11514, 11524 (XXI *Rapax*).

18. *ILS* 129. It was again restored under Severus in AD 202, as a second inscription on the façade reports.

Chapter 4 (pp. 25–9)

1. *ILS* 347 = *G* 67.

2. Dio 65.20.3; cf. A.R.Birley, *Liverpool Classical Monthly*, 1.2(1976), 11–14.

3. R.P.Wright and I.A.Richmond, *The Roman Inscribed and Sculptured Stones in the Grosvenor Museum, Chester* (Chester, 1955), no. 199; *Britannia* 2(1971), 292, no. 17.

4. *RIB* 1638. The genitive case here (lines 1–2) is unusual, in place of the normal dative. In line 4 *Aug(usti)* is

omitted after *leg(ato)*, for lack of space; cf. below, p. 72.

5. Notice especially the 'Romulus' stone found below a pavement in the Forum, Rome; *ILS* 4913 = G 4.
6. Quintilian, *Inst. Orat.* 1.7.26.
7. Suetonius, *Claud.* 41.3; Tacitus, *Ann.* 11. 13–14; R.P. Oliver, *AJA* 53(1949), 249–57.
8. *ILS* 210 = G 41; G 43.
9. The ending -*os* is found for -*us* in the nominative singular; -*eis* for -*is* in the dative or ablative plural; *xs* for *x* in words such as *exs* ('from/out of'); *oe* instead of *u* in words such as *coeravit* ('saw to it'); see Figs. 60, 32.
10. Notice -*ae* replaced as a case-ending by -*e* (e.g. on Fig. 56); *domnus* for *dominus* (Fig. 80).
11. SHA, *Hadrian* 19.9; cf. Augustus, *Res Gestae* 20.
12. K.K.Carroll, *The Parthenon Inscription* (Durham, N.C., 1982); Greek Roman and Byzantine Monographs, no. 9.
13. Strabo, *Geog.* 14.1.22.

Chapter 5 (pp. 30–5)

1. *RIB* 2273–74, 2290–92.
2. *Tusc. Disp.* 5.65–66.
3. Ausonius, *Epitaphs* 32.
4. XIV 4764, 4936, 4977; *Notizie degli Scavi* 1923, 408.
5. *RIB* 1909, 1912; *Durham University Journal* 26.5 (March 1930), 305ff with pl.
6. See Thucydides, 1.93, on the construction of the Athenian Long Walls to the Piraeus.
7. R.P.Wright and I.A. Richmond, *Catalogue of the Roman Inscribed and Sculptured Stones in the Grosvenor Museum, Chester* (Chester, 1955), 4ff.
8. J.C.Balty, *JRS* 78(1988), 91–104.
9. C.Hill, M.Millett, T.F.C.Blagg, *The Roman Riverside Wall and Monumental Arch in London; London and Middlesex Arch. Soc. Special Paper* 3(1980).
10. W.Selzer, *Römische Steindenkmäler: Mainz in Römischer Zeit* (Mainz, 1988), nos. 79, 26.
11. R.Fellmann, *Das Grab des Lucius Munatius Plancus bei Gaeta* (Basel 1957); *ILS* 886 = *EJ* 187.
12. *Inscriptiones Italiae* 10, fasc. 4 (Tergeste), Roma 1951, no. 94; V 579.
13. Notice at Lincoln a gravestone (*RIB* 262) set into the wall of the church of St Mary-Le-Wigford, which has a five-line Anglo-Saxon inscription added in its gable angle.
14. *AE* 1902, 230.
15. *RIB* 2216.
16. R.P.Duncan-Jones (ed.), *The Economy of the Roman Empire* 2 ed. (Cambridge, 1982), 360–62.
17. *RIB* 1634, 1637, 1638, 1666, ?1852, ?1702.
18. J.Kastelić, *Enciclopedia dell'arte antica* 7(1968), s.v. *Šempeter*; J.Korosec, *Archaeology* 10(1957), 117–22; J. and A.Šašel, *Situla* 5(1963), nos. 370–77 for the inscriptions. The late Dr Jaroslav Šašel kindly took me to visit the site in 1984.
19. G.Gherardini, *Notizie degli Scavi* 1905, 219–25. I am grateful to Dr Debra Pinkus for establishing its whereabouts, and to Prof. Jane Crawford and Prof. Bernard Frischer for confirming this in Venice.
20. *Britannia* 17(1986), 429, no. 3.

21. *Britannia* 20(1989), 331 no. 5.
22. *RIB* 2187; L.J.F.Keppie, *Glasgow Archaeological Journal* 5(1978), 19–24.
23. E.g. to the university museums at Johns Hopkins, Baltimore, and Ann Arbor, Michigan.

Chapter 6 (pp. 36–41)

1. J.Sparrow, *Visible Words* (Cambridge, 1969), 20f. with a photograph of the chapel.
2. See *CIL* V, p. 427; P. Kristeller, *Andrea Mantegna* (London, 1901), 472.
3. For a list of all *CIL* volumes and supplements, with full details of their editors, contents and publishers, see Gordon, *Introduction*, p. 50ff.; F.Bérard et al., *Guide de l'Épigraphiste* (Paris, 1986), 74ff.
4. For collections of Christian inscriptions, see chapter 16.
5. Other periodicals are *Zeitschrift für Papyrologie und Epigrafik* (Bonn), *Tyche* (Vienna), *Epigraphica Anatolica* (Bonn), *Gerión* (Madrid) and the series *Epigraphische Studien* (Bonn).
6. This work is reviewed in *JRS* 67(1977), 209–11; *Classical Philology* 75(1980), 269–73.
7. See now *Actes du colloque 'Épigraphie et informatique' (26–27 mai 1989)* (Lausanne, 1989), passim, published under the auspices of the Association Internationale d'Épigraphie Grecque et Latine (AIEGL).
8. Several museums and institutions have important collections of squeezes; e.g. the Berlin Acad. of the Sciences (for *CIL*); Ashmolean Museum, Oxford (for *RIB*), the Austrian Academy of the Sciences, Vienna (for material from Ephesus and elsewhere) and the Meritt library of the Institute for Advanced Study, Princeton (for *IG*).
9. D.J.Smith, *Museums Journal* (Dec. 1957), 215–19.
10. *Classical Review* 100(1986), 280.
11. *ILS* 9013; cf. Birley, *Fasti of Roman Britain* (Oxford, 1981), 301–2.
12. *Mitteil. Deutsches Arch. Inst. (Ath. Abt.)* 33(1908), 150.
13. I have to thank Dr David French for enquiring about the stone (in vain) during a recent visit to Konya Museum.
14. *RIB* 91; cf. *Britannia* 10(1979), 243–54.

Chapter 7 (pp. 42–51)

1. *ILS* 244 = *MW* 1 (the *lex de imperio Vespasiani*) is a bronze tablet detailing some of the powers conferred by the Senate on Vespasian at his accession, and precedents for the awards.
2. XIV 112 (Ostia), now in the Cortile della Pigna (Vatican Museums).
3. Suetonius, *Claud.* 1.3.
4. Cassius Dio 60.22.
5. Later developments in titulature are described in Chapter 17.
6. VI 945 = *ILS* 265; G 50; *TDAR* I, 133 with bibliog.; M.Pfanner, *Die Titusbogen* (Mainz, 1983) has fascinating information on the history of the Arch through the ages. There was another Arch of Titus in Rome, at the Circus Maximus.

7. F.Magi, *Röm.Mitt.* 82(1975), 99–116; M.Pfanner, *Arch.Anzeiger* 1981, 519–20.

8. VI 920 = *ILS* 216, cf. *ILS* 217. E.Nash *TDAR* I, 102–3; G.Castagnoli, *Bull.Comm.Arch. Rome* 70(1942), 58–73; A.Degrassi, *Scritti vari de antichità* (Roma/Trieste, 1962–71) I, 350–51.

9. F.Koeppel, *Röm.Mitt.* 90(1983), 103ff.

10. By A.A.Barrett, in a forthcoming article, to be published in the Journal *Britannia*.

11. *RIB* 665.

12. On the dating of Trajan's tribunician power, see M.Hammond, *MAAR* 15(1938), 23–61; 19(1949), 45–57. It is clear from inscriptions and coins that Trajan must have been awarded the power well before he actually became emperor. Hammond argues that Trajan held *trib.pot.* I from his adoption by Nerva in October 97, becoming *trib.pot.* II in October 98, and *trib.pot.* III in December 98; so that he was *trib.pot.* XII from Dec. 107 to Dec. 108.

13. A familiar restoration is on a line-drawing by I.A.Richmond, *Sheldon Memorial Lecture* (York, 1959), frontispiece; repr. as Royal Commission on Historic Monuments, *Eboracum* (HMSO, 1962), vol. I, p. 111; in line 5 Richmond gives IMP V, but IMP VI is to be read; *RIB* 665 is correct.

14. *ILS* 425 = *G* 73; Nash *TDAR* I, 126–30.

15. ET (line 3) was altered to read *P*(*atri*) *P*(*atriae*).

Chapter 8 (pp. 52–9)

1. *ILS* 6085–6089.

2. J.Gonzales, *JRS* 76(1986), 147–243.

3. On a visit to the village of Montefusco, south of Benevento, in 1982, I and others saw a painted slogan VIVA BADOGLIO, in support of the Italian marshal, briefly in power after the fall of Mussolini, and then still legible.

4. *ILS* 2637 = XIV 3472 = *EJ* 248. The plain slab, broken but restored, is beside an internal stairway in the Palazzo Cenci-Bolognetti at Vicovaro.

5. Tacitus, *Ann.* 3.21; cf. Aulus Gellius, *Noct.Att.* 5.6.14.

6. E.g. *ILS* 5053 = *EJ* 327.

7. X 802; cf. *ILS* 5619.

8. *ILS* 7730.

9. *ILS* 2229 = *EJ* 339.

10. Smallwood, *NTH* 508 = *ILS* 6841; cf. at Ancona, *ILS* 298; Lepcis, Smallwood, *NTH* 509.

11. *ILS* 287, 287a = Smallwood, *NTH* 389. Alcantara is Arabic for 'bridge'.

12. *ILS* 8897 = *EJ* 71.

13. *ILS* 5636 = *G* 17 = *ILLRP* 646

14. *ILRRP* 636.

15. *EJ* 236.

16. X 6306.

17. *ILS* 5724.

18. *Nat. Hist.* 34.17.

19. *ILS* 6446; cf. J.M.Reynolds and E.Fabbricotti, *PBSR* 40(1972), 127–34.

20. *ILS* 5373 = *EJ* 334.

21. *AE* 1979, 169. Here Lucius is a family name (*nomen*) rather than a forename (*praenomen*).

22. *EJ* 68–69 = *ILS* 139–40; *G* 31.

23. *MW* 445, 455ff, 461, 462. Cf. *ILS* 2735 = Smallwood, *NTH* 265 for a man who had 'hosted the emperor Hadrian' in his house at Camerinum in Umbria.

24. J.M.Reynolds, *Aphrodisias and Rome* (London, 1982), 35ff. For a sequence of edicts found at Cyrene, see *EJ* 311; R.P. Oliver, *MAAR* 19(1949), 105–14.

25. A.R.Birley, *The People of Roman Britain* (London, 1988), 193ff; cf. *Britannia* 1 (1970), 308, no. 14.; ibid. 19(1987), 367, no. 5.

26. *RIB* 288.

27. S.S.Frere, *Verulamium Excavations* II (London, 1983), 69–72; *MW* 434. *AE* 1957, 169. Close inspection suggests there were two texts, one on either side of an archway.

28. Tacitus, *Agr.* 21.

29. *ILS* 5946ff; *ILLRP* 476ff.

30. A. Piganiol, *Les documents cadastraux de la colonie romaine d'Orange*, Gallia Suppl. 16 (Paris, 1962).

31. *ILLRP* 467–75.

32. *ILS* 6509 = Smallwood, *NTH* 435 = *G* 53; *ILS* 6675 = Smallwood, *NTH* 436.

Chapter 9 (pp. 60–9)

1. Tacitus, *Hist.* 1.27.

2. Suetonius, *Aug.* 30; Augustus, *Res Gestae* 20; Dio 53.22.2.

3. *EJ* 286 = *ILS* 84.

4. X 6849, 6839.

5. *ILS* 5866 = Smallwood, *NTH* 408a.

6. *ILS* 296 = Smallwood, *NTH* 408b; F. Hassel, *Der Trajansbogen in Benevent* (Mainz, 1966).

7. *ILS* 296; cf. *ILS* 5866.

8. *ILS* 5892 = *G* 18; Nash, *TDAR* II, 189f. It was repaired in 21 BC.

9. *ILS* 7204; *IGLS* 39–44.

10. Pliny, *Epist.* 6.25; *ILS* 8504–8508; cf. II 3479.

11. *ILS* 4850a; G.Walser, *Summus Poeninus* (Wiesbaden, 1984), Katalog no. 19.

12. *ILS* 7478 (now in the Musée du Louvre, Paris); P.Flobert, 'A propos de l'inscription d'Isernia (*CIL* IX 2689)', in *Hommages à la memoire de Pierre Wuilleumier* (Paris, 1980), 121–28.

13. *Inst.Orat.* 4.5.22.

14. IX 6021.

15. *ILS* 6002–6013.

16. *ILS* 208 = *EJ* 363a.

17. *ILS* 5863 = Smallwood, *NTH* 413. *ILJug* 63 for an improved text.

18. *ILJug* 468; J. Šašel, *JRS* 63(1973), 80. *AE* 1973, 475. On soldiers who carried out the work, M.Gabricević, *Arh.Vestnik* 23(1972), 408–16 with plate.

19. Smallwood, *NTH* 424; *EJ* 290.

20. Smallwood, *NTH* 307b.

21. *ILS* 5834 = Smallwood, *NTH* 420. The stone illustrated on Fig. 38 marked the 54th mile along the road.

22. Smallwood, *NTH* 411 = *RIB* 2265.

Chapter 10 (pp. 70–9)

1. *ILLRP*, passim; *ILS* 1–69; *CIL* vol I².
2. *ILS* 1–10; *ILLRP* 309–17.
3. *ILLRP* 309 = *ILS* 1 = *G* 5.
4. *ILLRP* 323 = *G* 9.
5. *ILS* 43ff, esp. 50ff.
6. *ILS* 1052 = *G* 59 = Smallwood, *NTH* 229; A.R.Birley, *The Fasti of Roman Britain* (Oxford, 1981), 100ff.
7. The sequence (in descending order) could have been, 1 legate of a legion; 2 curator of roads; 3 praetor; 4 tribune of the People; 5 quaestor of Macedonia; 6 military tribune; 7 member of the board of three.
8. *SHA, Hadr.* 4.2, 15.2, 23.4.
9. *ILS* 8971 = *MW* 316; *Forschungen in Ephesus* (München/Wien 1944), V, 1, pp. 62–66.
10. *ILS* 1374 = *MW* 336; V.A.Maxfield, *Epigr.Stud.* 9(1972), 242–45.
11. Tacitus, *Agr.* 42.1.
12. *AE* 1963, 104; *AE* 1971, 477; *G* 38; H.Volkmann, *Gymnasium* 75(1968), 124–35. Below was a fifth line, its presence indicated now only by an *apex*-accent, which could have read FECIT or FECIT DEDICAVIT ('Built' or 'built and dedicated').
13. Tacitus, *Ann.*15.44.
14. *RIB* 12; Tacitus, *Ann.*14.38.
15. Fig. 44 follows the restoration offered at the British Museum. The 'replica' of this monument in the Museum of London omits C F in line 3, and offers INFELIX in place of INDIANA in line 5.
16. *AE* 1957, 250. Neither text survives complete, but the overlap is sufficient to allow the wording to be securely known. If the other gateway was similarly adorned with texts, there must have been four identical inscriptions.
17. *AE* 1963, 52; H.-G.Kolbe, *Bonner Jahrbücher* 162(1962), 407–20.
18. *SHA, Vit.Pert.*1.4–5.

Chapter 11 (pp. 80–90)

1. *ILS* 2288.
2. G.Pontiroli, '*T. Aponius signifer legionis IX Hispaniensis* nel territorio cremonese' *Rend.Ist.Lomb.* 105(1971), 149–56.
3. Livy 27.2.9.
4. Appian, *Bellum Civile* 2.82.
5. *ILS* 2244.
6. Tacitus, *Ann.* 1.61–62.
7. *ILS* 2082 = *EJ* 251; *ILS* 2300 = Smallwood, *NTH* 305.
8. On soldiers' wills, see J.B.Campbell, *The Emperor and the Roman Army* (Oxford, 1984), 210ff; on marriage, idem, *JRS* 68 (1978), 153–66.
9. *RIB* 200; E.J.Phillips, *Britannia* 6 (1975), 102–5.
10. *RIB* 492.
11. A.R.Burn, *Past & Present* 4(1953), 2–31; J.F.Gilliam, *AJP* 82(1961) 225–51.
12. *AE* 1955, 238; A.A.Aly, *Annals of the Faculty of Arts, Ain Shams University, Cairo*, 3(1955), 113–46; J.F.Gilliam, *AJP* 77(1956), 359–75; G.Forni and D.Manini, 'La base eretta a Nicopolis', in *Studi di storia antica in memoria di Luca de Regibus* (Genova, 1969),

177–210. For a document usefully listing soldiers of the Augustan age serving in Egypt; see *EJ* 261 = *ILS* 2483.
13. M.M.Roxan, *Epigraphische Studien* 12(1981), 265–86; see also Bibliography at p. 151.
14. *CIL* XVI 160 = Smallwood, *NTH* 344.
15. *ILS* 8502, 2309, 2307, 2308, etc.
16. *Classical Review* 85(1971), 329f.
17. Notice a crown inscribed beside names of soldiers on VI 32624, a.5 and d.15.
18. *AE* 1969/1970, 583; M.P.Speidel, *JRS* 60(1970), 142–53.
19. The suicide is featured also on a decorated samian bowl at La Graufesenque, now in the Archaeological Museum, Millau, France.
20. Suetonius, *Aug.* 18; Dio 51.1.3.
21. W.M.Murray and P.M.Petsas, 'The Spoils of Actium', *Archaeology* Sept./Oct. 1988, 28ff.
22. Tacitus, *Ann.* 2.22; cf. Plutarch, *Sulla* 19.5.
23. *ILS* 9107; A.G.Poulter in C.Unz (ed.), *Studien zu den Militärgenzen Roms* III (Stuttgart, 1986), 519–28; E.Dorutiu, *Dacia* 5(1961), 345–63; F.B.Florescu, *Monumentul de la Adamklissi* (Bucureşti, 1960).
24. Pliny, *Nat.Hist.* 3.136–37; *EJ* 40; J.Formigé, *Le Trophée des Alpes (La Turbie)*, Gallia Suppl. 2 (Paris, 1949) fig. 47.
25. *ILS* 2701 = Smallwood, *GCN* 282; L.J.F.Keppie, *Britannia* 2(1971), 149–55.
26. Tacitus *Ann.*15.50, 60, 61, 71.
27. *ILS* 2487, 9133–35a; Smallwood, *NTH* 328; Cagnat, *L'armée romaine l'Afrique* (Paris, 1913), 146ff; M.Le Glay, *Mélanges d'histoire ancienne offerts à W. Seston* (Paris, 1974), 277–84 for new readings.
28. *ILS* 5795.
29. A.Negev, *Israel Exploration Journal* 14(1964), 237–49, D.Barag, ibid., 250–51; A.Negev, ibid., 22 (1972), 52f.
30. *ILS* 3452–57. Notice also *ILS* 2609–2611 where soldiers at a stone quarry in Egypt painted up messages praising their n.c.o.
31. D.Baatz, *Röm.Mitt.* 87(1980), 283–99; *ILLRP* 1088–1120.
32. R.MacMullen, *AJA* 64(1960), 23ff.
33. *CIL* VII 495.
34. E.g. at Pompeii, IV 4310, 4311, 2145, 1994, 1711. For the ostraca at Bu Ngem, see *CRAI* 1979, 206, 436; P.Le Roux, *Epigraphica* 45(1983), 66–77.
35. R.O.Fink, *Roman Military Records on Papyri* (Case Western Reserve, 1971), no. 117, with translation; J.F.Gilliam, *HTR* 47(1954), 183–96.
36. *ILS* 9122; It can be viewed from a special viewing room in the Tatra Hotel. The inscription had been known since the sixteenth century, but was long misinterpreted, or considered a forgery. The commander of the detachment is reported on *AE* 1956, 124.
37. *MW* 369; F.Grosso, *Epigraphica* 16(1954), 117–79.
38. *ILS* 4795 with *RE* 12 1427f.
39. *EJ* 260 = *ILS* 2305; *ILS* 2259; Smallwood, *NTH* 302.
40. *ILS* 2641 = *MW* 357.
41. *RIB*, pp. 431ff; C.E.Stevens, *The Building of Hadrian's Wall* (Kendall, 1966).
42. *RIB* 2139 etc. L.Keppie, *Roman Distance Slabs from the Antonine Wall* (Glasgow, 1979).

43. *AE* 1979, 412; G.Precht, *Das Grabmal des L. Poblicius* (Köln, 1979).
44. A.K.Bowman and J.D.Thomas, *Vindolanda: the Latin Writing Tablets* (London, 1983); id., 'New Texts from Vindolanda', *Britannia* 18(1987), 125–41.

Chapter 12 (pp. 91–7)

1. V 18 = *ILS* 110.
2. XII 3156 = *ILG* 417; R.Amy and P.Gros, *Le Maison Carrée de Nimes*, Gallia suppl. 38(1979), vol. 1, 177ff, vol. 2, pl. 41, 44.
3. XI 5378. The original inscription in bronze letters honours two brothers as dedicators, who had been chief magistrates of the town.
4. VI 1005 = *ILS* 348.
5. X 1613, 1614 = *ILS* 7731a; P.Sommella, *Forma e urbanistica di Pozzuoli romana* = *Puteoli* 2 (Napoli, 1978), 72.
6. C.Daremberg, V.Saglio, *Dictionnaire des Antiquités* II. 2 (Paris, 1896), 1194, s.v. *focus*.
7. Horace, *Odes* 1.19; Ovid, *Tristia* 5.5.9, etc., with R.G.M.Nisbet and M.Hubbard, *Commentary on Horace Odes I* (Oxford, 1970), 242.
8. *AE* 1922, 116; see D.Courteault, *JRS* 11(1921), 101–7.
9. The dedication was initially interpreted as being to *Dea Tutela Boudig(a)*, the last name being a version of the Celtic word *Boudica*, meaning Victory; but see now R. Etienne, *Bordeaux antique* (Bordeaux, 1962), 173ff; L.Valensi, *Presentation d'oeuvres gallo-romaines* (Bordeaux, Musée d'Aquitaine, 1964–65).
10. *RIB* 2139; E.J.Phillips, *Proc.Soc.Antiq.Scot.* 105(1972–74), 176–82.
11. M.G.Jarrett, *Maryport, Cumbria, a Roman fort and its garrison* (Kendal, 1976).
12. E.Schallmayer, 'Ein Kultzentrum der Römer in Osterburken', in D.Planck (ed.), *Der Keltenfürst von Hochdorf* (Stuttgart, 1985), 378–407.
13. E.L.Bowie, *ZPE* 8(1971), 137–41.
14. Tacitus, *Ann.* 14.32.
15. *ILS* 6367.
16. I.A.Richmond and J.P.Gillam, *The Temple of Mithras at Carrawburgh* (Newcastle, 1951).
17. *RIB* 1544–46.

Chapter 13 (pp. 98–109)

1. Suetonius, *Tib.* 37.
2. *AE* 1959, 146 = *G* 20. Fig. 60 is based on Gordon, *Introduction*, plate 12.
3. M.Grant, *Cities of Vesuvius* (London, 1971), p.57; at the Herculaneum Gate.
4. ILLRP 309–17; Nash TDAR II, 352ff; see Cicero, *Tusc.Disp.* 1.7.13 on the tombs of the aristocracy on the fringes of Republican Rome.
5. *Satyr.* 71.
6. Suetonius, *Nero.* 41.2.
7. VI 2120; VIII 688; VIII 10712; XII 1751; VI 8686 (referring to Augustus' tomb in Rome).
8. Siculus Flaccus, 139.23–140.6L.
9. *Elegies* 4.7. 1–4, 83ff.
10. Tacitus, *Ann.* 14.14.
11. When Elagabalus in the early third century drove a chariot drawn by four elephants here, some nearby tombs had to be demolished to facilitate access; SHA, *Vit. Eleg.* 23.1.
12. *ILS* 881 = *G* 23.
13. XIV 3605–8; *EJ* 200 = *ILS* 921; *ILS* 986 = *MW* 261; *G* 49; L.R.Taylor, *MAAR* 24(1956), 9–30.
14. Aulus Plautius, the first governor of Roman Britain, belonged to a separate branch of the same family, and is unlikely to have been buried here.
15. *ILS* 917, cf. 917a; *G* 26; Nash, *TDAR* II, 321ff. A.Roullet, *Egyptian and Egyptianizing Monuments of Imperial Rome* (Leiden, 1972), no. 94, cf. no. 95.
16. In antiquity the word is used epigraphically to mean individual niches within a communal tomb, rather than the tomb itself.
17. XII 3637 = *MW* 519.
18. VI 10332.
19. *Satires* 1.8; *ILS* 8208.
20. The so-called *Laudatio Turiae*; *ILS* 8393 = *EJ* 357 = *G* 28. See Appian, *Bellum Civile* 4.44; Valerius Maximus 6.7.2. Valuable discussion by N.Horsfall, in *Bull.Inst.Class.Studs.* 30(1983), 85–98.
21. VI 22513; cf. VI 3636 'he bought this meadow and here made a place for himself to be buried and left it for his freedmen and their descendants, none to be allowed to sell it.'
22. XII 4501, 4533. θ is the first letter of the Greek words for 'death' and 'dead'.
23. *AE* 1945, 136; *G* 62. Paradoxically, Ulpius' tomb failed to survive the Constantinian landscaping of the site; for which see p. 102.
24. Suetonius, *Aug.* 101.
25. *Epist.* 2.1, 6.10, 9.19.1. The tomb was at or near Verginius' retirement villa on the coast north of Rome.
26. Seneca, *Epist.* 77.20. Cf. Pliny, *Nat.Hist.* 7.158; Martial, *Epigrams* 3.93.20.
27. Pliny, *Epist.* 7.29, 8.6.
28. Pliny, *Epist.* 9.19.
29. III 3241.
30. *ILS* 7671.
31. *ILS* 8524.
32. *ILS* 8527; cf. V 1710, *ILS* 8529a (a bride-to-be dies four days before her wedding).
33. *ILS* 8521.
34. *ILS* 8514.
35. *ILS* 8519.
36. *ILS* 8510.
37. *ILS* 8516–17.
38. *ILS* 8506.
39. *ILS* 8512.
40. *ILS* 8520.
41. *ILS* 8518.
42. VI 20905; *ILS* 5228 of an actor-manager: 'I died often (on the stage) but never like this!' Cf. Martial, *Epigrams* 9.15: 'Chloe done it!' (i.e. built tombs for, and also caused the deaths of, her seven husbands). Much less certainly, VI 29149 with a possible double meaning, on the length of a marriage.

43. *ILS* 9494 = *EJ* 252.
44. II 4314; G. Alföldy, *Die römische Inschriften von Tarraco* (Berlin, 1975), no. 444; taf. cii.2. The stone incorporates a small relief sculpture of the deceased, holding the palm of victory.
45. *ILS* 935 = *EJ* 206 (last of his family).
46. *ILS* 8364 phrase in full; cf. *ILS* 8205.
47. *ILS* 8172ff.
48. *ILS* 8207, cf. 8206, 8205.
49. *ILS* 8207b; cf. 8203, 8202.
50. IV 8899.
51. *ILS* 8199, cf. *ILS* 8201.
52. VI 29847a.
53. *ILS* 8212ff.
54. *ILS* 8220, 8221.
55. *Satyr.* 62.
56. Martial, *Epigrams* 1.34, 3.93.15.
57. Appian, *Bellum Civile* 4.44.
58. *Epist.* 3.12.

Chapter 14 (pp. 110–15)

1. *ILS* 7211ff.
2. *ILS* 7480f.
3. *ILS* 8627ff.
4. *ILS* 6147, 5590–91, 5603, 5612–13.
5. F.Haverfield, *Arch.Aeliana* ser.3, 13(1916), 85–102.
6. Haverfield's view that it really held almost 20 *sextarii*, and so was designed to cheat local farmers when they presented their produce for sale to the state, has been challenged; see A.Berriman, *Arch.Ael.* 4, 34(1956), 130; and now R.P.Duncan-Jones, *ZPE* 21(1976), 43–52; ibid., 53–62.
7. J.M.Reynolds and J.B.Ward-Perkins, *Inscriptions of Roman Tripolitania* (Rome/London, 1952), nos. 490, 590, 319, 468.
8. J.Hatzfeld, *Bull. Corresp. Hell.* 36(1912), 5–218; *ILLRP* 747–62.
9. *Satyr.* 76.3.
10. C.Humann et al., *Altertümer von Hierapolis* (Berlin, 1898), p. 92, no. 51; *CIG* 3920.
11. *ILS* 7518.
12. *ILS* 7519.
13. *ILS* 7479.
14. *CIL* XIV 4549, pp. 661ff. Fig. 70 is XIV 4549, no. 21.
15. See K.Greene, *The Archaeology of the Roman Economy* (London, 1986), 25f.
16. D.Manacorda, *JRS* 68(1978), 122–31; E.L.Will, *Journ. Field Arch.* 6(1979), 339–50.
17. *ILS* 7504–07.
18. Suetonius, *Vesp.* 1.2–3.
19. *ILS* 426; J.Madaule, *MEFR* 41(1924), 111–50; D.E.L.Haynes and P.E.D.Hirst, *Porta Argentariorum* (*PBSR*, Suppl.Pap) (London, 1939); M.Pallottino, *L'arco degli Argentari* (Roma, 1946).
20. *ILS* 7501; J.Andreau, *La vie financière dans le monde romain* (Rome, 1987), 111 with pl.2.
21. *CIL* IV, *Suppl.* 1; J.Andreau, *Les affaires de monsieur Jucundus* (Rome, 1974); IV 3433; cf. *ILS* 6404a, 3640.
22. Smallwood, *GCN* 433b.

23. An amphora bearing the painted inscription POPPAEAE SECVNDO ('For Secundus, ?slave of Poppaea') was found there; see A. de Franciscis, in B.Andreae and H.Kyrieleis (eds.), *Neue Forschungen in Pompeji* (Recklinghausen, 1975), 9–38.
24. See reports in *Rend.Acc.Nap.* 41(1966) onwards.
25. For a now much outdated, but still useful, list of stamps, M.H.Callender, *Roman Amphorae* (London, 1965).
26. *ILLRP* 1207ff.
27. B.Galsterer-Kröll, *Die Graffiti auf der römischen Gefässkeramik aus Haltern* (Münster 1983).
28. D.Atkinson, *JRS* 4(1914), 27–64.
29. I.A.Richmond, *Trans. Cumb & West.*, n.s. 36(1936), 104–25.
30. *ILS* 8734ff; V.Nutton, *Epigr.* 34(1972), 16ff.
31. *ILS* 8621; M.W.Frederiksen, *PBSR* 27(1959), 109.
32. X 8058/18. Others are to be seen in the Rheinisches Landesmuseum, Mainz.
33. *ILS* 8613–16; W.V.Harris, *JRS* 70(1980), 126–45.
34. *ILS* 8726ff.
35. *ILS* 8706ff.
36. *RIB* 998ff; *ILS* 3452ff.
37. *ILS* 8646ff.
38. *ILS* 642 (preamble only) = *G* 81.

Chapter 15 (pp. 116–18)

1. E.g. IV 10697: 'Portunnus loves Amplianda'.
2. IV 1904, 2487.
3. IV 10675–78.
4. IV 10005, 10030, 10195 etc.
5. IV 10619.
6. Plautus, *Rudens* 1294–96.
7. Suetonius, *Dom.* 13.2.
8. *ILS* 1046a; Cassius Dio 53.23.5.
9. Pliny, *Nat. Hist.* 36.58; Strabo, *Geog.* 17.1.46; Juvenal, *Sat.* 15.5.
10. A. and E. Bernand, *Les inscriptions grecques et latines du Colosse de Memnon* (Le Caire, 1960), no. 16, pp. 57–58 = III 39.
11. Bernand, *op.cit.*, no. 7 = III 34 = *ILS* 8759b.
12. Bernand, *op.cit.* no. 56f = III 49.
13. *SHA, Vit.Sev.* 17.4.
14. Petronius, *Satyr.* 58.
15. *ILS* 8626a; Ch. Hülsen, *Röm.Mitt.* 19(1904), 142f.
16. *ILS* 8746–8757; *ILLRP* 1144–50. A. Audollent, *Defixionum Tabellae* (Paris, 1904); M.Besnier, *Revue de Philologie* 44(1920), 5–30. A new corpus is in progress.
17. Annual reports of new finds in the journal *Britannia*.
18. IV 813.
19. *ILS* 6409.
20. *ILLRP* 1122.
21. *Satyr.* 28–29.

Chapter 16 (pp. 119–24)

1. Minucius Felix, *Octavius* 32.1.

2. *Matthew* 27.37; *Mark* 15.26; *Luke* 23.38. According to *John* 19.20 the text was in Hebrew, Greek and Latin. On artistic representations from the Middle Ages onwards the text is abbreviated to I N R I.
3. *ILCV* 3754ff.
4. *ILS* 9480; cf. W.M.Calder, *Klio* 10(1910), 232f with fig.; A.Wilhelm, ibid. 11 (1911), 388–90.
5. *ILCV* 4429a (Sousse, Tunisia).
6. O.Marucchi, *Christian Epigraphy* (Cambridge, 1912), no. 409; cf. *ILCV* 1293, 3848ff.
7. *ILCV* 3863; cf. above, p. 109 (Sidonius Apollinaris' grandfather).
8. *ILCV* 1516.
9. *ILCV* 1980–2187.
10. *ILCV* 1477–1509.
11. *ILCV* 2149, 2163, 3681a.
12. *G* 91; Marucchi, *op.cit.*, 340ff. The texts were inscribed in ornate lettering by a master stonemason, Furius Dionysius Philocalus.
13. *ILS* 1738.
14. *ILCV* 1752ff.
15. V 1583–1616; V 365–67; *Inscriptiones Italiae* x.2 (Parentium), nos. 57–86.
16. *Epist.* 2.10.3.
17. J.M.C.Toynbee, *Journal Brit. Arch. Assoc.* 16(1953), 1–24; D.Fishwick, *HTR* 57(1964), 39–53.
18. W.O.Moeller, *The Mithraic Origin and Meanings of the Rotas-Sator Square* (Leiden, 1973). The word-square recurs on an amphora sherd from a second-century context at Manchester; see *Britannia* 10(1979), 353n.

Chapter 17 (pp. 125–30)

1. T.Frank, *Economic Survey of Ancient Rome* 5 (Baltimore, 1940), 305–421; *ILS* 642 = *G* 81 (above, p. 115).
2. *Die Inschriften von Ephesus* Ia. 42; cf. 43.

3. *Die Inschriften von Ephesus* II.305–06.
4. E.g. *ILS* 1281, Acilius Glabrio Sibidius, '*vicarius* of the seven provinces of Gaul.'
5. V 8721–8771; *CIL* V, p. 1058ff.
6. *ILS* 1286 = *G* 87; also *AE* 1953, 239 for further fragments.
7. *PLRE* I, 155, *Bassus* 15.
8. H.-G.Horn, *Bonner Jahrbücher* 189(1989), 139–60.
9. Martial, *Epigrams* 14.16.
10. *ILS* 799 = *G* 94; Nash *TDAR* II, 401 with fig.

Chapter 18 (pp. 131–4)

1. *Boswell's Life of Johnson*, ed. by G.B.Hill, rev. by L.F.Powell (Oxford, 1934), II, p. 407.
2. Suetonius, *Aug.* 101.4; *EJ* 1 = *G* 34. Somewhat similar documents were erected by two Persian kings, Darius I at Behistun, and Sapor I at Naqs-i-Rustam near Persepolis. Livy 28.46.16 notes a text dedicated in Punic and in Greek by Hannibal in southern Italy, detailing his achievements.
3. *ILS* 8995 = *G* 22.
4. *ILS* 212 = Smallwood, *GCN* 369 = *G* 42.
5. *Ann.* 11.23–25.
6. See Bibliography at p. 153 for modern discussions.
7. Information on the discovery from Prof. B.H.Isaac, Tel Aviv.
8. *Monticola* = Highland; *Colpica* (from Greek *kolpos*, a bay open to the sea) = Seaforth. Col. A.A.Fairie provided details of its erection and reported the identity of the classical scholar who composed the text, Major John Muirhead.

BIBLIOGRAPHY

On such a broad subject, a bibliography can only be selective. Listed here are 'standard works', together with those publications in book or article form which deal with specific topics discussed in the text.

Chapter 1 (pp. 9–11)

Almar, K.P. *Inscriptiones Latinae: eine illustrierte Einführung in die lateinische Epigraphik* (Odense, 1990).

Barrow, R.H. *A Selection of Latin Inscriptions* (Oxford, 1934).

Bengston, H. *Introduction to Ancient History* (Berkeley/London, 1970).

Berard, F. *et al.*, *Guide de l'épigraphiste: bibliographie choisie des épigraphies antiques et médiévales* (Paris, 1986).

Bloch, R. *L'épigraphie latine* (Paris, 1952).

Cagnat, R. *Cours d'épigraphie latine* (1st ed., Paris, 1886; 4th ed, Paris, 1914).

Calderini, A. *Epigrafia* (Torino, 1974).

Chevallier, R. *Épigraphie et litterature à Rome* (Faenza, 1972).

Clauss, M. 'Ausgewählte Bibliographie zur lateinischen Epigraphik der römischen Kaiserzeit, 1.–3. Jh.', in H.Temporini (ed.), *ANRW* II.1 (Berlin/New York, 1974), 796–855.

Gordon, A.E. *Illustrated Introduction to Latin Epigraphy* (Los Angeles/London, 1983).

Guarducci, M. *Epigrafia greca*, 4 vols. (Cambridge, 1967–78).

Guarducci, M. *L'epigrafia greca dalle origini al tardo impero* (Roma, 1987).

Batle Huguet, P. *Epigrafia latina* (Barcelona, 1963).

Calabi Limentani, I. *Epigrafia latina*, 3rd ed. (Milano, 1974) – extensive bibliography by A. Degrassi.

Manzella I. de Stefano *Mestiere di epigrafia: guida alla schedatura del materiale epigrafico lapideo* (Roma, 1987).

Meyer, E. *Einführung in die lateinische Epigrafik* (Darmstadt, 1973).

Millar, F.G.B. 'Epigraphy', in M.H.Crawford (ed.), *Sources for Ancient History* (Cambridge, 1983), 80–136.

Robert, L. *Die Epigraphik der klassischen Welt* (Bonn, 1970).

Sandys, J.E. *Latin Epigraphy*, 2nd ed. rev. by S.G. Campbell (Cambridge, 1927).

Schumacher, L. *Römische Inschriften* (Stuttgart, 1988).

Stein, A. *Römische Inschriften in der antiken Literatur* (Prag, 1931).

Susini, G. *Epigrafia Latina* (Roma, 1982).

Thylander, H. *Étude sur l'épigraphie latine* (Lund, 1952).

Wachter, R. *Altlateinische Inschriften: sprachliche und epigraphische Untersuchungen zu den Dokumenten bis etwa 150 v. Chr.* (Berne, 1987).

Walser, G. *Römische Inschrift-Kunst: römische Inschriften für den akademischen Unterricht und als Einführung in die lateinische Epigraphik* (Stuttgart, 1988).

Woodhead, A.G. *The Study of Greek Inscriptions* (Cambridge, 1981).

Chapter 2 (pp. 12–16)

Filtzinger, P. *Hic Saxa Loquuntur* (Stuttgart, 1980).

Gordon, A.E. and J.S. *Contributions to the Palaeography of Latin Inscriptions* (Los Angeles, 1957).

Grasby, R. *Lettercutting in Stone* (Oswestry, 1989).

Ireland, R. 'Epigraphy', in M. Henig (ed.), *Handbook of Roman Art* (London, 1983), 220–33.

Susini, G. *The Roman Stonecutter* (Oxford, 1973).

Chapter 3 (pp. 17–24)

Forni, G. *Le tribù romane* (Roma, 1985), III.1 *le pseudo-tribù*.

Gordon, J.S. and A.E. *Contributions to the Palaeography of Latin Inscriptions* (Los Angeles, 1957).

Kajanto, I. *The Latin Cognomina* (Helsinki, 1965).

Mallon, J. *Paléographie romaine* (Madrid, 1952).

Mallon, J. *De l'écriture* (Paris, 1982).

Solin, H. and Salomies, O. *Repertorium nominum gentilium et cognominum Latinorum* (Hildesheim, 1988).

Taylor, L.R. *The Voting Districts of the Roman Republic* (Rome, 1960).

Taylor, L.R. 'Freedmen and freeborn in the epitaphs of imperial Rome', *AJP* 82(1961), 113–32.

Chapter 4 (pp. 25–9)

Degrassi, A. *I fasti consolari dell'impero romano* (Roma, 1952).

Degrassi, A. *Fasti et Elogia* (= *Inscriptiones Italiae*, 13.3, Roma, 1937–63).

Degrassi, A. *Inscriptiones Latinae Liberae Rei Publicae: Imagines* (Berlin, 1965).

Gordon, A.E. and J.S. *Album of dated Latin Inscriptions* (Berkeley, Cal., 1958–65).

Hübner, A. *Exempla scripturae epigraphicae Latinae* (Berlin, 1885).

Chapter 5 (pp. 30–5)

Ashmole, B. 'Ciriac of Ancona', *Proc.Brit.Acad.* 45(1959), 25–41.

Donati, A. (ed.) *Il museo epigrafico* (Colloquio AIEGL), Faenza 1984.

Greenhalgh, M. *The Survival of Roman Antiquities in the Middle Ages* (London, 1989).

Mitchell, C. 'Felice Feliciano *Antiquarius*', *Proc.Brit.Academy* 47(1961), 197–221.

Modonesi, D. (ed.) *Nuovi Studi Maffeiani: Scipione Maffei e il Museo Maffeiano* (Verona, 1985).

Sparrow, J. *Visible Words* (Cambridge, 1969).

Springer, C. *The Marble Wilderness* (Cambridge, 1987).

Weiss, R. *The Renaissance Discovery of Classical Antiquity* (Oxford, 1969).

Chapter 6 (pp. 36–41)

(For handbooks to epigraphy, see above, p. 148.)

Braund, D. *Augustus to Nero: a Sourcebook on Roman History, 31 BC–AD 68* (London, 1984).

Bücheler, F. *Anthologia Latina: carmina epigraphica* (Leipzig, 1886; suppl. ed. E. Lommatzsch, 1926).

Cagnat, R. *Inscriptiones Graecae ad Res Romanas pertinentes* (Paris, 1906–27); repr. Chicago 1975.

Degrassi, A. *Inscriptiones Latinae Liberae Rei Publicae* (Firenze, 1963–65).

Ehrenberg, V. and Jones, A.H.M. *Documents illustrating the Reigns of Augustus and Tiberius* (Oxford, 1949, ed. 2, 1976).

Ephemeris Epigraphica (Berlin, 1872–1913).

Frey, P.J.-B. *Corpus Inscriptionum Judaicarum* (New York, 1975).

Levick, B. *The Government of the Roman Empire: A Sourcebook* (London, 1985).

McCrum, M. and Woodhead, A.G. *Select Documents of the Principates of the Flavian emperors* (Cambridge, 1961).

Reynolds, J. 'Inscriptions and Roman Studies, 1910–1960', *JRS* 50(1960), 204–9.

– 'Roman Epigraphy, 1961–5', *JRS* 56(1966), 116–21.

– 'Roman Inscriptions, 1966–70', *JRS* 61(1971), 136–52.

– 'Roman Inscriptions, 1971–5', *JRS* 66(1976), 174–99.

Reynolds, J., Beard, M., Duncan-Jones, R., Roueché, C. 'Roman Inscriptions, 1976–80', *JRS* 71(1981), 121–43.

Reynolds, J., Beard, M., Roueché, C. 'Roman Inscriptions, 1981–5', *JRS* 76(1986), 124–46.

Smallwood, E.M. *Documents illustrating the Principates of Gaius, Claudius and Nero* (Cambridge, 1967).

Smallwood, E.M. *Documents illustrating the Principates of Nerva, Trajan and Hadrian* (Cambridge, 1966).

Ziebarth, E. 'De antiquissimis inscriptionum syllogis', *Ephemeris Epigraphica* 9(1905), 187–332.

Some national and regional surveys

Alföldy, G. *Die römische Inschriften von Tarraco* (Berlin, 1975).

Allason-Jones, L. *A Guide to the Inscriptions and Sculptured Stones in the Museum of Antiquities . . . of Newcastle upon Tyne* (Newcastle, 1989).

Barkóczi, L., Mócsy, A., Soproni, S., Burger, A., Fulep, F. *Römische Inschriften Ungarns* (Amsterdam, 1972–84).

Ben Abdallah, Z.B. *Catalogue des inscriptions latines païennes du Musée du Bardo* (Rome, 1986).

Biró, M. 'The Inscriptions of Roman Britain', *Acta Arch. Acad. Scient. Hung.* 27(1975), 13–58.

Burn, A. R. *The Romans in Britain: an Anthology of*

Inscriptions (2nd ed., Oxford, 1969).

Cagnat, R. *Inscriptions latines d'Afrique* (Paris, 1923).

Cepas, A. *The North of Britannia and the North-West of Hispania: an epigraphic comparison, British Archaeological Reports* (Oxford, 1989).

Chatelain, L. *Inscriptions latines du Maroc* (Paris, 1942).

Collingwood, R.G. and Wright, R.P. *The Roman Inscriptions of Britain* vol.i (Oxford, 1965); vol.ii (Gloucester, 1990–).

Deman, A. and Raepsaet-Charlier, M.-Th. *Les Inscriptions latines de Belgique* (Bruxelles, 1985).

Espérandieu, E. *Inscriptions Latines de Gaule* (Paris, 1929).

Galsterer, H. and B. *Die römische Steininschriften aus Köln* (Köln, 1975).

Guarducci, M. *Inscriptiones Creticae* (Roma, 1935–50).

Hoffiller, V. and Saria, B. *Antike Inschriften aus Jugoslavien* (Zagreb, 1938).

Inschriften griechische Städte aus Kleinasien (Bonn, 1972–).

Inscriptiones Italiae (Roma, 1932–).

Jalabert, L., Mouterde, R. *Inscriptions grecques et latines de la Syrie* (Paris, 1929–).

Merlin, A. *Inscriptions latines de la Tunisie* (Paris, 1944).

Mirković, M., Dušanić, S., Dragojević-Josifovska, B., and Petrović, P. *Inscriptions de la Mésie Supérieure* (Beograd, 1976–82).

Moretti, L. *Inscriptiones Graecae Urbis Romae* (Roma, 1968–79).

Panciera, S. (ed.) *Supplementa Italica* (Roma, 1981–).

Pippidi, D.M. and Doruţiu-Boilă, E. *Inscripţiile din Scythia Minor greceşti şi latine* (Bucureşti, 1980–88).

Reynolds, J.M. and Ward-Perkins, J.P. *The inscriptions of Roman Tripolitania* (Rome, 1952).

Russu, I.I., Florescu, G. and Petolescu, C.C. *Inscripţiile Daciei Romane* (Bucureşti, 1975–84).

Šašel, A. and J. *Inscriptiones Latinae quae in Jugoslavia inter annos MCMXL et MCMLX repertae et editae sunt* (Ljubljana, 1963)

– *Incriptiones Latinae quae in Jugoslavia inter annos MCMLX et MCMLXX repertae et editae sunt, Situla* vol. 19 (Ljubljana, 1978).

– *Inscriptiones Latinae quae in Jugoslavia inter annos MCMII et MCMXL repertae et editae sunt*, ibid. vol. 25(Ljubljana, 1986).

Šašel-Kos, M. *Inscriptiones Latinae in Graecia repertae: additamenta ad CIL III* (Faenza, 1979).

Selzer, W. *Römische Steindenkmäler: Mainz in römischer Zeit* (Mainz, 1988).

Vives, J. *Inscripciones Latinas de la España Romana* (Barcelona, 1971).

Walser, G. *Römische Inschriften in der Schweiz* (Bern, 1979).

Wuilleumier, P. *Inscriptions Latines des trois Gaules* (Paris, 1963).

Epigraphic Congresses

1 (not published).

2 *Actes du IIe congrès international d'épigraphie grecque et latine, 1952* (Paris, 1953).

3 *Atti III congresso internazionale di epigrafia greca e latina, Roma, 1957* (Rome, 1959).

4 *Akte des IV Internationalen Kongresses für Griechische und lateinisches Epigrafik, Wien, 1962* (Wien, 1964).

5 *Acta of the Fifth International Congress of Greek and Latin Epigraphy, Cambridge, 1967* (Oxford, 1971).

6 *Akten den VI internationalen Kongresses für griechisches und lateinisches Epigraphik, München, 1972* (München, 1973).

7 *Actes du VIIe congrès international d'épigraphie grecque et latine, Costanza 1977* (Bucureşti/Paris, 1979).

8 *Praktika tou 8 Diethnous Synedriou Hellenikes kai Latinikes Epigraphes, Athena, 1982* (Athena, 1984).

Recording and reproduction of inscriptions

Beck, C.W. 'Synthetic Elastomers in Epigraphy' *AJA* 67 (1963), 413–16.

Ducrey, P. et al. (eds.), *Actes du Colloque "épigraphie et informatique"* (Lausanne, 1989).

Krummrey, H. 'Tradition und Fortschritt der Inschriftenreproduktion: Polyvinylchlorid zum Nützen der Epigraphik', *Helicon* 6(1966), 685–93.

Pritchett, W.K. 'Liquid Rubber for Greek Epigraphy', *AJA* 56(1952), 118–20.; id., 'Further Notes on Liquid Rubber, ibid. 57(1953), 197–8.

Smith, D.J. 'Cleaning Inscriptions and Sculptures in Stone', *Museums Journal*, Dec. 1957, 215–19.

Walser, G. 'Die Reproduktion von Meilenstein-Inschriften', in *Acta 5th Epigr.Congr., 1967* (Oxford, 1971), 437–42.

Chapter 7 (pp. 42–51)

Grant, M. *The Roman Emperors* (London, 1985).

Hammond, M, *The Augustan Principate* (Cambridge, Mass., 1933).

Hammond, M. 'The Tribunician Day from Domitian through Antoninus: a Re-examination', *MAAR* 19(1949), 36–76.

Hammond, M. *The Antonine Monarchy* (Rome, 1959).

Kniesse, P. *Die Siegestitulatur der römischen Kaiser* (Göttingen, 1969).

Millar, F.G.B. *The Emperor in the Roman World* (London, 1977).

Yavetz, Z. *Plebs and Princeps* (New Brunswick, 1988).

Chapter 8 (pp. 52–9)

Castrén, P. *Ordo Populusque Pompeianus* (Roma, 1975).

Crook, J. *Law and Life of Rome* (London, 1967).

Franklin, J.L. *Pompeii: The Electoral Programmata, Campaigns and Politics, A.D. 71–79* (Rome, 1980).

Galsterer-Kröll, B. 'Untersuchungen zu den Beinamen der Städte des Imperium Romanum', *Epigr. Stud.* 9(1972), 44–105.

Hardy, E.G. *Three Spanish Charters* (Oxford, 1912).

Mason, H.J. *Greek Terms for Roman Institutions: a Lexikon and Analysis = Amer. Stud. Papyrology* 13 (Toronto), 1974).

Patterson, J.R. 'Crisis, What crisis? Rural change and urban development in imperial appennine Italy', *PBSR* 55(1987), 115–46.

Piganiol, A. *Les documents cadastraux de la colonie romaine d'Orange = Gallia Suppl.* 16 (Paris, 1962).

Reynolds, J.M. *Aphrodisias and Rome* (London, 1982).

Sherk, R.K. *Roman Documents from the Greek East* (Baltimore, 1969).

Sherk, R.K. *The Municipal Decrees of the Roman West* (Buffalo, N.Y., 1970).

Visscher, F. de *Les édits d'Auguste découverts à Cyrène* (repr. Osnabrück, 1965).

Williamson, C. 'Monuments of Bronze: Roman legal documents on bronze tablets', *Classical Antiquity* 6(1987), 160–83.

Chapter 9 (pp. 60–9)

Carettoni, G. *et al.*, *La pianta marmorea di Roma antica*, *Forma Urbis Romae* (Roma, 1960).

Casson, L. *Travel in the Ancient World* (London, 1974).

Chevallier, R. *Roman Roads* (London, 1976).

Dilke, O.A.W. *Greek and Roman Maps* (London, 1985).

French, D. *Roman Roads and Milestones of Asia Minor*, fasc.1 (Oxford, *British Archaeological Reports*, 1981).

Gounaropolou, L. and Hatzopoulos, M.B. *Les milliaires de la Voie Egnatienne entre Héraclée des Lyncestes et Thessalonique* (Athènes, 1985).

Hagen, V.W. von *The Roads that Led to Rome* (London, 1967).

Isaac, B.H. and Roll, I. *Roman Roads in Judaea*, fasc. 1 (Oxford, *British Archaeological Reports*, 1982).

Itinera Romana (Bern, 1967 onwards).

Sitwell, N.H.H. *The Roman Roads of Europe* (London, 1981).

Tabula Imperii Romani (1931–   ).

Chapter 10 (pp. 70–9)

Alföldy, G. *Fasti Hispanienses* (Wiesbaden, 1969).

Birley, A.R. *The Fasti of Roman Britain* (Oxford, 1981).

Birley, E.B. 'Senators in the emperors' service', *Proc. Brit. Academy* 39(1954), 197–214.

Broughton, T.R.S. *The Magistrates of the Roman Republic* (New York, 1951–52; suppl. 1986).

Eck, W. *Senatoren von Vespasian bis Hadrian* (München, 1970).

Jarrett, M.G. 'An album of the equestrians from North Africa in the emperor's service', *Epigr. Stud.* 9(1972), 146–232.

Panciera, S. (ed.), *Epigrafia e ordine senatorio* (Colloquio AIEGL) Roma, 1982.

Pflaum, H.G. *Les carrières procuratoriennes équestres sous le haut-empire romain* (Paris, 1960–61).

Prosopographia Imperii Romani, 1st ed. (Berlin, 1897–98); 2nd ed. (Berlin/Leipzig, 1932–   ).

Sherwin-White, A.N. 'The *tabula* of Banasa and the *Constitutio Antoniniana*', *JRS* 63(1973), 86–98.

Syme, R. *Roman Papers* (Oxford 1979–88).

Thomasson, B.E. *Laterculi Praesidum* (Göteburg, 1972–1984).

Chapter 11 (pp. 80–90)

Anderson, A.S. *Roman Military Tombstones* (Princes Risborough, 1984).

Bagnall, R.S. *The Florida Ostraca: Documents from the Roman Army in Upper Egypt = Greek Roman and Byzantine Monographs* 7 (Durham, N.C., 1976).

Bellen, H. *Die germanische Leibwache der römischen Kaiser des julisch-claudischen Hauses* (Wiesbaden, 1981).

Birley, E.B. *The Roman Army Papers, 1929–1986* (Amsterdam, 1986).

Bowman, A.K. and Thomas, J.D. *Vindolanda: The Latin Writing Tablets* (London, 1983).

Campbell, J.B. *The Emperor and the Roman Army* (Oxford, 1984).

Daris, S. *Documenti per la storia dell'esercito romano in Egitto* (Milano, 1964).

Devijver, H. (ed.), *Prosopographia Militiarum Equestrium quae fuerunt ab Augusto ad Gallienum* (Leuven, 1976–80).

Domaszewski, A. von *Die Rangordnung des römischen Heeres*, 2nd ed., rev. by B. Dobson (Köln/Graz, 1967).

Fink, R.O. *Roman Miltary Records on Papyrus* (Cleveland, Ohio, 1971).

Forni, G. *Il relutamento delle legioni da Augusto a Diocleziano* (Milano-Roma, 1953).

Gilliam, J.F. *Roman Army Papers* (Amsterdam, 1986).

Keppie, L. *The Making of the Roman Army: From Republic to Empire* (London, 1984).

McMullen, R. 'Inscriptions on armour and the supply of arms in the Roman Empire', *AJA* 64(1960), 23–40.

Mann, J.C. *Legionary Recruitment and Veteran Settlement during the Principate* (London, 1983).

Maxfield, V.A. *The Military Decorations of the Roman Army* (London, 1981).

Picard, G.-Ch. *Les Trophées Romains* (Bibl.Éc.fr. Ath. et Rome, vol.187; Paris, 1957).

Roxan, M.M. *Roman Military Diplomas, 1954–77* (London, 1978).

– *Roman Military Diplomas 2, 1978–1984* (London, 1985).

Saddington, D.B. *The Development of the Roman Auxiliary Forces from Caesar to Vespasian* (Harare, 1982).

Saxer, R. *Untersuchungen zu den Vexillationen des römischen Kaiserheeres von Augustus bis Diokletian* (Köln/Graz, 1967) = Epigr.Studien 1.

Schleiermacher, M. *Römische Reitergrabsteine* (Bonn, 1984).

Speidel, M.P. *Die Equites Singulares Augusti* (Bonn, 1965).

Speidel, M.P. *Roman Army Studies I* (Amsterdam, 1984).

Starr, C.G. *The Roman Imperial Navy* (New York, 1941).

Webster, G. *The Roman Imperial Army* (London, 1985).

Chapter 12 (pp. 91–7)

Birley, E.B. 'The Deities of Roman Britain', *ANRW* 18.1 (Berlin/New York, 1986), 3–112.

Duthoy, R. 'Les 'Augustales', *ANRW* 16.2 (Berlin/New York, 1978), 1254–1309.

Fishwick, D. *The Imperial Cult in the Latin West* (Leiden/New York, 1987).

Helgeland, J. 'Roman Army Religion', *ANRW* 16.2 (Berlin/New York, 1978), 1470–1505.

Henig, M. *Religion in Roman Britain* (London, 1984).

Merkelbach, R. *Mithras* (Königstein, 1984).

Price, S.R.F. *Rituals and Power: The Roman Imperial Cult in Asia Minor* (Cambridge, 1984).

Stambaugh, J.E. 'The Functions of Roman Temples', *ANRW* 16.1 (Berlin/New York, 1978), 554–608.

Syme, R. *Some Arval Brethren* (Oxford, 1980).

Taylor, L.R. *The Divinity of the Roman Emperor* (Middletown, Conn., 1931).

Vermaeseren, C. *Corpus Inscriptionum et Monumentorum Religionis Mithriacae* (Den Haag, 1956–60).

Vidman, L. *Sylloge Inscriptionum Religiosae Isiacae et Sarapicae* (Berlin, 1970).

Webster, G. *The British Celts and their Gods under Rome* (London, 1986).

Chapter 13 (pp. 98–109)

Altmann, W. *Die römische Grabaltäre der Kaiserzeit* (Berlin, 1905).

Calza, G. *La necropoli del Porto di Roma nell'Isola Sacra* (Roma, 1940).

Cumont, F. *Recherches sur le Symbolisme funéraire des Romains* (Paris, 1942).

Frischer, B. 'Monumenta et arae honoris virtutisque causa: Evidence of Memorials for Roman Civic Heroes', *Bull. Comm. Arch.Rome* 88(1982–83), 51–86.

Geist, H. *Römische Grabinschriften* (München, 1976).

Hesberg, H. von and Zanker, P. (eds.), *Römische Gräberstrassen* (München, 1987).

Hopkins, K. *Death and Renewal* (Cambridge, 1983).

Jashemski, W.F. *The Gardens of Pompeii* (New York, 1979).

Jones, R. 'Burial Customs of Rome and the Provinces', in J. Wacher (ed.), *The Roman World* (London, 1987), II, 812–37.

Kockel, V. *Die Grabbauten vor dem herkulaner Tor in Pompeji* (Mainz, 1983).

Lattimore, P. *Themes in Greek and Latin Epitaphs* (Urbana, 1942).

Reece, R. (ed.), *Burial in the Roman World* (London, 1977; Council for British Archaeology Res.Rep. 22).

Saller, R.P. and Shaw, B.D. 'Tombstones and Roman Family Relations in the Principate: Civilians, Soldiers and Slaves', *JRS* 74(1984), 124–56.

Toynbee, J.M.C. *Death and Burial in the Roman World* (Oxford, 1971).

Toynbee, J.M.C. and Ward Perkins, J.B. *The Shrine of St. Peter and the Vatican Excavations* (London, 1956).

Väänänen, V. *Iscrizioni della necropoli dell'autoparco vaticano* (Roma, 1973).

Walker, S. *Memorials to the Roman Dead* (London, 1985).

Chapter 14 (pp. 110–15)

Andreau, J. *La vie financière dans le monde romain* (Rome, 1987).

Andreau, J. *Les affaires de monsieur Jucundus* (Rome, 1974).

Bemont, C. and Vernhet, A. *La Graufesenque: village de potiers gallo-romains* (Paris, 1987).

Bloch, H. *I bolli laterizi e la storia edilizia romana* (Roma, 1938–39).

Callender, M.H. *Roman Amphorae* (London, 1965).

D'Arms, J.H. *Commerce and Social Standing in ancient Rome* (Cambridge, Mass., 1981).

Duncan-Jones, R.P. *The Economy of the Roman Empire: Quantitative Studies* (2nd ed., Cambridge, 1982).

Greene, K. *The Archaeology of the Roman Economy* (London, 1986).

Hatzfeld, J. *Les trafiquants italiens dans l'Orient hellénique* (Paris, 1919).

Lauffer, S. *Diokletians Preisedikt* (Berlin, 1971).

Meiggs, R. *Roman Ostia* (2nd ed., Oxford, 1973).

Paterson, J. '"Salvation from the Sea": Amphorae and Trade in the Roman West', *JRS* 72(1982), 146–57.

Peacock, D.P.S. and Williams D.F. *Amphorae and the Roman Economy* (London/New York, 1986).

Rickman, G. *The Corn Supply of Ancient Rome* (Oxford, 1980).

Rodriguez-Almeida, E. *Il Monte Testaccio* (Roma, 1984).

Rostovtzeff, M. *The Social and Economic History of the Roman Empire* (2nd ed., rev. by P.M. Fraser; Oxford 1957).

Ruyt, C. de *Macellum: marché alimentaire des Romains* (Louvain, 1983).

Schlippschuh, O. *Die Händler im römischen Kaiserzeit* (Amsterdam, 1974).

Setälä, P. *Private domini in Roman brick stamps of the Empire* (Helsinki, 1977).

Waltzing, J.P. *Étude historique sur les corporations professionelles chez les Romains* (Louvain, 1895–1900).

Chapter 15 (pp. 116–18)

Audollent, A. *Defixionum Tabellae* (Paris, 1904).

Bernand, A. and E. *Les inscriptions grecques et latines du Colosse de Memnon* (Le Caire, 1960).

Besnier, M. 'Recents traveaux sur les *defixionum tabellae* latines', *Revue de Philologie* 44(1920), 5–30.

Cipriotti, P. 'De cottidiano Romanorum sermone ex Latinis Inscriptionibus', *Latinitas* 9(1961), 6–16.

Gigante, M. *Civiltà delle forme litterarie nell'antica Pompei* (Napoli, 1979).

Guarducci, M. *I graffiti sotto la confessione di San Pietro* (Vatican City, 1958).

Harris, W.V. 'Literacy and Epigraphy, 1', *ZPE* 52(1983), 87–111.

Harris, W.V. *Ancient Literacy* (Cambridge, Mass./London, 1989).

MacMullen, R. 'The Epigraphic Habit in the Roman Empire', *AJP* 103 (1982), 233–46.

Mann, J.C. 'Spoken Latin in Britain as evidenced in the Inscriptions', *Britannia* 2(1971), 218–44.

Mann, J.C. 'Epigraphic Consciousness', *JRS* 75(1985), 204–6.

Rawson, B. 'Family life among the lower classes at Rome', *Classical Philology* 61(1966), 71–83.

Sabbatini-Tumolesi, P. *Gladiatorum paria: annunci di spettacoli gladiatorii a Pompeii* (Roma, 1980).

Tomlin, R.S.O. and Walter, D. *The Temple of Sulis Minerva at Bath*, vol. 2, *The Finds from the Sacred Spring* (Oxford, 1988).

Treggiari, S. 'Family life among the staff of the Volusii', *Trans. Amer. Phil. Assoc.* 105(1975), 393–401.

Väänänen, V. *Graffiti del Palatino* (Helsinki, 1966–1970).

Weaver, P.R.C. *Familia Caesaris* (London, 1972).

Chapter 16 (pp. 119–24)

Carletti, C. *Iscrizioni cristiane a Roma: testimonianze di vita cristiana* (Firenze, 1986).

Diehl, E. *Inscriptiones Latinae Christianae Veteres* (Berlin, 1925–31); suppl. ed. J.Moreau, H.I.Marrou (Dublin/Zürich 1967).

Dyggve, E. *History of Salonitan Christianity* (Oslo, 1951).

Ennabli, L. *Les inscriptions funéraires chrétiennes de Carthage* (Rome, 1975/82).

Feissel, D. *Recueil des inscriptions chrétiennes de Macedoine du IIIe au VIe siècles* (Paris, 1983).

Ferrua, A. *Epigrammata Damasiana* (Città del Vaticano, 1942).

Ferrua, A. 'L'epigrafia cristiana prima di Costantino', *Atti IX Congr. di Arch. Christ., Roma, 1975* (Città del Vaticano, 1978), 583–613.

Ferrua, A. *Nuove correzioni alla silloge del Diehl* (Città del Vaticano, 1981).

Hertling, L. and Kirschbaum, E. *The Roman Catacombs and their Martyrs* (London, 1960).

Inscriptiones Christianae Italiae (Bari, 1985–)

Kajanto, I. *Onomastic studies in the early Christian inscriptions of Rome and Carthage* (Helsinki, 1963).

Kaufmann, C.M. *Handbuch der altchristlichen Epigraphik* (Freiburg/Br., 1917).

Knott, B.I. 'The Christian "Special Language" in the Inscriptions', *Vigiliae Christianae* 10(1956), 65–79.

Le Blant, E. *Inscriptions chrétiennes de la Gaule antérieure au VIIIe siècle* (Paris, 1856–65); suppl. 1892.

Marrou, H.I. *Prosopographie chrétienne du Bas-Empire* (Paris, 1982–   ).

Marrou, H.I. *Recueil des inscriptions chrétiennes de la Gaule* (Paris, 1975).

Marucchi, O. *Christian Epigraphy* (Cambridge, 1912, Repr. Chicago, 1974).

Osborne, J. 'The Roman Catacombs in the Middle Ages', *PBSR* 53(1985), 278–328.

Silvagni, A. *Inscriptiones Christinae Urbis Romae* (Città del Vaticano, 1922–64).

Stevenson, J. *The Catacombs* (London, 1978).

Zilliacus, H. *Sylloge Inscriptionum Christianarum Veterum Musei Vaticani* (Helsinki, 1963).

Chapter 17 (pp. 125–30)

Barnes, T.D. *The New Empire of Diocletian and Constantine* (Cambridge, Mass., 1982).

Berchem, D. van *L'armée de Dioclétian et la réforme constantinienne* (Paris, 1952).

Chastagnol, A. *La préfecture urbaine à Rome sous le Bas-Empire* (Paris, 1960).

Clauss, M. *Der Magister Officiorum in der Spätantike* (München, 1980).

Donati, A. (ed.) *La terza età dell'epigrafia* (Colloquio AIEGL; Faenza, 1988).

Jones, A.H.M. *The Later Roman Empire* (Oxford, 1964).

Jones, A.H.M., Martindale, J.R. and Morris, J. (eds.), *Prosopography of the Later Roman Empire*, vol. 1 (AD 260–395) (Cambridge, 1971); vol. 2 (AD 395–527), ed. J.R.Martindale (Cambridge, 1980).

Shaw, B.D. 'Latin funerary epigraphy and family life in the Later Roman Empire', *Historia* 33(1984), 457–97.

Tomlin, R. 'The Late-Roman Empire', in Hackett, Sir J. (ed.) *Warfare in the Ancient World* (London, 1989), 222–49.

Williams S. *Diocletian and the Roman Recovery* (London, 1985).

Chapter 18 (pp. 131–4)

Beard, M. 'Writing and Ritual: a study of diversity and expansion in the Arval Acta', *PBSR* 53(1985), 114–62.

Billanovich, M.P. 'Falsi epigrafici', *Italia medievale e umanistica* 10(1967), 25–110.

Brunt, P.A. and Moore, J.M. *Res Gestae divi Augustus: The Achievements of the divine Augustus* (Oxford, 1967).

Fabia, P. *La Table Claudienne de Lyon* (Lyon, 1929).

Gagé, J. *Res Gestae divi Augusti* (Paris, 1935).

Griffin, M.T. 'The Lyons tablet and Tacitean hindsight', *Classical Quarterly* 76(1982), 404–18.

Wellesley, K. 'Can you trust Tacitus?', *Greece & Rome* n.s. 1(1954), 13–33.

INDEX